BUYING THE BEST

BUYING THE BEST

COST ESCALATION IN ELITE HIGHER EDUCATION

Charles T. Clotfelter

PRINCETON UNIVERSITY PRESS PRINCETON, NEW JERSEY

Copyright © 1996 by Princeton University Press
Published by Princeton University Press, 41 William Street,
Princeton, New Jersey 08540
In the United Kingdom: Princeton University Press,
Chichester, West Sussex
All Rights Reserved

Library of Congress Cataloging-in-Publication Data
Clotfelter, Charles T.
Buying the best : cost escalation in elite higher education /
Charles T. Clotfelter.
p.   cm.
Includes bibliographical references and index.
ISBN 0-691-02642-4 (alk. paper)
1. College costs—United States.   2. Education, Higher—United
States—Finance.   3. Educational surveys—United States.   I. Title.
LB2342.C56   1996
378′.02—dc20   95–26061

Publication of this book has been aided by a grant from
The Andrew W. Mellon Foundation.

This book has been composed in Baskerville

Princeton University Press books are printed on acid-free paper
and meet the guidelines for permanence and durability of the
Committee on Production Guidelines for Book Longevity of the
Council on Library Resources

Printed in the United States of America by Princeton Academic Press

1   3   5   7   9   10   8   6   4   2

Relation of the Directors to the Work and Publications of the National Bureau of Economic Research

1. The object of the National Bureau of Economic Research is to ascertain and to present to the public important economic facts and their interpretation in a scientific and impartial manner. The Board of Directors is charged with the responsibility of ensuring that the work of the National Bureau is carried on in strict conformity with this object.

2. The President of the National Bureau shall submit to the Board of Directors, or to its Executive Committee, for their formal adoption all specific proposals for research to be instituted.

3. No research report shall be published by the National Bureau until the President has sent each member of the Board a notice that a manuscript is recommended for publication and that in the President's opinion it is suitable for publication in accordance with the principles of the National Bureau. Such notification will include an abstract or summary of the manuscript's content and a response form for use by those Directors who desire a copy of the manuscript for review. Each manuscript shall contain a summary drawing attention to the nature and treatment of the problem studied, the character of the data and their utilization in the report, and the main conclusions reached.

4. For each manuscript so submitted, a special committee of the Directors (including Directors Emeriti) shall be appointed by majority agreement of the President and Vice Presidents (or by the Executive Committee in case of inability to decide on the part of the President and Vice Presidents), consisting of three Directors selected as nearly as may be one from each general division of the Board. The names of the special manuscript committee shall be stated to each Director when notice of the proposed publication is submitted to him. It shall be the duty of each member of the special manuscript committee to read the manuscript. If each member of the manuscript committee signifies his approval within thirty days of the transmittal of the manuscript, the report may be published. If at the end of that period any member of the manuscript committee withholds his approval, the President shall then notify each member of the Board, requesting approval or disapproval of publication, and thirty days additional shall be granted for this purpose. The manuscript shall then not be published unless at least a majority of the entire Board who shall have voted on the proposal within the time fixed for the receipt of votes shall have approved.

5. No manuscript may be published, though approved by each member of the special manuscript committee, until forty-five days have elapsed from the transmittal of the report in manuscript form. The interval is allowed for the receipt of any memorandum of dissent or reservation, together with a brief statement of his reasons, that any member may wish to express; and such memorandum of dissent or reservation shall be published with the manuscript if he so desires. Publication does not, however, imply that each member of the Board has read the manuscript, or that either members of the Board in general or the special committee have passed on its validity in every detail.

6. Publications of the National Bureau issued for informational purposes concerning the work of the Bureau and its staff, or issued to inform the public of activities of Bureau staff, and volumes issued as a result of various conferences involving the National Bureau shall contain a specific disclaimer noting that such publication has not passed through the normal review procedures required in this resolution. The Executive Committee of the Board is charged with review of all such publications from time to time to ensure that they do not take on the character of formal research reports of the National Bureau, requiring formal Board approval.

7. Unless otherwise determined by the Board or exempted by the terms of paragraph 6, a copy of this resolution shall be printed in each National Bureau publication.

(Resolution adopted October 25, 1926, as revised through September 30, 1974)

For James and John

Contents

List of Figures

List of Tables

Chapter 6

Chapter 7

Foreword

William G. Bowen and Harold T. Shapiro

As OBSERVERS of American higher education, and as staunch believers in the importance of evidence, we are delighted to introduce this important study of trends in institutional costs prepared so thoughtfully and meticulously by Charles Clotfelter. Concern about ever-rising costs runs like a thread through the myriad critiques of higher education that have been published in recent years. It is easy to understand why. Families recognize, on the one hand, the enormous and increasing importance of access to higher education for their children; at the same time, they worry if family resources will be adequate to pay the bills. Also, consistent with the skeptical nature of Americans, they wonder if anyone is "managing the store." _Why_ are costs rising so rapidly? What are the major sources of increases in costs? How are tuition charges for undergraduates affected by the rising costs of scientific research? And on and on.

Unfortunately, most existing studies of trends in institutional costs have been unhelpful in answering such questions. Researchers have felt obliged to rely on national data so highly aggregated that they obscure rather than clarify the basic issues. And, even then, the data are unaudited and of dubious quality.

This study breaks new ground in that it starts from the assumption that the essential unit of analysis is the academic department in an identifiable university. Hard as it is to assemble data at such a highly disaggregated level of inquiry, we are persuaded that it is only by working in the "trenches" that one can hope to understand the forces shaping trends in costs. Charles Clotfelter has the great advantage of being both a highly respected economist and an individual with practical experience in making budgetary decisions for a leading university (Duke). As a result, he is in the rare position of having both the requisite analytical skills and an understanding of how institutions actually work.

Professor Clotfelter has chosen to study intensively the experiences of typical departments in the humanities, social sciences, and sciences at three leading research universities (Chicago, Duke, and Harvard), as well as the contrasting experiences of a leading liberal arts college (Carleton). The presence in this study of a fine liberal arts college serves as a kind of "control" in that costs at Carleton are not affected directly by the demands of doctoral programs and associated research expenditures. Professor Clotfelter's time frame is the period from 1976/77 to 1991/92. The budgets of selected academic and administrative departments, including student services, have been analyzed in detail in order to compare costs of sub-units. In addition to examining financial records (including capital spending projects and start-up costs as well as operating costs), Professor Clotfelter has looked very carefully at data on course enrollments and faculty teaching loads.

This is, we believe, the first time that the changing costs of university activities have been derived, documented, and presented in such anatomical detail. Clotfelter's analysis certainly yields new insights regarding the cost-escalation experiences of the particular institutions he has studied; even more important, it provides a framework within which this important subject can continue to be studied throughout higher education.

It is not the purpose of this Foreword to summarize the findings, but we will note several recurring themes. First, Clotfelter does not believe that rising costs are due principally to incompetence or, as he puts it more delicately, to "an increase in inefficiency." Why, then, have expenditures risen at what most of us perceive as a rapid rate? One straightforward explanation is "increases in the prices of inputs" (most notably faculty salaries), which did indeed go up fast enough to repair some of the damage done to real faculty compensation in the 1970s. This is, however, but a minor part of the story, especially when one recognizes that salaries of other professional occupations rose even more rapidly. Clotfelter is left with three other explanations: (1) unavoidable increases in various classes of expenditures, including those associated with the technological revolution in computing; (2) "compensating" increases in outlays for student aid and for other expenditures (especially the capital costs) related to scientific research, needed to offset decreases in government support; and (3) what Clotfelter refers to as "the nature of competition that exists among institutions."

It is this last phenomenon that deserves the most careful consideration (even though, as Clotfelter notes, outlays for student aid have risen faster than any other type of expenditure). We certainly do not want vital institutions to be passive, and so, at least at one level, no one should object to what Clotfelter calls "unbounded aspirations." Such aspirations do lead, however, to intense competition for the most respected faculty and then to all sorts of associated costs beyond just salaries (equipment, reduced teaching schedules, and so

on). Of the four institutions in this study, Duke was the most affected during the 1980s by the force of this felt imperative to "get
better," and it is no coincidence that total expenditures went up
faster at Duke than at the other three institutions. Yet, as Clotfelter
notes in quoting Hanna Gray, who was President of the University
of Chicago during the period covered by this study, there are real
questions concerning, at the minimum, the "degree of comprehensiveness" that should be sought by a leading university. These institutions may be, in her words, "burdened by too many tasks, too
many demands, and too great a confusion of expectations." We
agree. And we also know that, as this study reveals, making the hard
choices implied by such a formulation is not easy.

One of the great contributions of Clotfelter's work is to dismiss
easy explanations for the problems that worry us. With some of the
scales removed from their eyes, both those with responsibility for the
future of higher education and observers who continue to expect an
ever-wider scope of effort from particular colleges and universities,
can now adjust their focus. Armed with this original and extremely
useful analysis, we can confront more directly (and with less roman-
ticism) the real choices before us as we seek to employ limited resources most effectively in the service of teaching and research. The
present work is the first in a series of studies of higher education
commissioned by the Mellon Foundation and featured at "The Conference on Higher Education, March 21–23, 1996" celebrating
Princeton University's 250th anniversary.

Preface

DURING the 1980s, higher education came under what Derek Bok calls a "torrent of criticism."[1] The charges against colleges and universities included insufficient attention to teaching, intellectual conformity in the form of "political correctness," financial abuses connected with federally funded research, conspiracy to fix financial aid offers, and irresponsibly high rates of increase in costs and tuition rates. Although the loudest of these complaints originated outside higher education, those within it shared a growing concern over the problem, and more than a few presidents subjected their institutions to serious introspective criticism. The present study arises from this spirit of self-examination on the part of several university officers as well as others closely associated with research on higher education. It is directed especially to those university administrators and policy analysts who must address in one way or another the issues raised in this book. In an effort to make the analysis as accessible as is reasonable, virtually all equations and some detailed tables are relegated to footnotes and appendices, while leaving considerable graphical and tabular material in the text for the reader to digest.

Among those who conceived of a project on this subject were William Bowen, Martin Feldstein, Jerry Green, and Neil Rudenstine. The project would not have been possible, however, without the cooperation of each of the four sample institutions. I am grateful, therefore, to Jeremy Knowles and the above-named officials at Harvard, to Keith Brodie, Thomas Langford, Malcolm Gillis, and Charles Putman at Duke, to Hugo Sonnenschein at Chicago, and to Stephen Lewis at Carleton for permitting me unfettered use of detailed information on their institutions.

Beyond securing permission, I had to call on many administrators at the four institutions to obtain data and to receive guidance on the use and interpretation of those data. The study required the collection of several kinds of information for academic years, most of it spaced at five-year intervals over the period 1976/77 to 1991/92, a time period that typically pushes to the limit most institutions' computerized record keeping. The most complex data are detailed financial records of expenditures; other data include records of class enrollment, faculty teaching, and capital spending projects, some limited to a few departments and some collected on an annual basis. Because of the variety of sources from which these data were generated in any single institution, a critical aspect of the research project was the organization and documentation of numerous data sets and their translation into computer-readable form. For their assistance in collecting and interpreting these data sets, I am particularly grateful to Candace Corvey, Marilyn Fitzgibbon, Doug Funkhouser, Jane Hill, Elizabeth Huidekoper, Nolan Huizenga, Dorothy Lewis, Marilyn Shesko, and Jeff Wolcowitz at Harvard; to Judy Argon, Bill Auld, Harry DeMik, David Jamieson-Drake, Thomas Mann, Dan Parler, Lynn Pinnell, Kendrick Pleasants, James Roberts, and Richard Siemer at Duke; to Andrew Lyons, Caren Skoulas, and Henry Webber at Chicago; and to David Brodigan, Beverlee DeCoux, Clement Shearer, and Carol Spessard at Carleton.

I owe a large debt of gratitude to Christopher Giosa, who worked assiduously and effectively as a research associate on the project during the 1993/94 academic year. I am also very grateful to Marshall Adesman, Adrian Austin, Merrick Bernstein, Lei Ellingson, David Goetzl, and Paul Harrison, all of whom provided valuable research assistance over the course of the project.

For their suggestions and other helpful discussions at the outset of the project during the spring and summer of 1993, I owe thanks to William Bowen, Martin Feldstein, Bert Ifill, and Harriet Zuckerman. In the ensuing months, I received many helpful comments from colleagues, including Philip Cook, Ronald Ehrenberg, Irwin Feller, Malcolm Getz, W. Lee Hansen, James Hearn, Henry Levin, Allen Kelley, Larry Litten, William Massy, Charles Putman, and Michael Rothschild.

The project was supported financially by the Andrew W. Mellon Foundation, through a grant to the National Bureau of Economic Research. Duke University provided significant support as well. However, the views expressed here are not necessarily those of any of these organizations.

List of Abbreviations

AAUP	American Association of University Professors
COFHE	Consortium on Financing Higher Education
CBO	Congressional Budget Office
CPI	Consumer Price Index
EEOC	Equal Employment Opportunity Commission
FTE	Full-time-equivalent
GDP	Gross Domestic Product
HEGIS	Higher Education General Information Survey
HEPI	Higher Education Price Index
IPEDS	Integrated Postsecondary Education Data System
NIH	National Institutes of Health
R&D	Research and Development
ROTC	Reserve Officer Training Corps
SAT	Scholastic Aptitude Test

BUYING THE BEST

CHAPTER 1

The Problem of Rising Costs

Simply put, the cost of what we are doing at
universities is rising quickly.
Harold Shapiro, 1993[1]

EXPENDITURES by American colleges and universities increased rapidly during the 1980s, markedly so among private institutions. Tuition charges rose sharply as well, making the rate of inflation in private college tuition even worse than the much-heralded run-up in medical costs. The aim of this study is to examine these increases, particularly as they have affected private research universities, and to consider their possible causes. This initial chapter begins by providing some background on the increases, describing the increases in spending and tuition and noting how they came to play a central role in the larger debate on the direction of and policy toward higher education. It then presents an overview of the book, by addressing the general importance of rising costs, previewing the book's conclusions, and outlining the organization of chapters.

AN EXPLOSION IN SPENDING AND TUITIONS

Higher education in the United States is a costly enterprise. Measured by aggregate statistics, the expenditures by all 3,400 colleges and universities amounted to some $164 billion in the 1991/92 academic year, or about 2.9 percent of the gross domestic product (GDP).[2] From the perspective of a family sending a child to college, it no longer is uncommon for the financial burden of a four-year program to reach six digits, making college the second largest lifetime expense for many families, after the purchase of a house.

Beginning around 1980, these costs, measured in real, inflation-adjusted dollars, began to rise rapidly. Growth was especially rapid at private institutions. Figure 1.1 shows trends in spending over time in colleges and universities, using information on educational and general expenditures per full-time-equivalent (FTE) student and adjusted for inflation.[3] After holding steady between 1929/30 and

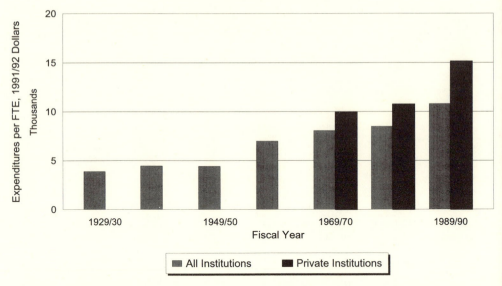

Figure 1.1 Expenditures per FTE, Constant Dollars.

Sources: (a) 1929/30–1969/70: U.S. Department of Education (1989), Table 281, p. 304; 1979/80: U.S. Department of Education (1989), Table 278, p. 301; 1989/90: U.S. Department of Education (1992), Table 332, p. 327.

(b) 1969/70–1989/90: U.S. Department of Education (1992), Table 187, p. 197; 1929/30–1959/60: Bowen (1980), Table 41, p. 261.

(c) 1969/70: U.S. Office of Education (1973), Table 130, p. 114; 1979/80: U.S. Department of Education (1990), Table 280, p. 303; 1989/90: U.S. Department of Education (1992), Table 324, p. 329.

(d) U.S. Department of Education (1992), Table 187, p. 197.

Note: Expenditures refer to general and educational expenditures.

1949/50, average cost rose rapidly after 1950, exhibiting the sharpest increases during the 1950s and the 1980s. Between 1979/80 and 1989/90, spending per student in all institutions grew at an annual real rate of 2.4 percent, and at a 3.4 percent rate in private institutions alone. In their study of costs in higher education during the period 1979 to 1988, Getz and Siegfried (1991) found that costs per student rose especially fast in private research universities and private liberal arts colleges.[4]

Tuitions rose sharply as well, with particularly steep increases in the private sector. Throughout most of the past three decades, the average tuition and fees charged by colleges and universities in the United States tended to increase faster than the overall rate of inflation. While the rise was modest for state-supported institutions, it was more rapid among private institutions, accelerating dramatically during the 1980s. Figure 1.2 charts average tuition, room, and

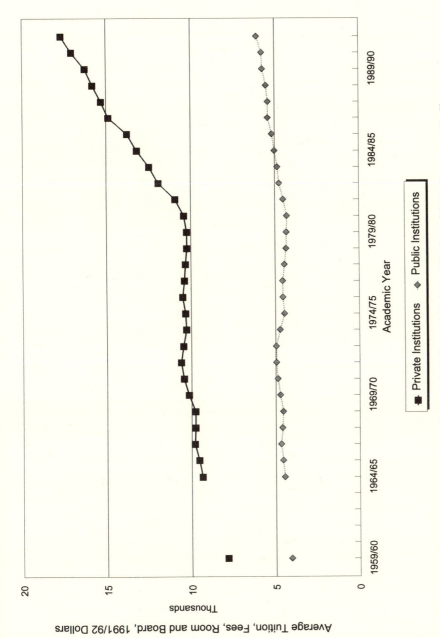

Figure 1.2 Average Cost of Attendance, Public and Private Universities, Constant Dollars.
Source: U.S. Office of Education (1969), Table 120; U.S. Department of Education (1992), Table 301.

board in constant dollars for public and private universities over the last three decades. During the 20 years from 1959/60 to 1979/80, average real tuition and fees rose at a scant 0.3 percent average annual rate in public universities and at a 1.3 percent rate in private universities. After 1979/80, however, the growth rate in the public universities increased to 2.8 percent; among the private universities, it jumped even more, to 4.5 percent per year.

To be sure, the tuition figures cited here refer to the "sticker price," before financial aid is netted out. In fact, during the 1980s, institutions devoted a growing share of their own funds to pay for scholarships, in effect giving students a larger discount from the stated tuition rates.[5] These effective discounts moderated the growth in net tuition slightly, by an average of 0.6 percent per year in private institutions and 0.1 percent per year in public institutions. Nevertheless, even correcting for this expansion of aid, the rates of growth in net tuition remained high—about 2.7 percent annual real growth in the public sector and 3.9 in the private sector. In fact, during the period between 1975/76 and 1991/92, the inflation in the net-of-aid cost of attending private universities exceeded not only the overall rate of inflation but also inflation in medical costs.[6]

Increases such as these attracted particular attention in one very visible group of private institutions: the handful of nationally known private "elite" research universities and liberal arts colleges. Enrolling only a tiny fraction of all undergraduates, this group of institutions is distinguished by its disproportionate share of the nation's top students, most-prominent scholars and scientists, and basic and applied research.[7] As measured by the percentage of applicants accepted for undergraduate admission and the qualifications of those admitted, these colleges and universities boast the most competitive admissions standards in all of higher education. The very names of the research universities in this group—Columbia, Johns Hopkins, Stanford, and Yale, among others—bespeak world-class research, academic selectivity, and social prestige. These names also have come to be associated with high tuitions and, in the view of many critics, excessive spending.

To illustrate how the increase in costs has manifested itself in the tuition at one of these prestigious institutions, consider the case of the University of Chicago, whose impressive gothic campus in Hyde Park was built near the end of the 19th century. Imagine a student preparing to enroll for a year's study in the year 1900. This student would have faced a bill for the year's tuition and fees that is laughably small by today's standards: $120. When translated into dollars corresponding to the 1991/92 academic year, the bill still would be a downright cheap $2,340. Eight decades later, in the fall of 1980, a student beginning a year at Chicago would face a bill for tuition and fees of $5,100, or $8,090 in 1991/92 dollars. Over this 80-year span, tuition had grown an average of 1.6 percent per year faster than had overall price inflation. But during just the next 11 years, Chicago's tuition and fees would double again in constant dollars, rising to $15,945. The average annual growth rate during this most recent period was a breathtaking 6.2 percent over inflation. As dramatic as this escalation in tuition and fees at the University of Chicago was during the 1980s, however, it was by no means unusual among America's most prestigious private colleges and universities. In Figure 1.3, the century-long rise in Chicago's tuition is compared in graphical form with that of Duke's. Although Duke's tuition remained below that of Chicago's for most of the period, it is clear that tuition at both institutions followed almost the same trajectory.

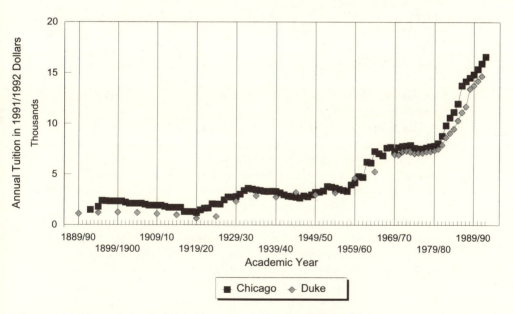

Figure 1.3 Trends in Tuition Rates at Chicago and Duke.

Source: Tuition data: Duke University Annual Reports and unpublished data; unpublished data, University of Chicago. Price data: before 1939, U.S. Department of Commerce (1960), Table F 1-5, p. 139; 1938 to 1959, U.S. Council of Economic Advisers (1991), Table B-3, p. 290; after 1959, U.S. Council of Economic Advisers (1994), Table B-3, p. 272.

Note: Nominal figures are deflated using the GNP price deflator.

COSTS AND CONTROVERSY

A headline on page 1 of the *New York Times* in May 1987 announced, "Tuitions Hit New Peak, Igniting a Bitter Debate."[8] The rapid rise in costs and tuitions during the 1980s became a flash point that intensified an ongoing debate over the direction of higher education itself, serving as evidence for critics of the inefficiency, misdirection, and even greed of institutions of higher education. Some critics viewed the run-up in costs as a direct result of an increasing emphasis on research at the expense of teaching. Others pointed to what they saw as excessive spending on frills and bloated bureaucracies.

The criticism of rising costs came from many quarters. For example, in editorials, the *Washington Post* called higher education "a machine with no brakes" and criticized in particular "the reckless escalation of tuition" and the "outsized demands of the richest and most famous universities."[9] *Business Week* described higher education as "a huge, sprawling enterprise with sclerotic bureaucracies."[10] One op-ed piece in the *Wall Street Journal* charged that "productivity is a dirty word when it comes to higher education."[11] Highly critical books denounced various aspects of higher education. One book described faculty as "overpaid, grotesquely underworked, and the architects of academia's vast empires of waste" (Sykes 1988, p. 5). Another stated, "As increasingly vast sums of money have poured into colleges and universities over the past half-century, one of the most striking results has been that professors have taught fewer and fewer classes, and have done more and more research."[12] Critics also blamed rising costs on new spending for recruitment and student amenities, a proliferation of courses and departments, and increases in administrative bureaucracies.[13] Professors themselves criticized the growth of administration, with the president of the American Association of University Professors (AAUP) claiming, "Huge amounts have been devoted to funding administrative positions that a few years ago would have been thought unnecessary" (Bergmann 1991, p. 12).

This critical attitude also found a home in Washington's corridors of power. Ronald Reagan's Secretary of Education, William Bennett, was outspoken in his criticism of higher education, citing among other faults its "greedy" pricing policies.[14] In a widely noted speech during Harvard's 350th anniversary celebration, he stated, "American higher education simply refuses to acknowledge the obvious fact that, in general, it is rich." He went on to criticize, among other things, what he saw as decreased attention to undergraduate education (Bennett 1986, p. 29). Similar ideas were expressed on Capitol Hill as well. One House subcommittee held hearings entitled, "College Education: Paying More and Getting Less" (U.S. House of Representatives 1992b). Not only was new funding for university research receiving careful scrutiny, there appeared to be a growing inclination to take some action to restrain cost increases, such as conditioning federal aid on cost containment. In 1992, the President's Council of Advisors on Science and Technology (1992, p. 19) summarized the situation in this way:

> Public confidence in universities is eroding. Although studies show that the economic value of an advanced education has increased substantially in the last decade, there is nevertheless a growing concern that tuition and related costs are rising too quickly and that the teaching programs of the research-intensive universities should receive more attention.

Because of their prominence as well as their high cost, the elite private research universities were subject to a large share of this critical scrutiny. One defining moment was the chilly reception given to Stanford president Donald Kennedy in hearings about overhead rates on federal grants; the hearings produced embarrassing disclosures about Stanford's financial practices, one of which was the inclusion of a yacht and other luxuries in the base used to calculate the amount the university charged for indirect costs on its federal grants and contracts expenditures.[15] Even more attention was focused on the elite institutions by the Justice Department's antitrust case against several groups of institutions, the most prominent of which was the "Overlap Group," an informal consortium that included MIT and the Ivy League schools. The Overlap Group held annual meetings to share information about the financial need of individual students, which had the effect of removing price differentials among schools for most recipients of aid and, therefore, the further effect of preventing a bidding war among institutions for prized applicants.[16]

Beyond the very serious implication that these institutions were running a cartel for the purpose of fixing prices, the Justice Department case also focused attention on the role of financial aid in the cost escalation. Conceived in large part by these institutions during the 1960s, the financial aid system, operated by institutions and supported by federal aid programs, was based on a definition of a student's financial need as the difference between the cost of attendance and an amount supposedly indicating what that student's family reasonably could pay. This system had two effects: (1) to entitle students at the most expensive institutions to the largest amounts of government aid, and (2) to create within each institution an apparent "Robin Hood" transfer from rich students to poor students.[17] Thus, not only were the prestigious institutions being accused of running a cartel to fix prices, they were receiving a disproportionate share of government student aid funds and were viewed by their more affluent customers as running redistribution programs among their own students. That their tuitions were rising at breakneck speed simply poured gasoline on this firestorm of criticism.

The escalation in costs did not go unnoticed, or undefended, by the institutions themselves. University presidents routinely expressed concerns about rising costs, particularly about those related to scientific research and instrumentation, and about how these increases might affect the ability of their institutions to conduct pathbreaking research. In defense of the increases, universities pointed to outside pressures on budgets, including increases in needed purchases of scientific equipment, the rapid rise in the cost of books and academic journals, rising faculty salaries, a growing reliance on institutionally funded student financial aid, the need to attend to the physical deterioration of physical plants, and increasingly burdensome varieties of government regulation.[18]

As is evident from its themes, much more is at stake in the controversy over the rise in costs than just the mechanics of financing a major college or university. Especially as it pertains to the group of elite colleges and universities, the issue of rising costs carries with it implications for several important functions in which these institutions are involved. One of the most important functions of research universities, and of the well-known private research universities in particular, is the creation, extension, and development of knowledge, both basic and applied. The research carried out in these institutions, some of which is financed by government, contributes materially to the economic well-being of the nation and the world, spurring economic growth and, in many different ways, enhancing human welfare.[19] Although industry carries out research and development on a large scale, the research conducted in universities is recognized as having a special role, as it often is more basic or generalizable than research that can be justified by individual firms. Because of the economic usefulness of university research, anything that affects its cost to the nation is by definition a matter of some concern.

A second function that may feel the impact of rising costs is, of course, the education of students, a function that can be seen perhaps most clearly in the advanced training that universities offer.

Not only is this training central to the continued economic growth of the United States, university education increasingly has become one of the country's major export industries, sending an ever-growing number of graduates back to their native countries. How the increases in costs will affect the ability of American universities to retain this preeminent position is unclear.

Still another reason for concern about increasing costs arises from the role of higher education, in particular, the role of the group of selective private institutions, in influencing the transmission of affluence and power from one generation to the next in this country. Although American higher education offers to the aspiring young person a larger number of avenues to success than is afforded in other countries,[20] the fact remains that admission to one of the 50 most selective colleges and universities tends to confer on a young person the chance at a credential of enduring economic and social value. Given the importance in the American civic tradition of the principle of equal opportunity and its embodiment in discussions of higher education policy in the emphasis on "choice" as a primary goal of student financial aid,[21] it should not be surprising that the affordability of college, especially of these elite institutions, is a question of no mean policy significance. Indeed, the ability of a talented young person to rise from the poverty of an urban neighborhood or depressed rural area to attend Harvard stands as something of a symbolic litmus test of equal opportunity in America. Thus, rising tuitions and their impact on the affordability of the best college education are significant for this reason as well.

ARE RISING EXPENDITURES A PROBLEM?

As it and similar terms are employed in public debate on higher education, the term "escalating costs" invariably is meant to convey something undesirable, whether the writer has in mind tuition charges or some measure of per-student spending. Before proceeding in a study of either tuition or spending, it is important to understand the significance of rising expenditures. A moment's reflection will make clear that an increase in spending is not, by itself, cause for alarm. Consider, for example, one of the simplest types of spending units, a family. By definition, the family's expenditures, like those of a firm or a university, reflect the amounts of various items purchased and the cost per unit of those items. If expenditures rise from one year to the next, the increase may reflect decisions that are discretionary, such as increases in the amount of groceries, clothes, or electricity purchased, or may reflect forces over which the family has no control, such as an increase in the price of these items. A third possibility is that the increase might reflect inefficiency, such as leaky insulation or a car that needs tuning. We worry about the impact of forces of the second kind on the well-being of families, as measured in increases in the Consumer Price Index (CPI), because inflation represents an increase in the cost of attaining the same real level of consumption. Likewise, inefficiencies are a concern because they decrease the attractiveness of the entire menu of possible consumption choices. One's evaluation of rising expenditures must be quite different, however, if the increase occurs simply because a decision has been made to buy more of something, or to buy an item of higher quality. Such decisions may be wise or unwise, but there is no reason to suppose that the decision-making unit is necessarily worse off for having made them.

These generic categories are useful for suggesting three possible explanations for rising costs in higher education. One possible cause can be laid generally to *exogenous forces*, any external influences that have the effect of changing the prices that institutions pay for inputs. For example, explanations stressing the market determination of faculty salaries, the high cost of computers and scientific equipment, the increase in cost sharing in government grants and contracts, or the growth in burdensome government regulation all relate to forces outside the influence of any one institution. Developments such as these imply higher costs and, therefore, a harsher economic environment in which existing functions are carried out. Note, however, that not all exogenous forces are unfavorable. Some, such as those in the form of technological improvements, may serve to decrease the cost of inputs. Whatever the direction or cause of changes in input prices, colleges and universities, like other firms, usually have some latitude for responding by changing the mix of inputs, for example, by substituting computers for labor.

A second possible explanation for rising costs is *output choices*, such as the increases in expenditures required for institutions to upgrade their faculty, add new programs, or diversify their student bodies by offering new scholarships. In these cases, expenditures may rise simply because a decision has been made to buy more of something, or to buy an item of higher quality. Rather than reflecting forces outside the control of decision makers, as in the first case, this explanation arises from the choices made by institutions. A third possible reason is *inefficiency*. Whenever a given set of inputs produces less output or lower-quality output than it could produce under ideal conditions, the cost per unit is higher than it could be; this is inefficiency. Explanations suggesting such factors as bureaucratic bloat or self-serving faculty behavior appeal to this theme.[22] If organizations and techniques fail to reflect "best practices," resources are being wasted. It is useful, although frustrating, to note in passing that the latter two explanations assume that the "output" of colleges and universities can be identified, if not actually measured. In fact, the services that these institutions produce are numerous, diverse, and not at all amenable to quantification.

The extent to which one need worry about rising expenditures depends on one's perception of the cause. To the extent that these increases arise from forces over which institutions have little control, sympathy and understanding are called for. To the extent that they arise because of decisions to expand missions or improve quality, the nature of the improvements must be weighed against the cost, as well as against whether the beneficiaries and payers are the same. If tuition from undergraduates is used to allow faculty more time to conduct research, for example, there may well be justification for raised eyebrows. In a survey focusing on expenditure increases during the 1980s, college and university financial officers most often reported that costs had risen faster than inflation in the following categories: insurance, government regulations, libraries, scientific and computing equipment and facilities, and development (and, in every case, the percentage noting the increases was greater than average in doctoral institutions) (Chaney and Farris 1990, p. A–13). These categories suggest a combination of rising input costs and deliberate decisions to do more things, or to do them better. To the extent that costs rise simply because of inefficiency, however, the concerns of critics may be well founded, and policies designed to force economies may be justified.

WHY DID SPENDING RISE SO FAST?

In considering this book's motivating question of why expenditures in private research universities rose so rapidly during the 1980s, it is important to examine particular aspects of these institutions, as well as of that decade. The economic conditions that developed around 1980 provided what amounted to a window of opportunity for the best private colleges and universities to improve, and to remain competitive with other elite institutions doing the same thing. To some extent, the rise in spending was forced by increases in the real cost of inputs, such as faculty and library books; however, these cost pressures do not explain the bulk of the spending increases. There is even less evidence of increasing inefficiency, unless shrinking class-room teaching loads by faculty are an indication of that trend. If the decrease in classroom teaching was replaced by research or adminis-trative work that contributed at least as much to the output of insti-tutions, then the bulk of the increases in spending therefore must be laid to the remaining category—that is, to an increase in output, in the form of more services, more faculty, more research, and higher levels of quality.

To understand how these increases occurred, it is necessary first to consider the nature of the beast that is the modern private research university. Lacking virtually any of the hierarchical structure of the modern corporation, the private research university operates more like a little democracy than an efficient firm. Because of the inde-pendence traditionally accorded to its most prominent workers—its faculty—it possesses neither the capacity to formulate a coherent corporate objective nor the ability to implement one, if it existed. By default, then, the operational objective of the research university is simply to "be the best." At the same time, each research university is locked in continual battle with its competitors, principally for faculty, research funding, and top students. Expenditures on salaries, facili-ties, and amenities are crucial to this competition, and therein lies the source of an ongoing, unsatisfied demand on the part of univer-sities for more revenue. In contrast to today's corporate managers, however, university administrators possess neither the ability nor the financial incentive to cut costs. As a result, every private research university worth its salt always has a list of worthwhile projects to fund but little prospect of funding them by cutting programs.

These institutional characteristics were as true in the 1970s as in the 1980s. What was different in the latter decade was the *opportunity* to achieve institutional objectives. Several fundamental economic changes occurred about this time, including increases in the wealth of the affluent, a dramatic improvement in the economic benefit from attending college, and a sudden slowdown in overall price in-flation. Applications to the nation's most selective colleges and uni-versities increased rapidly, suggesting strong demand for this kind of college education. Yet the capacity of the institutions barely in-creased, resulting in persistent excess demand. In this environment, the leaders of these institutions could not fail to realize that they *could* raise tuition without undue harm to their continued ability to make highly selective admissions decisions. Large increases in tuition would be a problem, of course, especially if they discouraged mid-dle-income students from applying. Nevertheless, worries about the effects on the poor could safely be put aside, owing to the social contract into which all selective colleges and universities had entered.

This social contract consisted of two promises: (1) to remove consideration of financial need from admissions decisions (so-called "need-blind" admissions); and (2) to provide financial aid to all matriculating students according to a standard formula that assesses families' ability to pay for college, based primarily on the families' income, net worth, and number of children in college.[23] Some commentators have taken the view that financial aid is primarily a means of price discrimination whereby applicants with more choices are given a discount.[24] While that characterization may be accurate for many less selective private institutions, for the selective institutions examined here, the commitment to this social contract made expenditures on financial aid a real cost of doing business. To play by these rules required spending money on a certain kind of need-based aid system, even if it meant dipping into institutional funds. That most of these institutions did in fact have to use institutional funds to pay for this commitment makes for an interesting implication: the policy objective of "choice" (that is, the idea that any qualified student should be able to choose to attend any college, even the most expensive one) was financed at the margin not by government but by the most selective institutions themselves. They did not do so necessarily out of altruistic motives, however. Subscribing to the social contract on student aid may simply be the best way to signal to the world that one's degrees are earned by merit, not by financial resources.

Thus, the increase in spending by the top private research universities can be understood as a result of the impact of some unprecedented economic changes on a set of institutions that featured a distinctive structure and operating style. Other factors, including a change in the nature of federal support and the advent of computerization, played a small part. But the bulk of the increases that occurred was the result of paying for more and better units of the educational services that these institutions always had produced.

THE APPROACH TAKEN IN THIS BOOK

Numerous studies conducted in recent decades have examined university expenditures, but most have relied on aggregated financial data for cross-section samples of institutions (for example, data based on U.S. Department of Education surveys of institutions).[25] These data are subject to two important drawbacks, however. The first drawback arises from the heterogeneity in missions that exists among institutions. Clearly, the functions of research universities and liberal arts colleges differ markedly, and almost any statistical comparison that could be made between a college and a research university would be of limited value in the absence of other information. In fact, most empirical work using such survey data takes this heterogeneity into account by analyzing groups of institutions separately, such as by the Carnegie classification.[26] Even within these classes, however, other important differences among institutions exist, for example, between research universities with medical centers and research universities without medical centers. While some of these differences can be taken into account by further dividing the groups,[27] comparisons even within subgroups may be skewed significantly by the presence of professional schools, differences in areas of emphasis in arts and sciences programs, or quality differences in otherwise similar programs.

A second drawback of federally collected survey data is, simply, their lack of reliability. Because the survey responses collected from institutions are not audited, both changes in classification and outright errors can produce data that are of little use. In their study using surveys for three recent years, for example, Getz and Siegfried (1991) provide several striking anomalies, including an increase in public service expenditures at Columbia from $0 in 1984 to $126 million in 1988, no expenditures by Harvard on libraries in 1988, and numerous fluctuations in enrollments that appeared implausible. Although it is possible simply to omit observations that are manifestly wrong, these problems highlight a more fundamental difficulty with survey data—the basic lack of comparability in accounting categories between one institution and the next. What is counted under student services at one university might very well be part of academic administration at another, either because of differences in administrative organization or simply because of the way that accounts traditionally have been maintained at each place.[28]

Largely in response to the problems posed by the use of survey data, the present study substitutes in-depth examinations of four institutions for the analysis of cross-section survey data. Three of the four (Duke University, Harvard University, and the University of Chicago) are private research universities, and one (Carleton College) is a private liberal arts college. In an effort to increase comparability, the study focuses within each institution solely on the arts and sciences, excluding both medical centers and professional schools. The remainder of this section describes the approach taken in more detail.

Case Studies

This study differs from previous, mostly cross-section analyses of higher education finance in that its principal data come from only a small number of institutions. Rather than relying on comparisons between institutions, which is the raison d'etre of cross-section analysis, it focuses on *changes within these institutions over time*. Data within institutions are further divided; for some applications, information on individual departments is examined.

The only valid justification for this course of action is the belief that the disadvantages inherent in relying on any small group of examples, which, obviously, may be unrepresentative of a larger group of institutions, will be outweighed by the advantages. One obvious advantage to this approach is that it allows for a level of detail unattainable in studies using data that are aggregated at the institution level. A second clear advantage is comparability of data. Comparability has been sought in two ways. First, by obtaining and examining detailed data, particularly financial data, it has been possible to reconfigure information into categories that are much more similar in function across institutions than are the categories that each institution defines and uses for its own reporting purposes. Owing to differences in organization, mission, or quality, however, this kind of reconfiguring can go only so far. For example, whereas one university might have departments in both history and the history of science, another might have only a history department, with its historians of science split between history and other departments. Although two institutions might have departments of psychology, one might have a doctoral program and the other only a master's program, or one might have a higher-quality doctoral program than the other. It is not necessary to look very long or very hard to find differences such as these when comparing actual institutions.

A second step in seeking comparability is to take these categories, which have been adjusted to be as comparable as the available data will allow, and to examine changes in them over time within each institution. This step reflects the belief that any modifications over time in accounting definitions, the allocation of functions, basic institutional objectives, or quality within a given college or university will tend to be minor when compared with measurable changes in spending, enrollments, and other relevant quantities. In order to gauge trends in each institution over the recent period in which costs have risen rapidly, data were collected over a 15-year period at five-year intervals, for academic years 1976/77, 1981/82, 1986/87, and

1991/92; the 1991/92 academic year was the most recent one for which detailed information was readily available for each institution. In some cases in which information was not available for those four years, information was collected for other years. In order to simplify the comparison of trends in quantities of all kinds, especially where the time intervals are not the same, changes generally are expressed in terms of annual growth rates.[29] As in any comparison of quantities over time, if growth is not smooth, measured growth will be sensitive to the choice of beginning and ending years.

In a further effort to peel the onion of detail, several of the most detailed analyses in the study, presented in chapters 7 and 8, use case studies within the case studies, usually studies of particular departments. For example, the calculation of classroom teaching loads requires information on the status and activities of individual faculty members. The volume of information required to make calculations for an entire institution made it impractical to examine more than a few departments. Therefore, detailed calculations on classroom teaching loads, staffing, and course characteristics that are presented in various chapters are based on the same three academic departments at each of the institutions, one each in the humanities, social sciences, and natural sciences. The departments were selected as being roughly representative of three different traditions of research and teaching, with the humanities department relying on books, library research, and writing; the social sciences department more heavily dependent on computing and quantitative research; and the natural sciences department using laboratories outfitted with expensive equipment and training graduate students largely through hands-on research. At Duke, which contains a separate school of engineering, a fourth department, in engineering, also received special scrutiny. To guard against the possibility that the calculations in the present study could be used to identify individuals or small groups of individuals, the identities of the sample academic departments are not given. Particular departments that are identified, for example, in the listing of course offerings, are not necessarily the same departments as those used to make the detailed calculations mentioned here.

This approach is not without drawbacks of its own. The most glaring weakness is, of course, the small sample. No four institutions can be representative of higher education nor, for that matter, of highly selective private institutions. To a certain extent, it must be left to the reader to judge the extent of applicability of the present study's findings. The four institutions are anything but a random sample. As private, highly selective, and relatively well-endowed institutions, they are distinctive. Three of the four are among a group of only about 100 research universities in the country, with two among the very most prominent of this type. However, the set of institutions to which these four belong has considerable importance, for the share of the nation's research they conduct and for the disproportionate contribution of their undergraduate colleges to the training of leaders in many fields, if not for the rapidity of the escalation in their costs in recent years.

Another, probably less critical drawback to the approach is that using administrative records to make comparisons over time could introduce bias into the findings. One important criterion used in constructing time series of variables within institutions was, for obvious reasons, that comparable data be available over the period in question. This approach tends to make it difficult to follow changes in quantities that are increasing so rapidly that information on earlier years has not been recorded or has been buried in administrative structures that, perhaps because of the growth itself, have been modified over time. For example, owing to student interest or burgeoning research opportunities, a department of environmental studies could have been created during the period of study, perhaps drawing faculty from several different departments. A change in organization of this sort usually will mean that accounting and other administrative data will not be comparable over time; avoiding such cases because of lack of comparability might well bias the choice of cases toward less rapidly growing functions. At the very least, it must be recognized that, despite the steps taken to increase comparability of the time-series data, administrative or other changes over time will tend to corrupt the data, and attempts to avoid this corruption may bias the pattern of findings. Neither of these potential possibilities appears to be a serious problem, however.

Points of Methodology

Several aspects of the methodology are worth mentioning. First, for the purpose of considering the causes and implications of the increase in spending in universities, it is most useful to focus on expenditures that institutions find to be costly and over which they have control. This study therefore examines internally financed spending, that is, spending paid for by unrestricted revenues such as tuition, investment income, and return from endowments. Excluded from this category are expenditures tied to outside grants and contracts or to the self-financed operation of auxiliaries, such as dormitories and dining halls. Internally generated funds are used to finance institutions' core functions, including teaching, research, and much administration.

Second, a principal component of the study focuses on the analysis of expenditures. Throughout the study, however, every reasonable attempt was made to identify other quantifiable aspects that might be related to those expenditures, including enrollments, number of faculty, and measures of employment. Where possible, attempts were made to identify the portion of these changes in expenditures that can be attributed to increases in associated quantities. Although they may contribute little to our understanding of the behavioral aspects of expenditure increases, these decompositions offer a neutral way to separate increases.

A third point relates to the treatment of administration and other shared functions in the analysis of expenditures. A necessary step in determining an institution's expenditures for arts and sciences is to allocate some portion of central administration and other university-wide operations to the arts and sciences component. This methodological problem is much the same as that which arises in the negotiation of universities' overhead rates for grants. For this study, administrators at the institutions were asked to estimate the proportions of the expenditures in each departmental category that apply to arts and sciences. These proportions were then applied to the corresponding university totals in order to obtain an amount for each expenditure category for each year that reasonably can be associated with arts and sciences functions.

A fourth general point has to do with inflation. Following the standard practice in applied economics, virtually all monetary quantities are expressed in constant dollars, usually dollars corresponding to the 1991/92 academic or fiscal year. For most purposes, the price index used is the GDP implicit price deflator, a price index that reflects all goods and services produced in the economy, rather than the narrower group of retail goods and services covered in the other most commonly used price index, the CPI. In most cases, the difference between these two indices is small. Regardless of the choice of index, however, following this conventional practice does, in a sense, misrepresent the reality that the administrators, faculty, and consumers faced at the time they were making decisions underlying the data that we now examine, after the fact. In particular, unexpected changes in the rate of inflation caused actual increases to be larger or smaller than decision makers had intended. The role of expectations about inflation is discussed in greater detail in chapter 3.

PREVIEW

To lay the groundwork for the empirical study of the four institutions presented in this book, chapters 2 and 3 begin by providing some necessary background. Chapter 2 describes universities as an organizational form, emphasizing three characteristics that set them apart from most other modern firms and aspects that they have in common with firms. It then reviews the major explanations that have been offered for rising expenditures in higher education. The chapter concludes by briefly describing the sample institutions—Chicago, Duke, Harvard, and Carleton—touching on their history, characteristics of their students, and quality of their research and graduate programs. Chapter 3 turns from the institutions to the times, focusing on the years from the middle 1970s to the early 1990s that constitute the period covered by the study, and on the developments in those years that may have had an effect on colleges and universities, particularly on their expenditures.

Chapters 4 and 5 present a detailed examination of the expenditures in arts and sciences for each of the four sample institutions. In chapter 4, expenditures are classified according to administrative unit and type of expenditure, and increases in spending for these categories are compared. Chapter 5 focuses on several prominent expenditure categories in an attempt to explain the increases by reference to other quantifiable changes. To assess the importance of administrative functions and the effect of changes in the technology of the office, chapter 6 examines the staffing patterns of several selected administrative and academic units.

Because of the key role of faculty and teaching in colleges and universities, it is important to augment the analysis of expenditure patterns with information on staffing in academic departments and on the resulting characteristics of courses. Chapters 7 and 8 therefore examine the use of faculty in academic departments, using data for several illustrative departments within each institution. Chapter 7 focuses on the allocation of faculty time among various duties, which include, but are not limited to, classroom teaching, committee work, and research. It presents estimates of average classroom teaching loads in the sample departments for four academic years from 1976/77 to 1991/92. Chapter 8 considers the courses offered by these departments from the perspective of the student, noting the size of classes and the portion of courses taught by graduate students and nonregular faculty. The book's concluding chapter notes some of the implications of the study.

CHAPTER 2

A Peculiar Institution

The research university reeks of professional
dominance, with professors constantly sliding
from the role of employee into that of
salaried entrepreneur, going largely their own
way in managing their time, their research,
and their teaching.
Burton R. Clark, 1987[1]

FEATURING the size of a small city, the complexity of a major con-
glomerate, the technical sophistication of the space program, the
quaintness of a medieval monastery, and the political intrigue of a
Trollope novel, the modern private research university in this country is a peculiar institution indeed. As an organizational type, its origins date to the Middle Ages, making its European examples some
of the oldest continuously operating organizations other than the
Roman Catholic Church. Probably its most famous example in this
country, Harvard, founded in 1636, is today both among the very
oldest and the most influential of American institutions.

A logical first step in understanding the rise in expenditures in
private research universities is to consider the institutional context in
which the increase occurred. To this end, the first section of this
chapter describes universities as we know them in the United States,
focusing on four aspects that distinguish them from other large organizations. Universities are not distinctive in all their features, of
course. Therefore, it is essential to remember that universities, like
corporations and many other nonprofit organizations, retain significant flexibility in allocating resources, an issue discussed in the second section. Awareness of these characteristics is essential for assessing the explanations that recent research on higher education has
offered for the continual rise in expenditures, reviewed in the third
section. The chapter's last section briefly describes the four institutions that serve as case studies in this book. Note that the characterization of universities presented in this chapter is meant to apply first
and foremost to private, selective universities, such as those examined in this study. However, the discussion probably applies in many

respects not only to other research universities but also, with suitable modifications, to selective liberal arts colleges.

WHAT KIND OF FIRM IS A RESEARCH UNIVERSITY?

In the vernacular familiar to economists, a private college or research university is a firm, sharing the same essential elements as countless other firms, both nonprofit and for profit: employees are hired, physical capital is purchased and maintained, a service is produced, customers consume it, and revenues are collected. Yet these institutions constitute a distinctive class of firm, as even a brief visit to any campus will suggest. Employees and customers, often indistinguishable, may be seen making their way across parklike expanses, which separate imposing buildings of varying architectural design; inside these buildings may be found modern offices, labyrinths of laboratories, dining rooms, theaters, gymnasiums, and auditoriums. Beyond the areas of intense activity may lie acres of playing fields and parking lots, punctuated by the unmistakable silhouette of an outdoor stadium.

What Is the "Business" of the Private Research University?

To suggest the range of activities that are carried out on campuses, it is instructive simply to list them.[2] The first step in doing so is to recognize that a handful of activities are of paramount importance: they define the institution. These activities include the traditional trinity—teaching, research, and service—plus patient care in the universities with medical centers. Teaching takes place not only through formal instruction in classrooms and laboratories, but also in many less-formal interactions in such settings as offices, libraries, and local area communication networks. Service encompasses a wide variety of activities, from advising foreign governments to volunteering with local charities. Other activities, some of them almost as thoroughly identified with colleges and universities as the first three, support the defining functions. They include selecting among applicants; maintaining records on students; counseling students; and providing a range of campus services to students, such as dining, housing, and transportation. Another uniquely collegiate function is intercollegiate athletics, although how to classify it is not obvious. Part commercial enterprise, part student activity, it would, in recognition of its prominence, appropriately appear in the list of defining processes for many universities. There also are semicommercial activities, such as stores, theaters, and golf courses, which sell to customers both on and off the campus. A third group of activities comprises supporting functions not unique to higher education, for example, general administration, legal counsel, financial accounting, investment management, public relations, maintenance, and security. These functions, although essential to the operations of the university, also are routinely performed by most large corporations and nonprofit organizations. In assessing the rise in university outlays, it will be useful to divide total university expenditures into broad categories such as these.

Of the university's defining activities, most observers probably would agree that the two most important are teaching and research. However, it is not always easy to distinguish between the two in practice. One central activity of all the institutions examined in this study is undergraduate education. For liberal arts colleges, this activity is the primary, if not exclusive, aim. In contrast, the three universities examined here offer a variety of graduate and professional programs. In 1992, in addition to undergraduate baccalaureate programs, Chicago, Duke, and Harvard offered professional degrees in business, law, medicine, public policy, and divinity, and graduate training in numerous arts and sciences fields. At least one university offered graduate professional training in education, engineering, social work, public health, architecture, and environmental studies. In addition, the universities' operating units include museums, marine laboratories, departments of athletics, university presses, and a laboratory school featuring classrooms for school children of all ages. By focusing exclusively on arts and sciences, the present study simplifies comparisons among the institutions.

Although vast differences exist among disciplines in methods of inquiry as well as subject matter, it is not too great a simplification to say that the major difference between a college and the arts and sciences component of a university is the presence of graduate students, particularly doctoral students. Their presence radically transforms the relationship between faculty and undergraduate students. Graduate students assist in the teaching of undergraduates by acting as graders and instructors. Probably more important, they provide a competing object of attention for faculty. In particular, the process of doctoral training involves both classroom teaching and highly individualized supervision. The relationship between faculty and doctoral student has been described as symbiotic, because the faculty member typically benefits materially, as does the apprentice. Faculty gain from the intellectual challenge of teaching and overseeing the research of bright, energetic students as well as from students' services as laboratory and research assistants, as is evident from coauthorships and the acknowledgments found in faculty publications.[3]

Four Distinctive Features

As this short description makes clear, the functions of the research university can be readily distinguished from those of most other kinds of firms. Less readily observed, but perhaps more important, however, are the university's distinctive features as an organization. In his analysis of the modern university, Coleman (1973, p. 369) notes that the university is one of the few institutions in existence that traces its beginnings from the Middle Ages. In contrast to the hierarchical nature of the modern corporation, universities retain the nature of a community. As an organization, Coleman argues, the university displays three features that distinguish it from the modern corporation: (1) it has no corporate goal (other than to award degrees), (2) those who perform its central functions are not employees in the usual sense, and (3) it is governed along collective rather than hierarchical lines. This list suggests a useful outline for describing the distinctive institutional trademarks of universities. To these three institutional features, a fourth is added here relating to the nature of the commodity that colleges and universities provide to their customers, and to the implications this feature has for the market for higher education.

Mission: To Be "The Best"

In its purest conception, the modern corporation is the epitome of rational organization that is built around a central mission guiding all its decision making. Indeed, the crafting of "mission statements" has become a familiar part of contemporary corporate planning. Many colleges and universities, in their emulation of corporations' efforts to improve productivity, have undertaken similar planning exercises, often to discover that the process of crafting a mission statement is agonizingly difficult. The apparent reason for this difficulty, quite simply, is that the objectives of most universities are both varied and vague. Coleman's view that the university has no goal at all, except to award degrees, is hyperbole. More accurately, a university simply is many things to many people. This attribute explains the observation of Keohane (1993, p. 101) that a mission statement "sufficiently bland to encompass everyone's conception" is unsatisfying, whereas more specific statements quickly engender controversy. What is left, if it is actually put into words, is a general commitment to "excellence" or the aim to be "the best" (Cole 1993, p. 23). Using precisely these words, Duke provost Phillip Griffiths stated in an address to university trustees, "The goal for Duke University, clearly, is to be the best. More specifically, it is to strengthen Duke's position as the leading private teaching and research university in the Southeast and improve its national position among such universities" (Griffiths 1984). Such devotion to superlative achievement is by no means new, as Charles Eliot's inaugural as president of Harvard in 1869 illustrates (Morison 1965, pp. 329–30): "This University recognizes no real antagonism between literature and science, and consents to no such narrow alternatives as mathematics or classics, science or metaphysics. We would have them all, and at their best." To be sure, university mission statements often feature some specificity, usually organized into the traditional trinity of research, teaching, and service. What seems significant for the present analysis is the unconstrained nature of the stated aspirations.

Not surprisingly, the larger and more complex the institution, the more difficult it is to give a simple statement of purpose. At one end of the spectrum is the small liberal arts college. Offering neither graduate training nor professional training, not to mention the vast array of research and service activities included under the tent of the large state universities, the liberal arts college has the luxury of a distinct and widely shared objective. It is noteworthy that, among the four institutions examined in the present study, in only one—Carleton College—did the official catalog offer a statement of purpose: "Carleton College strives to provide a liberal education of the highest quality. The goal of such an education is to liberate individuals from the constraints imposed by ignorance or complacency and equip them broadly to lead rewarding, creative, and useful lives."[4]

Faculty: Autonomy and Divided Loyalties

Coleman's second distinctive feature is that those who perform the institution's central functions, the faculty, are not employees in the conventional sense, but rather, "semi-independent professionals" (Coleman 1973, p. 369). From this perspective, faculty have the best of the community and corporate worlds—privilege, pay, and security without the obligations of obedience within a chain of command. More precisely, this favored position is enjoyed by faculty who have passed the profession's most prominent professional hurdle: the virtual lifetime guarantee of employment known as tenure.

Tenure most often is justified in terms of protecting the freedom to express unpopular ideas, but McPherson and Winston (1993a) argue that it is an institutional response to the highly specialized duties that professors are hired to perform and to the easy portability of skills to other employers. Whatever its origins, academic tenure inevitably limits the degree to which central authority can be exercised within a university. Not only could he as dean not order faculty to do very much, complained Henry Rosovsky in a letter to the Harvard faculty, he found it difficult even to gather basic information, such as the number of hours of classroom teaching by faculty. Without a strong social contract spelling out obligations, he warned, this autonomy could result in a "society largely without rules" (Rosovsky 1991, p. 18). To be fair, it is necessary to note the readily apparent fact that, despite this freedom, faculty in general do appear to work a great deal. In 1988, faculty reported in a survey an average work week of 53 hours; for those in private research universities, the average was 57 hours (U.S. Department of Education 1991, p. 51).

In addition to tenure, two aspects of university culture are worth noting because both have the potential to influence expenditures. The first is the strong allegiance that most faculty members feel to their own disciplines or professions. Like guild members of old and members of other professions today, most faculty display strong attachment to that national or international group of scholars who share the same disciplinary training or who teach and conduct research in similar areas of inquiry. It is accepted as fact, and probably expected, that the loyalties of the chemists, linguists, and political scientists of any university faculty will be divided between institution and profession. Two surveys conducted in the 1980s revealed that twice as many faculty stated their academic discipline to be "very important" to them as stated their college or university to be that important (Boyer 1990, p. 56). To Gray (1992, p. 237), this "dual citizenship" is simply an unavoidable fact of university life. Indeed, research universities encourage an outward-looking disciplinary orientation through such policies as the use of external committees to review departments and other programs, the reliance on outside letters of reference and evaluations of peer-reviewed publications in promotion and tenure reviews for individual faculty, and university-financed subsidies for attendance at professional meetings. As research has received increasing emphasis in most universities, one's standing in one's discipline, rather than in one's institution, has become the coin of the realm.[5] Moreover, as the elite liberal arts colleges increasingly expect faculty to conduct research, one would expect to see a similar outward orientation develop there as well. This emphasis on research presents a dilemma for faculty, especially untenured ones, who come to realize that the *duties* of the job (especially teaching and advising) are largely distinct from the activities that will earn them advancement.[6]

The second noteworthy feature of the culture of the professorate is a live-and-let-live attitude toward disciplines (and thus departments) other than one's own. As noted by Cole (1993, p. 6) and Kennedy (1993, p. 137), the taboo against criticizing other disciplines in public is strong. Whether it arises out of a broader devotion to freedom of inquiry and expression or out of an appreciation of the vulnerability of all disciplines to attack from without, and whether this attitude is any more characteristic of academe than of other large organizations, it is not hard to see how this tolerance—combined with the participatory elements in university governance noted in the following section—could inhibit serious discussions of retrenchment in universities.

Governance: "Company of Equals"[7]

The third distinctive feature of the university highlighted by Coleman is the way that it governs itself. Coleman points out that the university more closely resembles a community than a hierarchically structured corporation. The decisions of major importance in any research university center around the approval and termination of programs, the requirements for degrees, the allocation of space and budgetary support among components, the hiring and promotion of faculty and senior staff, and the setting of institutional policy. Who actually makes these decisions? Within any institution, three obvious possibilities are the governing board, the administration, and the faculty. Private universities, like most nonprofit organizations, are governed ultimately by self-perpetuating boards of trustees, which have the legal responsibility to make all such decisions of consequence. Reporting to the governing board are the university's senior administrative officers (president, provost, vice presidents, and deans) who, subject to the board's approval, usually exercise broad powers over the day-to-day operation of the institution. Among the undeniably important decisions left largely to administrators are the setting of salaries, the allocation of space, the approval of positions, and the choice of enrollments and average class size that in turn determine faculty teaching loads. Although boards of trustees exert influence over the overall shape of policy, it is rare that these decisions are rejected at the level of the board.

The claim is sometimes heard that the faculty "run" the university.[8]

For most universities, this notion still seems to be an exaggeration; however, it may have more to recommend it than an organizational chart would suggest. The influence of the faculty is felt in two ways. First, most universities have established elaborate structures of deliberative committees to consider, review, or propose various decisions. The most prominent deliberative body is usually the faculty senate, although its role may be largely symbolic. Many institutions use committees composed of administrators, faculty, and, sometimes, students to deliberate over budgetary matters. Among the institutions examined in the present study, both Carleton and Duke have established such committees. In addition, faculty bodies appointed for the specific purpose of making recommendations often exert considerable influence. For example, faculty committees empaneled to review departments and other programs, to make recommendations on promotion and tenure cases, or to offer guidance on budget priorities have become an integral part of institutional decision making. To be sure, these arrangements, and the degree of influence they imply, differ from one institution to another.

Faculty appear to exert influence over university decisions in a second, informal way. Because most senior administrators come from the ranks of the faculty, they look to their colleagues for understanding, if not approval. This sensitivity is clear and understandable in the case of the departmental chairs, who typically anticipate returning to their previous roles as members of their departments. In the case of senior administrators, such as deans, provosts, and presidents, a similar influence is at work. As Feldstein (1993, p. 38) and Stigler (1993, p. 167) note, the incentives facing administrators are decidedly asymmetric: whereas policies of growth or maintenance of the status quo that require sacrifice from no one individual usually generate little if any dissent, proposals to cut programs can be expected to produce howls of protest and determined opposition. The participatory character of university decision making, and the faculty's role in it, ultimately lead to a form of governance that is difficult to model with precision. The observation of Caplow and McGee (1958, pp. 206–7) made more than 30 years ago still is descriptive: "The fundamental device by which stresses in the university are resolved is a kind of lawlessness, consisting of vague and incomplete rules and ambiguous and uncodified procedures."

Although it is difficult to quantify, the influence of the faculty, which also implies the influence of the disciplines and professional associations to which faculty feel allegiance, appears to be a real force in university governance. It may be a version of the old joke about who makes the important decisions in the family. The trustees and administrators make the "important decisions," such as how to invest the endowment and where to locate new buildings, but the faculty have substantial influence over the "unimportant" decisions, such as what the curriculum will be and who will receive tenure. As one unnamed political scientist said, "On the things that count to the faculty, the faculty have a lot of power."[9] The truth is perhaps murkier than usual. Not only is it difficult to determine the loci of influence in a single institution, with all its complexities, the reality itself surely differs from one institution to another.

Product: Essential, Ephemeral

The fourth distinctive aspect of research universities lies in the nature of the product that they sell and what that implies about the market in which they sell it. Whatever else can be said about them, the services that colleges and universities provide are ill-defined and virtually unmeasurable. Even ignoring research and service, the remaining teaching-related services are noteworthy on at least three grounds. First, as suggested by the use of the plural, they are multidimensional; they include training in specific subjects as well as skills and experiences that, taken together, are recognized as a college education. Second, as McPherson and Winston (1993b) have emphasized, the quality of these services is not easily assessed, either by customers or by experts in the industry. In the terminology of economics, the output is an "experience" good, the quality of which can be judged only after it is consumed, as opposed to a commodity that can be assessed adequately by inspection before purchase. Because useful information therefore is hard to come by, consumers will be influenced by observable signals of quality, including new programs, prestigious professors, or even a high price. Third, the customers of the output are also inputs to the production process. A student's experience is affected not only by faculty, staff, and buildings, but also by his or her own efforts, and by the presence of other students. The characteristics of students also no doubt affect the pleasure that faculty derive in teaching. In addition, characteristics of the student body may have reputational aspects of their own, for example, when average standardized test scores are used in college rankings. For these reasons, institutions care about both the average quality and diversity of the students who enroll in them.

Closely related to these aspects of the commodity that colleges and universities produce is the question of competition in the "market": do colleges and universities compete with one another? Even casual observation confirms that they do indeed, but, owing to the uncertainty about quality, it certainly is not carried out in the conventional model of price competition. As evidence presented here will illustrate, institutions are keenly aware of their competition, of the programs, rankings, prices, and admissions success of the institutions with which they compare themselves.

According to Gray (1992), competition impels institutions to match the programs offered elsewhere, pushing up spending and, in the process, making institutions more homogeneous. In the market for undergraduate students, quality-based competition may have perverse effects when expensive tuition, rather than acting as a deterrent to enrollment, serves as a signal of high quality.[10] Indeed, some commentators have argued that a policy of tuition restraint could have the ironic effect of damaging an institution's competitive position in attracting good students.[11] Although this seemingly perverse price effect might simply be one more modern example of the phenomenon of conspicuous consumption, it probably has more to do with consumers' inherent difficulty in making informed judgments about quality in this arena. Another potential force for higher spending arising out of the competition noted by these authors is the temptation to use scholarships in a bidding war to attract top students.[12]

OPERATIONAL FLEXIBILITY

Like ordinary households and firms, universities have considerable latitude in deciding what to buy and how much to spend. This flexibility is not absolute, of course. Universities, as with other economic actors, are subject to legal constraints and to the discipline of the markets in which they compete. For example, because the institutions examined in the present study compete for many of the same high school seniors, they will be understandably reluctant to make decisions that would undercut their ability to compete for their share of the students.

Within these constraints, however, institutions retain significant flexibility, chiefly along four dimensions: (1) input mix, (2) sources of funding, (3) intertemporal allocation, and (4) outputs. These dimensions are important because their implied latitude of operation will tend to frustrate attempts to assign specific causes to increases in spending. A university, like the textbook firm, has a choice of methods of producing many of its servies or outputs, each method implying a different mix of inputs. For example, it can teach introductory undergraduate courses by using small classes, large lectures, or a combination of large lectures and small sections; the classes can be staffed with regular faculty, adjunct and visiting faculty, or graduate students. Similar alternatives exist for other functions, such as advising, graduate instruction, residential housing arrangements, and library circulation.

Among the variables under the control of university administrators are enrollments, the number of faculty, the delegation of faculty to specific departments, the assignment of other duties, the relative size of graduate programs, the frequency of maintenance and repair, and the use of computers and other capital to substitute for labor. As is discussed at more length in chapter 7, administrators necessarily face trade-offs along all these dimensions, including such derivative measures as teaching loads and average class size. The "leveraging of faculty time" that Massy and others have highlighted (for example, the devolution of functions, such as advising and departmental administration, onto nonfaculty staff) may reflect the kind of factor substitution implied by these trade-offs.[13] As an example, institutions can minimize their need to hire relatively expensive faculty by shifting some tasks that faculty traditionally have performed, such as advising or departmental administration, onto other employees. The implication of this kind of flexibility for understanding rising expenditures is the same as in the textbook analysis of the firm: the university can blunt the effect of rising input costs by conserving on those inputs the costs of which are increasing most rapidly. As long as universities wish to conserve their resources, therefore, any rise in expenditures over time can be assumed to be occurring despite the best efforts of an institution to reduce those expenditures through factor substitution.

A second degree of latitude open to administrators is the real, but limited, fungibility of funds at their disposal. Although income from endowments and grants and contracts is restricted as to use, unrestricted funds are not. Thus, unrestricted funds can be used, for example, to continue a program that was begun with external funding; Ehrenberg, Rees, and Brewer (1993) found this to be the case when universities substituted unrestricted funding to support graduate students in the wake of cuts in National Science Foundation funding. Similarly, increasing endowment or external support for an activity already under way can free up unrestricted funds. Of course, donors and granting agencies may recognize this possibility and attempt to avert it. In the case of gifts, fund-raising sometimes takes on the appearance of an elaborate dance in which the donor tries to structure a gift that will "make a difference" by causing activities to be undertaken that would not otherwise have been implemented, and the institution tries not to commit to doing anything that it would not otherwise have done.[14] (By lumping together unrestricted and endowed funds as "internal," the present study carries with it the implicit assumption that the institutions are ultimately successful, because they have the option of refusing gifts when the conditions either will be too expensive to fulfill or are otherwise unacceptable.)

A third dimension of administrative flexibility, and an option open to almost any economic actor, is to save money in the short term by undertaking actions that may well be unwise in the long run. An institution can save money in the short term, for example, by deferring the maintenance of its buildings and other physical assets; there is evidence that many institutions followed this policy during the 1970s and 1980s. Similarly, an institution can increase its revenues in the short run by raising the spending rate from its endowment and other financial assets. It may also have some latitude in the extent to which it uses grants and contracts to cover what otherwise might be considered ordinary expenditures, such as faculty salaries. Or it may accept gifts that will generate costs in excess of the additional revenue generated.

A final dimension for maneuvering lies in the ability to change the mix or quality of the output. Programs can be added, eliminated, upgraded, or allowed to deteriorate. These shifts may be minor, for example, by not replacing a retiring historian specializing in British colonialism, or major, for example, by instituting a new department of women's studies. More subtly, an institution can allow the quality of what it produces slowly to decline, such as by increasing the size of courses with no concomitant improvements, by hiring less talented faculty, or by cutting financial aid awards. Or it may do so in a noticeable way, for example, by dropping its need-blind admissions policy or by ending its commitment to meet 100 percent of demonstrated financial need. Or it may try to raise quality gradually by increasing faculty salaries faster than the market. In light of these illustrative possibilities, it is useful to combine an analysis of changing expenditures with attention to other important changes in the institutions being studied—an aim of the present study.

EXPLAINING THE INCREASE IN EXPENDITURES

The phenomenon of rising expenditures in higher education is not new, so it should not be surprising that it has attracted the attention of scholars. In summarizing this previous analytical work, it is useful to distinguish analyses that seek to decompose the increases into identifiable parts from those that propose some behavioral explanation for the trends.

Decomposing the Increases

A first step to understanding why expenditures have risen in real terms is measurement. Two recent studies have used financial data on expenditures of a large set of institutions, from the Higher Education General Information Survey (HEGIS) and the Integrated Postsecondary Education Data System (IPEDS), to identify the sources of expenditure increases. In the more detailed of these two studies, Getz and Siegfried (1991) examine changes in spending between 1978/79 to 1987/88. Blasdell, McPherson, and Schapiro (1993) extend the period to 1988/89. Both studies examine expenditures, divided by FTE enrollment, and broken down by type, for various classes of institutions. These data cover entire institutions, each observation including an institution's professional schools and on-campus medical center, if any.

To separate the components of the increase in spending, Getz and Siegfried divided the increase in general expenditures per FTE into five components.[15] Table 2.1 shows these components for three groups of research universities over the period 1978/79 to 1987/88. For all research universities covered by the study, total general spending per FTE rose at a 3.08 percent annual rate. The largest contributor to this increase was the average faculty salary rate, which rose at a 1.91 percent rate. The second largest contributor was the increase in the nonfaculty share of instructional spending. The remaining two components served more or less to cancel each other out, with the relative growth in noninstructional spending boosting per-student spending somewhat, and a decline in the student-faculty ratio over the period reducing the growth in spending per student. Relative to all research universities, private research universities showed more-rapid growth in total expenditures, number of faculty, and noninstructional spending. Among all higher education institutions, the category showing the fastest growth in spending was Liberal Arts I colleges, with a 4.62 percent average annual growth rate in spending per FTE. In addition to the trends shown for all research universities, these colleges increased rather than decreased their faculty-student ratios and showed more-rapid growth in noninstructional expenditures (Getz and Siegfried 1991, p. 380).

In their comparison of expenditure increases of different types, Blasdell, McPherson, and Schapiro (1993) show that private institu-

TABLE 2.1

Components of Growth in Expenditure per FTE Student
in Research Universities, 1978/79 to 1987/88

	Research Universities			Liberal Arts I Colleges
		Private		
	All	No On-Campus Medical School	On-Campus Medical School	
Number of Observations	87	27	4	122
Real Growth Rates in:				
Instructional expenditures (I$)	3.53%	3.50%	3.82%	3.75%
Faculty salaries (F$)	2.33	2.99	3.22	2.65
Number of faculty (F)	0.42	0.95	0.78	0.82
Number of students (S)	0.67	0.32	1.13	0.40
General expenditures (E$)	3.76	4.50	4.74	5.02
Components of Growth Rate of General Expenditures per Student [r(E$/S)]				
Instruction as percentage of total general expenditures [−r(I$/E$)]	0.23%	1.00%	0.92%	1.27%
Faculty salaries as percentage of instructional expenditures [−r(F$/I$)]	1.20	0.50	0.60	1.10
Average faculty salaries [r(F$/F)]	1.91	2.04	2.43	1.83
Student/faculty ratio [−r(S/F)]	−0.25	0.64	−0.35	0.42
Total	3.08%	4.18%	3.61%	4.62%

Sources: Getz and Siegfried (1991), Tables 14.4 and 14.5, and pp. 360–85; and author's calculations.

Note: r( ) refers to the growth rate.

tions had very large increases in expenditures for plant additions over the period of study. They also highlighted the decline in the portion of private universities' revenues obtained from federal grants and contracts.[16]

External Forces

In an effort to go beyond a mere accounting of these increases, one useful distinction is to separate influences that are external to universities as a whole from those that may be said to occur within institutions themselves. For example, rising input prices require increases in total outlays just to maintain a given level of output. Thus, the Higher Education Price Index (HEPI), an index reflecting the inputs typically purchased by colleges and universities (mostly trained workers), rose during the 1980s at a rate slightly faster than the CPI.[17] (To be sure, these factor prices are affected by actions of the industry, but from the perspective of a single institution they are largely exogenous.) A similar external effect on higher education is that of rising costs associated with the expansion of knowledge and the increasing sophistication of scientific research. The growth in the sheer amount of knowledge to be dealt with, absorbed, recorded, and taught may be seen most clearly in its effects on library holdings and the increasing specialization within academic disciplines, the latter putting upward pressure on the numbers of faculty, courses, journals, and library holdings.[18] A related force is what has been termed "sophistication inflation" (President's Council of Advisors on Science and Technology 1992). This force can be seen in the rising cost of scientific instrumentation and, more generally, in the high cost of conducting scientific research.[19]

One external force on university costs noted by more than a few observers is government regulation.[20] Regulations covering such areas as student records, workplace safety, employee discrimination, handicap access, athletics, retirement, and federal grants, it is argued, necessitate increased administrative effort and expense. Another impact of government is the reduction in federal funding for research, training, and financial aid, and the increased pressure exerted on internal funding to make up for the reductions.

Internal Mechanisms Fostering Expenditure Growth

Perhaps the richest set of explanations that has been offered to explain the growth in expenditures in colleges and universities is that appealing to the internal dynamics of the decision-making mechanisms inside the institutions. As suggested in the preceding discussion, however, the inside/outside dichotomy is by no means a precise one.

Revenue-Driven Expenditures

Elegant in its simplicity, one of the most frequently cited explanations for rising expenditures is that of Howard Bowen (1980).

Bowen argues that, because of the imprecise but all-embracing striving for excellence motivating all research universities, there is no limit to the amount of money that a thriving, creative institution usefully can spend. Institutions therefore raise all the revenue they can, and they spend everything they raise. Quality increases, functions proliferate, and expenditures rise. Reminiscent of Parkinson's Law and more serious models of bureaucratic growth, this general concept underlies criticism of the growth in administrative bureaucracies and recently has been recast by Massy and his colleagues as the "growth force."[21] Although such increases are not necessarily wasteful, the interpretation usually given to this dynamic is an unfavorable one. Whatever the interpretation, however, this intuitively appealing notion provides little in the way of theory to explain why this dynamic might materialize.[22]

The "Cost Disease"

A second explanation focusing on forces within institutions is the idea from William Baumol and William Bowen that the production functions at work in universities, much like those in a chamber orchestra, are inherently inhospitable to technological progress.[23] In the unchanging technology of education, it is argued, teaching and research methods do not change, and faculty-student ratios are fixed. As Rosovsky (1992, p. 185) remarks, "techniques of instruction have changed relatively little in a thousand years: the professor still stands on the podium, lecturing to students." Meanwhile, advancing productivity in other parts of the economy raises the general level of wages, necessitating an increase in the real cost of producing output in the technologically frozen industries. Because of a method of production that is inherently resistant to productivity enhancements, this view argues, real costs will tend to rise over time.

Research Emphasis and Productivity

A mounting emphasis on research—probably motivated by forces external to universities but carried out by decisions within them—and rising standards for its performance, is another general cause that has been cited for increasing costs. The emphasis that universities place on research, as opposed to teaching, stands at the center of a controversy that continues unabated and is played out in institution after institution. That the emphasis on research in universities, at least in research universities, increased during the 1980s has been acknowledged. Bok (1992, p. 16), for example, has written: "What presidents and deans are held accountable for is improving the prestige of their institutions, and the prestige of their institutions comes from the research reputation of their faculties."[24] More amorphous is the effect on research and its costs of the rising capacity of scientific equipment. Shapiro (1993, p. 13) has argued that the dramatic increases in computational capacity have "changed the scholarly agenda and the way we approach it," making large capital expenditures on networks and computers essential. "Productivity gains, if any, have been taken in quality improvements and agenda expansion rather than cost reduction." Feeding on changes external to universities but manifesting itself in internal decisions about priorities, this set of effects implies rising costs for research, including the operation of research libraries. It also may manifest itself in a reduction in average classroom teaching loads.

Asymmetric Incentives

Several commentators explain rising expenditures in terms similar to the explanations of public-choice theorists for governmental growth.[25] The tradition of collegial decision making combined with a reluctance to criticize others sets the stage for logrolling, whereby faculty assent to the growth in the programs favored by colleagues in return for their reciprocal support. In this "politics of self-preservation" (Kennedy 1993, p. 139), cuts in any program are extremely difficult to achieve.[26] As Feldstein (1993, p. 38) notes, administrators have little incentive to achieve economies, because such economies can be achieved only at significant political cost.[27] Another form of asymmetric incentives, noted in the discussion of the competitive aspects of the higher education market, is the bias toward price hikes that arise from the function of price as a signal of quality.

Inertia

Add to these forces other mechanisms that impede change of any kind, particularly cost cutting. One quite visible manifestation of the heavy hand of the past is the enormous capital investment that is the campus. Given the sheer magnitude and functional specialization represented by the physical plant of campuses, it is little wonder that universities rarely move. Moreover, it is difficult to avoid the costs of operating and maintaining that capital. Another inertial force is of course academic tenure, which, barring financial disaster, means that a large share of an institution's personnel budget is virtually uncontrollable in the short run. In addition to these constraints, the time-honored tendency for favorable working circumstances to become seen as entitlements is yet another barrier to cost cutting.[28]

THE FOUR INSTITUTIONS

As noted in chapter 1, the present study uses as cases four institutions: the University of Chicago, Duke University, Harvard University, and Carleton College. A list alone is sufficient to highlight one enormous distinction among the four: whereas three are research universities, combining an undergraduate program with postgraduate training in professional schools and the arts and science, one is a liberal arts college, offering only bachelor's degrees. Furthermore, as shown in Table 2.2, among the research universities there exist sizable differences in relative weighting among baccalaureate, graduate, and professional training. At Duke, which is most similar to Carleton in terms of its relative emphasis on undergraduate education, undergraduates in 1991/92 accounted for 57 percent of all students, compared with only 37 percent at Harvard and at Chicago. Moreover, Duke's arts and science graduate enrollment was considerably smaller than those of the other two universities. One revealing statistic is the ratio of undergraduates to graduate arts and science students. The lower the ratio, the greater the use that can be made of graduate students in undergraduate instruction, and the more time that faculty will have to devote to their research and to the training of graduate students. In 1991/92, this ratio stood at 3.0 at Duke, compared with 2.0 at Harvard and 1.0 at Chicago. The institutions examined therefore differ in important ways.

This mix of dissimilar institutions was intentional. Because all four institutions compete for undergraduate students and offer undergraduate education, the hope was that including one institution specializing in that activity would provide an illuminating contrast along a number of dimensions. Before undertaking a detailed examination of the four institutions, it is useful to begin by providing some descriptive background on them.

Antecedents

Like the speaker who needs no introduction, Harvard is certainly one of the most celebrated universities in the world. Founded in 1636, it is the oldest and surely one of the most influential institutions of higher education in the United States. Although heavily in-

TABLE 2.2

Enrollments at the Sample Institutions, 1976/77 to 1991/92

	1976/77[a]	1981/82	1986/87	1991/92	Growth Rate, 1977–92[a]
University of Chicago					
Undergraduate students	2,442	2,867	3,166	3,447	2.9
Arts and sciences graduate students	2,693	2,504	2,886	3,395	1.9
Professional school and other students	2,262	2,323	2,554	2,601	1.2
Total	7,397	7,694	8,606	9,443	2.0
Percentage undergraduate	33	37	37	37	
Ratio of undergraduates to arts and science graduate students	0.9	1.1	1.1	1.0	
Duke University[b]					
Undergraduate students	5,805	5,849	6,068	6,001	0.2
Arts and sciences graduate students	1,480	1,191	1,497	2,028	2.1
Professional school and other students	2,076	2,178	2,356	2,557	1.4
Total	9,361	9,217	9,920	10,585	0.8
Percentage undergraduate	62	63	61	57	
Ratio of undergraduates to arts and science graduate students	3.9	4.9	4.1	3.0	
Harvard University					
Undergraduate students	6,439	6,497	6,620	6,677	0.2
Arts and sciences graduate students	2,358	2,318	2,604	3,391	2.4
Professional school and other students	6,400	7,238	8,074	8,205	1.7
Total	15,197	16,053	17,298	18,273	1.2
Percentage undergraduate	42	40	38	37	
Ratio of undergraduates to arts and science graduate students	2.7	2.8	2.5	2.0	
Carleton College					
Undergraduate students	1,736	1,832	1,825	1,798	0.2

Sources: University of Chicago: Unpublished table, entitled, "Table I-D, Enrollment by Department or Field of Studies, Degree Students"; Duke University: Office of the Registrar, *Annual Statistical Report*, table entitled, "Registrar's Enrollment Statistics;" Harvard University: Unpublished tables, and Office of Budgets, *Statistical Profile, 1991–92*; Carleton College: Unpublished tables.

[a]Data for Chicago are for 1979/80; growth rates for Chicago are based on 12 years.
[b]Full-time equivalents.

fluenced by American Protestantism and an early supplier of Puritan ministers in New England, Harvard from its beginning has been independent of any formal church ties. Over the years, its practices, including the lecture and the undergraduate major, have been emulated widely. Its house system, in which undergraduates live in largely self-contained residential units for three years, is another distinctive feature that Harvard shares with only a few other American institutions. Harvard is the largest of the four sample institutions, with a total enrollment of more than 18,000 in 1992. In addition to its undergraduate college, Harvard features a graduate school of arts and sciences and schools offering professional training in such fields as law, medicine, business administration, education, design, public policy, and public health. Harvard's endowment, at some $5 billion in 1992, is the largest of any American university.

Founded in 1892, the University of Chicago was from its beginning to be a center of graduate training as well as an undergraduate college. Its rapid rise to prominence was fueled by a series of gifts from John D. Rockefeller, amounting to $35 million by 1916; by what has been called "the greatest mass raid on American college faculties in history" (Rudolph 1962, p. 350); and by its application of innovative educational ideas. Among the distinctive features of Chicago's approach was coeducation, the quarter system, a general curriculum for students in their first two years of college, and a system of major and minor studies (Rudolph 1962, pp. 350–1). Ironically, its early prominence also arose from its success in football under the hand of famed coach Amos Alonzo Stagg, who had been hired away from Yale (McNeill 1991, pp. 4–6). Football is not what the University of Chicago is known for today, of course. Symbolic of its change in direction was the naming of Robert M. Hutchins as president in 1929. Under President Hutchins, Chicago established the four graduate divisions that remain today—physical science, biological science, social science, and humanities—and sought to offer a core curriculum to undergraduates (McNeill 1991, pp. 31–2). Among Chicago's contributions to research were the first department of sociology, the first artificially produced nuclear chain reaction, and the "Chicago school" of economics. Like Harvard, Chicago has an array of professional schools covering most of the fields offered by the largest private universities as well as social work.

In the same year in which the University of Chicago was founded, Trinity College, an institution with strong ties to the Methodist church, moved to Durham, North Carolina, from a rural county in the Piedmont. After receiving a gift from James B. Duke, it changed its name to Duke University in 1924 and quickly undertook a massive building program that resulted in two separate campuses, one of which was designated for the university's women's college. Duke's gift, like Rockefeller's to Chicago, enabled the university to establish nationally recognized programs quickly, particularly in medicine. Like Chicago, Duke also used football to gain early notoriety; it remains one of the few private, selective research universities to continue to compete in big-time intercollegiate athletics. Emphasizing professional training, Duke established, in addition to a school of medicine, schools of law, engineering, forestry, nursing, and divinity, adding business administration only in 1969. A major reallocation of resources occurred during the 1980s, when the undergraduate nursing school was dropped and those places were used to expand undergraduate enrollments in engineering and arts and sciences. Another program dropped during this period was education, which had accounted for a sizable portion of the doctorates awarded by Duke.

Founded in 1866 as one of 40 colleges sponsored by Congregationalists, Northfield College, in the Minnesota town of that name, became Carleton College in 1871 in honor of an early benefactor. Like the University of Chicago, it was coeducational from its beginning and it shared with Chicago the use of a quarter system, but its size, rustic surroundings, and lack of graduate training made it altogether different in most other ways. A century later, Carleton remains small, relatively isolated, and firmly dedicated to the mission of undergraduate education. It retains a Midwestern work ethic and an ethos of egalitarianism, symbolized by the prohibition of automobiles for students and a high proportion of students who work on campus.

Undergraduates

All four of these institutions display the objective indicators that are the hallmarks of selective undergraduate colleges: strong high school records of entrants, difficulty of admission, and low dropout rates. Among the classes of students who entered in the fall of 1991, the vast majority at each institution had ranked in the top 10 percent of their high school classes, this share ranging from 69 percent at Chicago to 95 percent at Harvard. Acceptance rates ranged from 57 percent at Carleton to 17 percent at Harvard, giving one indication of the difficulty of getting in. Applicants evidently valued these acceptances, as indicated by the relatively high percentages of accepted applicants who decided to enroll, ranging from Chicago's 31 percent to Harvard's 74 percent. Once enrolled, undergraduates at these colleges were very likely to stay on, as illustrated by the high percentage of first-year students who returned as sophomores, which ranged from 93 percent at Chicago to 99 percent at Duke.[29]

Although the clientele of selective colleges and universities tends to be affluent, enrollment statistics nevertheless suggest a significant degree of diversity on several scales. Table 2.3 reports on some characteristics of the undergraduate student bodies in 1981/82 and 1991/92. In terms of geographic diversity, Duke and Harvard showed the lowest representation from their states, but all drew from a national pool of applicants. The racial and ethnic diversity of the colleges increased during the decade; this development is particularly marked in the case of Asian-Americans, a group whose share at least doubled at each institution over the decade. Reflecting this growth, Carleton's president, Stephen Lewis, noted in his address to alumni in 1993 that the second most common surname in the first-year class was Yang (Lewis 1993). International students remained a small group in these undergraduate student bodies, except at Harvard, where they constituted 8 percent of undergraduates in 1991/92.

Once enrolled, the undergraduates at these selective institutions distributed themselves among disciplinary majors in similar ways. Table 2.4 lists the most popular majors among the undergraduates at the sample institutions at the beginning and the end of the period of study. The changes shown there reflect larger trends among undergraduates in this country, namely, a decline in the number of science majors and an end to the temporary boom in economics. By 1992, political science was among the top majors in all four institutions and English was in this place in three of the four undergraduate colleges sampled. Despite these similarities in favored fields of study, however, there was a significant difference among the graduates of three institutions (no information was available for Harvard) in their propensity to attend graduate school in an arts and sciences discipline as opposed to a professional school. Among Carleton and Chicago graduates, the number going to graduate school far exceeded the number going to law school or medical school. Duke's graduates were much more professionally oriented, with approximately equal numbers going into law, medicine, and graduate study.[30]

Research and Graduate Programs

Among the three universities included in the present study are two of the preeminent national research universities, Harvard and Chi-

TABLE 2.3

Characteristics of Undergraduates at Four Institutions, 1981/82 and 1991/92

	Carleton College		University of Chicago		Duke University[b]		Harvard University	
	1981/82	*1991/92*	*1981/82*	*1991/92*	*1980/81*[b]	*1991/92*	*1981/82*	*1991/92*
Percentage of Students Who Were:								
State residents	28	25	33	25	16	12	21	16
African-American	4	3	5	4	7	8	7	8
Native American	1	1	2	1	1	1	1	1
Hispanic	3	3	4	3	1	4	4	7
Asian-American[a]	4	8	8	19		8	5	19
Total minority	12	15	19	27	9	21	17	35
International	2	1	1	3	2	1	6	8

Source: Peterson's Guide to Four-Year Colleges, 1983 and 1993 (Princeton, NJ: Peterson's Guides).
[a]Not reported for Duke for 1980/81.
[b]Not reported for 1981/82.

TABLE 2.4
Largest Undergraduate Majors

	1976/1977	1991/1992
Carleton College	Biology (13.7) History (11.9) English (11.3)	History (12.3) English (12.1) Political science (11.5)
University of Chicago	Biological sciences (11.4) Economics (10.0) Political science (5.1)	Economics (7.9) Biological sciences (7.5) Political science (6.5)
Duke University	History (11.2) Economics (9.1) Zoology[a] (9.1)	English (11.0) Political science (10.3) History (9.8)
Harvard University	Economics (11.8) Biology (10.5) Government[b] (8.7)	Government (11.6) English[c] (8.0) Biology (7.7)

Sources: Carleton College, University of Chicago, and Harvard University: unpublished tabulations; Duke University: Office of the Registrar, *Annual Statistical Report*, 1976–77 and 1991–92.

Notes: Numbers in parentheses indicate percentage of students. Figures for Duke and Carleton refer to graduating seniors; figures for Harvard are for all those with declared concentrations.

[a]Duke had no biology major in 1976/77, only zoology and botany.

[b]Corresponds to political science at most institutions.

[c]English and American Literature and Language.

cago. The third, given its history and the relative size of its schools, stands between those two universities and a purely undergraduate college. Research and graduate training go hand in hand. In the terminology of economists, the production of research and the training of graduate students are joint products: the one is produced more or less as a by-product of the other. In describing the sample institutions, it is important to acknowledge probable quality differences in these outputs. Although virtually every academic scholar has an opinion on the ranking of universities in his or her discipline, there is little consensus on just how that quality should be measured. Two of the most common criteria used in the occasional studies on the subject are counts of faculty publications and subjective reputational rankings.

In their assessment of graduate programs, Jones, Lindzey, and Coggeshall (1982) gathered information on a number of different aspects of faculty research and graduate training. A sampling of their findings provides an illuminating comparison among the three universities examined here. Table 2.5 presents data on nine depart-

TABLE 2.5

Measures of Quality of Quality of Graduate Programs in Nine Disciplines, 1980

Field and University	Number of Faculty	Number of Graduate Students[a]	Percentage of Graduates with		Ratings of		Percentage of Faculty with Grants[d]	Number of Faculty Articles[e]
			Post-Graduate Employment[b]	University Employment[b]	Scholarly Quality[c]	Effectiveness in Teaching[c]		
History								
Chicago	46	125	59	23	4.5	2.3	—	149
Duke	35	83	60	13	3.7	2.1	—	82
Harvard	29	123	78	39	4.8	2.4	—	61
French								
Chicago	8	36	NA	NA	3.1	1.9	—	—
Duke	9	9	42	0	3.2	1.9	—	—
Harvard	9	21	50	18	3.2	1.6	—	—
English								
Chicago	33	72	65	40	4.4	2.4	—	—
Duke	21	76	52	18	3.2	1.9	—	—
Harvard	33	91	77	36	4.5	2.5	—	—
Physics								
Chicago	38	115	85	39	4.6	2.6	50	246
Duke	19	46	64	46	3.0	1.9	26	53
Harvard	28	93	88	41	4.9	2.8	68	337
Mathematics								
Chicago	30	77	91	63	4.8	2.7	60	69
Duke	21	21	50	21	2.8	1.5	52	39
Harvard	26	48	95	65	4.8	2.7	35	51
Chemistry								
Chicago	28	119	81	47	4.4	2.5	79	84
Duke	22	78	79	41	2.9	1.9	64	88
Harvard	24	174	86	51	4.9	2.8	75	114

Psychology							
Chicago	60	217	77	45	4.2	2.2	40	187
Duke	33	81	63	39	3.7	2.1	36	75
Harvard	27	82	71	51	4.6	2.3	52	173
Political Science							
Chicago	27	103	72	32	4.5	2.4	15	85
Duke	23	40	59	11	3.4	1.8	4	54
Harvard	23	158	81	41	4.7	2.4	9	68
Economics							
Chicago	27	120	93	44	4.8	2.7	22	94
Duke	22	60	80	21	3.0	1.8	18	90
Harvard	34	130	91	46	4.9	2.4	27	197

Source: Jones, Lindzey, and Coggeshall (1982).

Note: Figures refer to numbers of faculty and graduate students in December 1980.

[a] Number of full-time and part-time graduate students.

[b] Percentage of fiscal year 1975/76 program graduates who, at the time they completed requirements, had made definite commitments for postgraduate employment, total and in Ph.D.-granting institutions, respectively.

[c] Mean rating of the scholarly quality of program faculty and of the effectiveness of the program in education research scholars/scientists.

[d] Percentage of program faculty members holding research grants from the Alcohol, Drug Abuse, and Mental Health Administration, the National Institutes of Health, or the National Science Foundation at any time during the fiscal years 1978 to 1980.

[e] Number of published articles attributed to program faculty members, 1978–80.

—: no information gathered.

NA: no information available.

ments at the three universities for 1980. Measured by size of faculty or graduate enrollments, Harvard and Chicago's departments are consistently larger than Duke's—which is not surprising, given the institutions' graduate enrollment figures. Two measures gauge the success of students in finding employment after graduate school: (1) the percentage who landed any job, and (2) the percentage obtaining employment in universities. On these scales, Harvard's percentages tend to be slightly higher than those of Chicago's, but both clearly exceed Duke's. Much the same can be gleaned from the reputational ratings in the next two columns, which are based on national surveys of faculty. According to these data, Harvard ranked first in scholarly quality in all but one field and tied with Chicago in the other. The last two columns present information on faculty research, one on the percentage of faculty with grants and the other on the number of published articles attributed to faculty members between 1978 and 1980. The first tends to track the reputational rankings; the second is influenced by faculty size.

The more common means of comparing programs (again, quality measures for faculty research and graduate training become almost interchangeable) is through the use of rankings, which may be based on elaborate analysis or on simple tabulations of ratings or faculty publications. Table 2.6 summarizes the results of two rankings of graduate programs in 14 disciplines spanning the period covered in the present study; this summary allows some assessment of both the position and the change in position over time for departments in the three universities. The rankings are based on the qualitative ratings of a large sample of scholars on the quality of graduate faculty in the nation's graduate programs in a variety of disciplines. In most cases, the fields shown in the table were represented at all three of the sample universities. Although these rankings are certainly imperfect, they are a useful way of summarizing prevailing informed opinions about quality.

For the disciplines shown, the rankings clearly indicate that Harvard's position in most disciplines was unassailable over this period, and remained so although some slippage from the very high rankings of 1969 is apparent. With a few exceptions, Duke's departments are ranked behind those of both Chicago and Harvard in 1993. These rankings, like those in Table 2.5, leave little doubt about the scholarly verdict regarding relative quality in research and graduate training among the three universities over the study period. Some movement is evident, however, with Duke's ranking improving in a majority of the disciplines, whereas those of Harvard and Chicago generally fell.

TABLE 2.6
Rankings of Graduate Programs in Selected Fields, Harvard,
Chicago, and Duke, 1969 and 1993

	Harvard		*Chicago*		*Duke*	
Discipline	*1969*	*1993*	*1969*	*1993*	*1969*	*1993*
Classics	1	1	12	7	NR	44
Spanish	1	10	16	NR	17.5	2
Philosophy	2	3	9	12	26*	44
English	2.5*	2*	4.5*	10	23	5.5*
History	1.5*	4	8.5*	8	19*	15
French	3.5*	17	6	16	20.5*	3
Chemistry	1	3.5*	9.5*	10*	48.5*	44
Mathematics	1.5*	4	4	5	36*	34.5*
Physics	2*	1	9.5*	7	24.5*	42.5*
Biochemistry	1	5	17*	23.5*	11.5*	15
Sociology	1.5*	7	3	1	26*	20
Psychology	4	6	17.5*	18	25*	33
Economics	1.5*	1.5*	3	1.5*	24.5*	22
Political Science	2	1	4	6	27.5*	14

Sources: 1969: Roose and Anderson 1970; 1993: Goldberger, Maher, and Flattau 1995.

Notes: Ratings are based on assessments of the quality of graduate faculty by a national sample of scholars in each of the survey years. In cases in which institutions are tied for a given rank, the average of all the possible ranks of the tied institutions is given. For example, if an institution is one of four tied for 10th place, its average rank is 11.5 (the average of 10, 11, 12, and 13). These ties are indicated by an asterisk.

Their usefulness notwithstanding, ratings such as these inevitably hide a multitude of developments at each institution. During the period of study, each institution strenuously attempted to improve individual departments, sometimes devoting hundreds of person-hours to the recruiting of a single scholar. In the case of Duke, the administration pursued deliberate policies designed to improve the faculty and graduate school, including the hiring of prominent scholars and increasing the number of doctoral students. In pursuit of his objective "to be the best," Provost Phillip Griffiths argued that the size of both the faculty and the graduate student enrollment would have to increase. He stated, "A principal barrier to recruiting faculty of the desired level of excellence is the size and quality of Duke's graduate student body."[31] In fact, graduate enrollments increased, between 1976/77 and 1991/92 at an annual rate of 3.3 percent.[32]

Budgetary Issues: The View from Carleton

Despite their differences in size and mission, these and other private institutions faced many common issues during the period of study. It is illuminating to view these issues from the perspective of a single institution, and an opportunity for this is afforded by Carleton's open and inclusive budget process, which featured a budget committee composed of faculty, administrators, and students, whose regular meetings often were attended by members of the college community.[33] Meeting throughout the academic year, the committee discussed the impact of major budget decisions, including those concerning increases in tuition, faculty salaries, the size of the student body, financial aid policy, and other expenditure items. The budget committee submitted its recommendations to an administrative committee, which was the effective final decision-making body. The budget committee's deliberations, recorded in published minutes and covered by the student newspaper, provide a fascinating perspective on the economic environment of private selective institutions during this period.

Several recurrent themes recorded in the minutes illustrate the trade-offs that both colleges and universities faced. One trade-off was between raising tuition, with the additional revenue that this step would bring, and the potential dampening effect that this increase was thought to have on the decisions of potential students, particularly those with financial need. Recognizing that the cost of financial aid was a growing share of the budget, Carleton considered the possibility that it might have to abandon the policy of need-blind admissions (a policy, followed through the 1980s to some degree by virtually all selective colleges and universities in the country, whereby applicants are judged for admission without regard to their financial need). The committee set maximum limits for Carleton's financial aid expenditures, stated as percentages of tuition income; if reached, these limits determine the portion of an entering class that would be selected under the need-blind rule. In fact, these ceilings were not reached, so Carleton did not abandon the policy during the period under study. Another trade-off was between increasing the college's enrollment, again bringing in additional revenue, and the damage that this step might do to the intimate atmosphere made possible by the college's small size.

In its efforts to develop recommendations consistent with a balanced college budget, the committee also worried about a number of other issues that were not unique to Carleton, including the growth in administrative and support personnel, maintenance of its buildings, the cost and allocation of computing equipment, the spending rate from endowment, and, quite prominently, the competitiveness of its faculty salaries. One striking fact that emerges from a reading of the minutes of the committee is the very high degree of awareness at the college of its competitors' tuitions and faculty salaries. College administrators and committee members had information on average rates of increase for several groups of comparison institutions. In the case of faculty salaries, the AAUP's annual survey of faculty salaries, showing average salary, by rank, for individual institutions, is readily available to any institution. The committee examined salary comparisons between Carleton and several groups of comparable institutions. Among 30 colleges, for example, the committee was shown tabulations in 1987 in which Carleton was ranked 20th in compensation for full professors and 13th for assistant professors. Owing to the presence of faculty on the committee, it should not be surprising that the adequacy of faculty salaries was one of the committee's most frequent topics of discussion during the period of study; nevertheless, the administration itself appeared to regard Carleton's ranking on this score to be both important and largely outside the college's control. At one committee meeting in 1984, President Robert Edwards made an appearance to appeal for a higher-than-anticipated increase in faculty salaries, citing the "anarchy of competition" to which Carleton was subject and the difficulty the college was having in attracting faculty, especially at the junior level.[34] Information on tuition was likewise available for discussion, as noted in the next chapter.

SUMMARY

As institutions, universities are remarkable in their decentralization and diffusion of authority, if not in the outright disorganization that this decentralization might suggest. Owing to the institution of lifetime tenure among faculty and deep-seated traditions of tolerance, participation and consensual decision making, research universities are more akin to political jurisdictions than to corporations. Although universities may have general institutional objectives, these are seldom spelled out with much specificity. Nonetheless, there exists a general consensus within institutions that they should strive for excellence. Because standards of excellence are disseminated through the various academic disciplines and are widely accepted by faculty and administrators, each institution carries with it a set of goals that few could actually achieve. Consequently, room for improvement always exists, and university leaders always can produce lists of worthwhile projects for which money readily could be spent. As the next chapter shows, the decade of the 1980s offered a period in which some of these ambitious aims could be satisfied.

Appendix 2.1

A Simple Financial Model of a University

To CONSIDER the financial implications of decisions about expenditures, it is useful to examine a simple analysis of a university's revenues and expenditures. This analysis simplifies the situation faced by actual universities in several ways. It lumps undergraduate and graduate students together. In addition, the model, like the empirical work in the study, ignores professional schools. The model also ignores two financially important kinds of enterprises contained within universities that finance themselves largely with earmarked fees for services supplied: (1) so-called auxiliaries, typically consisting of dormitories, dining halls, health services, and book stores; and (2) university hospitals. Although it is not hard to argue that most of the functions of university hospitals are quite distinct from the rest of what occurs in research universities, it is more difficult to make this argument for auxiliaries. By tradition, however, auxiliaries are set up as break-even service operations and are treated separately in most analyses of higher education finances. I follow that convention in this study.

In the part of the university that remains, it is convenient to consider four major forms of revenue and four categories of expenditures. The sources of revenue include (1) tuition, which is equal to the tuition rate per student (T) multiplied by enrollment (E); (2) current gifts and endowment and investment income (G); (3) grants and contracts (C); and (4) federal and state support of university-administered financial aid (F). To relate these revenue sources to the internal–external split described in chapter 2, tuition, gifts, and endowment are internal means of financing, whereas grants, contracts, and federal support are external. Grant and contract revenue by definition is equal to the amount of direct costs associated with the grant (D) plus payments made for indirect costs, where i is the rate that is applied to direct costs, $C = (1 + i)D$.

Expenditures are divided into four categories: (1) instruction (I), (2) research (R), (3) student aid (S), and (4) general administrative and operating costs (A). (Including or excluding capital costs in these expenditures does not affect the basic points made here.) The institution's total research effort is assumed to increase with the amount of sponsored research but not to be identical to it. More specifically, the simple linear relation $R = a + bD$, where $b < 1$, implies that total research rises with sponsored research, but not dollar-for-dollar. It also implies that some research would be conducted in the absence of outside support.[35] Student aid is assumed to be need-based at the margin, which implies that the amount of aid required will be a function of the financial characteristics of the student population and tuition and other costs of attendance. The total aid bill is written simply as $S = (a_s + jT)E$, where a_s is a constant that depends on the income distribution of the student population and j is a constant related to the proportion of students receiving financial aid.

A balanced university budget can be written in terms of total revenues and expenditures:

$$TE + G + C + F = I + R + A + S. \tag{2.1}$$

Because of the differences in the importance of internally and externally funded expenditures, it is useful to split both the expenditures and revenues in this way. External funds abide by the budget function:

$$C - iD + F = D + S_f, \tag{2.2}$$

where S_f is the portion of student financial aid paid for by federal and state aid programs. Indirect-cost payments are treated as unrestricted revenue because they are not restricted as to specific expenditure object. As for internal funds, the budget equation is

$$TE + G + iD = I + (R - D) + A + (S - S_f), \tag{2.3}$$

which may be rewritten as

$$TE + G = [a - (1 + i - b)D] + [(a_s + jT)E - S_f] + I + A, \tag{2.3'}$$

where

T = tuition rate,
E = enrollment of undergraduate and graduate students,
G = current gifts and endowment and investment income,
C = grants and contracts = $D(1 + i)$,
I = expenditures for instruction,
R = expenditures for research = $a + bD$,
D = direct costs of sponsored research,

S = student aid = $(a_s + jT)E$,

A = other administrative and operating costs, and a, a_s, b, i, j = constants.

This equation may be rewritten further as

$$(1 - j)TE + G = [a - (1 + i - b)D] + [a_sE - S_f] + I + A. \quad (2.4)$$

This rewritten expression shows that, in order to raise another dollar for internally financed expenditures, such as administration, it would be necessary to increase tuition by $1/(1 - j)$, to compensate for the requisite increase in financial aid.

With these alternative forms of the budget constraint as background, one can consider a basic question for this study: In which expenditures are we interested, and why? One obvious possible answer is "all of them." If we simply were interested in a measure of the total activity of universities, then we would want to consider all the items on the right-hand side of equation (2.1), which correspond to the sum of internally and externally funded expenditures on the right-hand sides of equations (2.2) and (2.3). (Of course, as noted, the logic of total output would have us include auxiliaries as well; however, they are being ignored here, as is normally the practice, because dedicated fees are used to finance them separately and because their functions are fairly distinct from others we are considering in universities.) But, as "complete" a view as this method might yield, it is likely to miss a basic source of concern about rising expenditures in higher education—the fear that escalating costs either will cause vital functions to be curtailed or will price some students out of the market. If this concern is the dominant one, then it is clear that not all expenditures are equally important. Increases in sponsored research will have quite different implications from increases in items financed by tuition or other forms of unrestricted revenue. For example, if a faculty member is awarded a grant that pays to refit a laboratory with new equipment and to hire several research personnel, there is no necessary diminution of resources to pay for the ongoing functions of instruction and administration. In contrast, an increase in staff and faculty salaries must be matched either by increases in unrestricted income or in appropriately designated gift or endowment income or by decreases in some other category of internally funded expenditure. If these concerns motivate the interest in rising outlays, which I believe is the case, then it is not very helpful to look only at total spending.

The approach taken in this study is to place primary emphasis on internally funded spending, on the principle that externally funded expenditures bring with them earmarked sources of revenue and therefore have a limited impact on the "core" functions of the university. The impact of externally funded spending is said to be limited, rather than nonexistent, because this spending affects the level of unrestricted spending in several ways. One obvious way is through substitution. For example, government funding for scholarships will reduce the amount of internal funds needed to pay for financial aid. A second, more general way that restricted expenditures might affect unrestricted spending is through substitution by donors. The campaign to raise funds for a new library may well reduce the university's receipt of unrestricted gifts.

A third form of interaction between restricted and unrestricted expenditures occurs in the important area of funding research. The model presented in equation (2.3) reflects the facts that sponsored research is a subset of all research conducted in universities, research has widespread costs as well as easily attributable (direct) costs, and sponsoring agencies taken together reimburse universities for more than the direct costs of research. Figure 2.1 illustrates the financial impact of sponsored research. The university's total research costs (R) are shown as a function of the direct costs of sponsored research (D) by the line $R = a + bD$. The assumption that the slope b is less than one implies that cuts in sponsored research will result is less than dollar-for-dollar reductions in total research expenditures. This would be the case, for example, if universities acted toward research in the same way that they do regarding the funding of graduate students, where Ehrenberg, Rees, and Brewer (1993) found considerable substitution between external and internal financing. The revenue received to cover sponsored research is shown in the figure by the line $C = (1 + i)D$; the higher the indirect cost rate i, the steeper this line.[36] At a level of sponsored research D^*, grants and contracts would theoretically pay for all the university's research costs, although this level presumably exceeds the actual level achieved by virtually all universities. The relationship between the costs and revenues associated with research represented here offers one good reason why it is misleading to look only at a university's total expenditures: a decrease in grants and contracts reduces the university's total spending but *increases* the net cost of research—a net cost that must be covered either by an increase in internally generated revenues or by a decrease in other expenditures.[37]

In summary, a sensible analysis of rising outlays must do more than simply measure total expenditures of universities. Not all expenditures have the same implications for the well-being of univer-

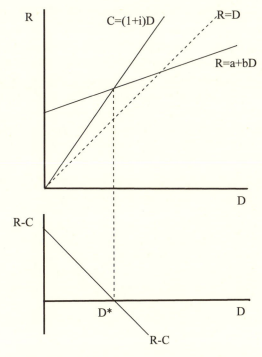

Figure 2.1 The Net Costs of Research.

R = cost of research
D = direct cost of sponsored research
$R - C$ = net cost of research

sities. As the logic of omitting auxiliaries suggests, increases in expenditures that are "tied" to a particular revenue stream may well have different implications than increases in expenditures that are not. Spending associated with grants and contracts, or at least the portion that is a direct cost, is attached to a dedicated revenue source. Likewise, growth in undergraduate financial aid that arises from increases in tuition may be viewed simply as a reduction in the net tuition that is received. Some view internally financed scholarships simply as "price discounts" (as I explain elsewhere, I do not take this approach).

Although it may be helpful in identifying relevant concepts of expense, the simplified accounting framework discussed here does not address some quite important issues of institutional behavior. For example, should one want to predict a university's response to such changes as a reduction in federally funded graduate fellowships or a cut in the allowable rate of overhead on federal grants, it would be necessary to develop a more fully specified model of behavior. This model would have to consider institutional objectives, such as the relative emphasis on undergraduate and graduate instruction, as well as to posit a mechanism by which decisions, such as the setting of tuition, are made. Some research on institutional behavior has been conducted[38]; however, I am not attempting to undertake any in this book.

Appendix 2.2

Decomposing Rates of Growth in Expenditures

IN THEIR 1991 study of costs, Getz and Siegfried (Clotfelter et al. 1991) decompose the annual growth rate in general expenditures per student into four components, based on the identity:

$$E\$/S = (E\$/I\$) \, (I\$/F\$) \, (F\$/F) \, (F/S), \qquad (2.5)$$

where

- $E\$$ = general expenditures,
- S = number of FTE students,
- $I\$$ = instructional expenditures,
- $F\$$ = faculty salaries,
- F = number of faculty.

Because the exponential growth rate $r(\ )$ of a product is equal to the sum of the growth rates of each component, and the growth rate of a quotient is the difference in the growth rates,[39] equation (2.5) implies:

$$r(E\$/S) = r(E\$/I\$) + r(I\$/F\$) + r(F\$/F) + r(F/S), \qquad (2.6)$$

which can be rewritten using more familiar quantities:

$$r(E\$/S) = -r(I\$/E\$) - r(F\$/I\$) + r(F\$/F) - r(S/F), \qquad (2.6')$$

where $I\$/E\$$ is the share of general spending devoted to instruction, $F\$/I\$$ the share of instructional spending constituting faculty salaries, $F\$/F$ the average faculty salary, and S/F the overall student-faculty ratio.

CHAPTER 3

Boom Times for Selective Institutions

The economy bloomed like a plant that had
been cut back and could now grow quicker
and stronger. Our economic program brought
about the longest peacetime expansion in our
history: real family income up, the poverty
rate down, entrepreneurship booming, and an
explosion in research and new technology.
Ronald Reagan, 1989[1]

THE FACT THAT motivates the present study is the extraordinary increase in per-student expenditures and tuition levels in private colleges and universities beginning about 1980. The preceding chapter
reviews a number of explanations for this escalation, but the question that remains unanswered is, Why did the escalation happen
when it did? Before examining in detail the four institutions in this
study, it is necessary to focus on the time period during which these
dramatic increases in spending and tuition occurred. Was this period
unusual in any way? To what extent are the trends observed in the
sample institutions likely to be characteristic of private institutions in
general?

In order to provide a historical context for the detailed analyses to
follow, this chapter begins by noting several developments that
occurred over the period covered by the current study, roughly corresponding to the decade of the 1980s. Following this review is a
detailed examination of the increases in tuitions at the four sample
institutions, and comparisons with a broader range of similar colleges and universities. A brief concluding section notes the connec-
tion among these various developments.

WHAT WAS DISTINCTIVE ABOUT THE 1980s?

As higher education officials entered the 1980s, they anticipated that
a dominant theme of the decade would be demographic decline,

with the number of 18-year-olds expected to fall by 25 percent between 1979 and 1992. To almost everyone's surprise, owing to increases in the enrollment rates of most demographic groups, enrollments did not decline.[2] Moreover, the decade turned out to be a prosperous one indeed, buoyed by a confluence of several largely independent favorable trends in the economy. Private colleges and universities as a whole enjoyed a surge in demand, as measured by the number of applications they received.[3] In setting the context for the empirical analysis that follows, it is useful to review several of the most important developments of the 1980s that affected higher education in general and private research universities in particular. Six developments are noted: (1) the improvement in the economic well-being of the most affluent households, (2) the increase in the economic returns to college training, (3) the concentration of top students in selective colleges and universities, (4) the slowdown in overall inflation in the economy, (5) the rise in real faculty salaries, and (6) the change in the nature of federal support for university research and student financial aid.

Economic Gains Among the Affluent

The 1980s was an especially good decade for those on the top rungs of the economic ladder. In the words of Phillips (1990, p. xii), the decade witnessed "the triumph of upper America." The most prominent bellwether of this improvement was a robust increase in incomes at the top of the income distribution. During the 15-year period covered in the present study, between 1977 and 1992, the mean income of families in the top quintile of the income distribution increased at an annual rate of 1.1 percent, after inflation. By comparison, the incomes of the remaining four-fifths of families barely grew, increasing at only 0.2 percent per year.[4] As illustrated in Figure 3.1, the success enjoyed by those at the top of the income distribution began well before the 1980s. Although the trajectory of the top quintile's average income was not an unbroken string of increases, the overall pattern was one of strong growth, which contrasts markedly with the stagnation of everyone else's incomes during this period.

The well-being of the affluent also received a boost from the tax cuts of 1981 and 1986; the marginal tax rate in the highest income classes dropped over the decade from 70 percent to 28 percent.[5] These reductions partly were offset by a broader definition of taxable income, but it appears that the net effect of the tax changes was

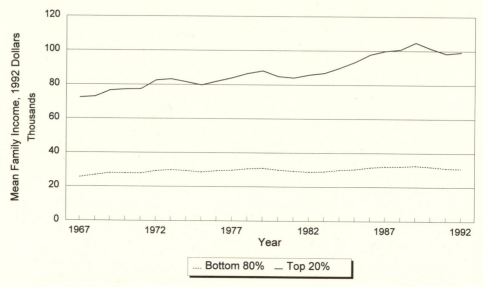

Figure 3.1 Mean Incomes, Top 20 Percent and Others, 1967–1992.
Source: Table 3A.1.

to reduce the effective average tax rates for those in upper-income classes.[6]

A similar increase in the relative well-being of the most affluent households occurred in wealth holding. The 1980s was a decade of solid gains in both stocks and owner-occupied housing, two of the most important sources of wealth for households. After a decade of tepid advance, stock prices rose rapidly during the 1980s: the S&P 500 increased by 181 percent during the 1980s, compared with only 43 percent during the previous decade (U.S. Council of Economic Advisers 1993, p. 453). House prices rose as well, spectacularly in a few metropolitan areas.[7] Another form of wealth the value of which skyrocketed during the decade was art, with Sotheby's aggregate art index increasing more than threefold from 1980 to 1989 (Phillips 1990, Appendix J). In the midst of these advances, the wealthiest households appear to have done especially well. Data from the Survey of Consumer Finances suggest that the share of total net worth held by the wealthiest 1 percent of households increased from 31.5 percent in 1983 to 37.1 percent in 1989 (U.S. House of Representatives 1992a, p. 1566).

Not only were the incomes and wealth of the most affluent families increasing, their average family size fell disproportionately, further increasing their ability to bear the financial burden of college for their children. Between 1977 and 1992, the average size of all families fell 5.1 percent, from 3.33 persons in 1979 to 3.16 in 1992. Over the same period, the average size of families with incomes of $65,000 or more in 1992 dollars (roughly the lower bound for the top quintile of families) fell from 3.72 to 3.38, a decrease of 9.1 percent.[8] With fewer children to put through college, these affluent families had even more resources to finance the college educations of those children whom they did send.

These facts have special relevance for the set of selective institutions that constitute the main focus of the present study. In addition to having unusually high average test scores and strong high school records, the students at these colleges and universities tend to be more affluent than the average college student, and considerably more so than the average high school graduate.[9] Thus, the improvement in the well-being of those at the top of the income distribution fueled their demand for consumption of many kinds, including elite higher education.

Increase in the Economic Returns from College

Among the benefits of attending college is the likelihood that a student's lifetime earnings will increase as a result. On average, college graduates earn more than similarly situated individuals who do not have a college degree. Although it is not a simple matter to determine what portion of this earnings advantage is attributable directly to college education, as distinct from other personal characteristics possessed by college graduates, movements in this earnings advantage do reflect variations over time in the financial rewards of college training. Like other investments that require financial sacrifices in order to reap future rewards, a college education can be said to pay off for most students and, to the extent that higher earnings signify greater productivity, for society. One ready indicator of the rate of return to a college education is the earnings advantage that college graduates enjoy over high school graduates. During the 1970s, this earnings advantage fell noticeably, leading to concerns that America was "overinvesting" in college education.[10] After hitting its nadir around 1980, however, the college earnings advantage rebounded sharply, rising more or less steadily through the decade.[11]

Table 3.1 presents earnings data for the four years examined in the present study, comparing mean earnings of high school graduates with those of college graduates holding only a bachelor's degree. For men, the percentage difference in the two earnings levels, corre-

TABLE 3.1

Mean Earnings, by Education, for Full-Time, Year-Round Workers,
Ages 25–34, Selected Years

	1977	*1982*	*1987*	*1992*
Men				
High school graduates ($)	14,086	19,036	22,990	24,441
College graduates ($)	16,818	24,773	32,555	37,612
Percentage difference (%)	19	30	42	54
Women				
High school graduates ($)	8,983	13,408	16,237	18,918
College graduates ($)	11,207	17,586	24,080	28,979
Percentage difference (%)	25	31	48	53

Source: Data are from U.S. Bureau of the Census, *Current Population Reports*, Series P–60, *Money Income of Households, Families, and Persons in the United States* (Washington, DC: U.S. Government Printing Office). For data for 1977: No. 118 (1979), Table 47; for data for 1982: No. 142 (1984), Table 47; for data for 1987: No. 162 (1989), Table 35; and for data for 1992: No. 184 (1993), Table 29.

Note: High school graduates include those with four years of high school or a high school diploma only. College graduates include those with four years of college or a bachelor's degree only.

sponding roughly to the college earnings advantage, increased from 19 percent in 1977 to an impressive 54 percent by 1992. The pattern for women was much the same, with the difference growing from 25 to 53 percent. The size of the gap in 1992 is the highest recorded in 25 years. Although this rebound may have had more to do with a decline in the earnings of high school graduates than with an increase in those of college graduates, it nevertheless highlights one aspect of the increase in the demand for college. The extent to which this growing earnings gap increased the demand for elite colleges and universities such as those studied in this book is unclear.

Growing Concentration of Top Students

Not only did a college degree become a more valuable commodity during the 1980s, but places at elite, mostly private colleges and universities apparently became relatively more attractive as well. Cook and Frank (1993) present data suggesting that these elite institutions enrolled an increasing share of the nation's best students. As an illustration, they calculated the share of freshmen with high SAT verbal scores who enrolled in a group of highly selective colleges and universities, a group that together enrolled about 25,000, or about 2.5

percent of all freshmen in the country. Between 1979 and 1989, this group's share of all freshmen with SAT verbal scores of 700 or higher increased markedly, from 32 to 43 percent. Similarly, the finalists in the Westinghouse Science Talent Search increasingly became concentrated in a small number of elite institutions. Using the results of previous econometric analyses of college applications, Cook and Frank show that the probability of a high school senior with a high SAT score applying to at least 1 of a group of 33 private selective institutions increased between 1976 and 1987. For example, the probability that a hypothetical student with a combined score of 1300 would apply to one of these institutions increased from .36 to .56 (Cook and Frank 1993, pp. 131–3). Although the average number of applications per student also was increasing over time, this increase is another indication of the apparent growth in the attractiveness of places in selective institutions, particularly among the strongest applicants.

A Surprising Slowdown in Inflation

One feature of the rosy economic environment of the 1980s was a marked deceleration in the overall rate of inflation. As the 1970s ended, inflation had accelerated sharply, for the second time in the decade. In the three years beginning with 1979, buffeted by sharp increases in the cost of fuel, the CPI experienced annual jumps of 9.0, 13.3, and 12.5 percent, respectively. As suddenly as it had begun, however, this inflation cooled: from 1982 to 1990, the CPI grew at an annual rate of only 3.8 percent (U.S. Council of Economic Advisers 1994, pp. 335, 339).

How might this slowdown in inflation have affected colleges and universities? Faculty certainly had little trouble comparing their salary increases with the inflation rate; as the figures presented below indicate, faculty lost ground during the late 1970s. What may be of more importance for higher education finance is the extent to which changes in inflation—both the acceleration and the subsequent slowing—were unanticipated. Not only was the inflation of the late 1970s severe, but it exceeded the rates predicted by most macroeconomic models. Then, for most of the 1980s, the reverse pattern occurred: widely accepted forecasts of inflation were too pessimistic, and consistently so. This pattern of persistent overestimation of inflation is illustrated in Figure 3.2, which compares two-year averages of actual inflation with forecasts that had been published by the Congressional Budget Office (CBO) for the corresponding periods. For example,

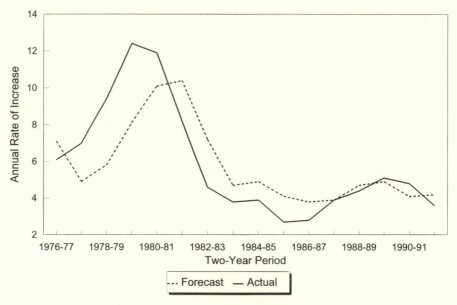

Figure 3.2 Forecast Versus Actual Inflation.
Source: Table 3A.2.

the CBO's forecasts of inflation for the calendar years 1976 and 1977, each made 12 months before the corresponding year was to begin, averaged 7.1 percent. Actual inflation for the two years averaged 6.1 percent, for an overstatement of one percentage point. As the figure shows, forecasts of inflation were too low for the period from 1977–78 through 1980–81 and were too high until 1987–88. The average error in the period of underestimation was 3.0 percent; the average error in the period of overestimation was 1.5 percent.

That this pattern of forecast errors, resulting in consistently pleasant inflation surprises, may have affected the real increases in spending is a reasonable supposition, especially if institutions tended to be slow to respond. Administrators developing budgets for a fiscal year necessarily must begin to work at least 12 months before that year begins and therefore must rely on forecasts of inflation. Any attempt to target expenditures in terms of real levels will necessitate adding expected inflation. This behavior certainly would apply to the setting of such important parameters as the overall increases for wages and salaries and the increase in tuition and fees. If budgets were set, year after year, using inflation projections that consistently overestimated actual inflation, real spending would tend to rise faster than intended. Whether such surprises would have similar effects for a number years running is unclear, but evidence shows that, for at least one of the institutions covered in the present study, the impact of consistent overestimates of inflation did not go unnoticed. The minutes of Carleton College's budget committee reveal a recurrent complaint by students on the committee—that budget projections using inflation assumptions that subsequently proved to be too high had the effect of increasing tuition more than planned. In 1986, the committee agreed that inflation assumptions thereafter would be adjusted if such overestimates occurred.[12]

The Rebound in Real Faculty Salaries

Owing to their large share of university budgets, faculty salaries inevitably exert a prodigious influence on overall university costs. After a decade during which they lost ground to inflation, faculty salaries moved ahead in real terms throughout the 1980s. The relatively high rates of inflation in the 1970s eroded real faculty salaries. As shown in Figure 3.3, general price inflation outstripped the annual increases in average faculty salaries between 1971/72 and

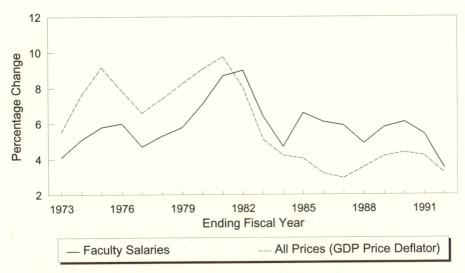

Figure 3.3 Annual Increase in Faculty Salaries and Prices.

Source: Academe (March/April 1992) Table 1; and U.S. Council of Economic Advisers (1993) p. 352.

Note: The years shown on the horizontal axis refer to the change from the previous academic year. For example, 1973 refers to the change between the 1971/72 and 1972/73 academic years.

1980/81, leading to a 16 percent decline in the average faculty salary over the period. However, this relationship was reversed beginning with the 1981/82 academic year. Whether a result of an effort to restore the buying power lost during the recent inflationary period or of the surprisingly low inflation that now characterized the economy, or a combination of the two factors, real faculty salaries rebounded smartly, as shown in Figure 3.4. Between 1980/81 and 1991/92, both the average faculty salary and the salary of full professors alone increased in real terms by 18 percent. For assistant professors, the increase was 20 percent. By 1992, these average salaries, when calculated in real terms, stood roughly where they had been 20 years before.[13]

As significant as it was, when compared with the trajectories of earnings in other professional groups, this improvement in the real salaries of faculty was by no means extraordinary. For example, in the period from 1980 to 1992, when the earnings of full professors increased at an average annual rate of 1.3 over inflation, the real earnings of nonsupervisory attorneys increased at a 1.1 percent annual rate, those of chief legal officers at 1.4 percent, and those of physicians at 2.3 percent.[14] According to Bok (1993, Figure 4–1,

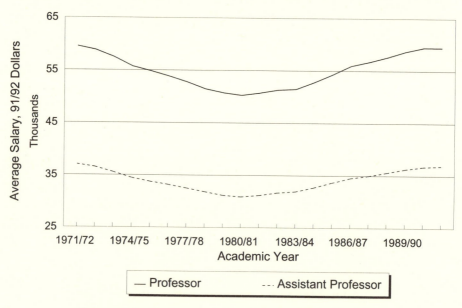

Figure 3.4 Average Faculty Salaries, Two Levels.
Source: Table 3A.4.

p. 66), some groups fared even better, notably surgeons, Wall Street lawyers, and chief executive officers of Fortune 500 companies.

The rebound in faculty salaries is reflected in the broader index of input prices measured in the HEPI, shown in Figure 3.5, which gives substantial weight to faculty salaries and other wage payments.[15] From the perspective of a given college or university, are faculty salaries and the prices of other important inputs properly viewed as an exogenous force to be reckoned with, as in the textbook firm, which purchases inputs in competitive factor markets? Certainly this model of competitive factor markets appears to fit the bill when it comes to buying most manufactured equipment or to the hiring of new faculty in the national market for academic labor. For these inputs, the institutions wishing to hire or purchase have little choice but to pay the salaries and other prices set by the market. But, because they are among the largest firms in their local markets, many colleges and universities hold some of the power of the monopsonist, particularly in the case of faculty and staff who are tied to a locality; to this extent, an institution can exert some control over the salaries and prices that it pays for some inputs.[16]

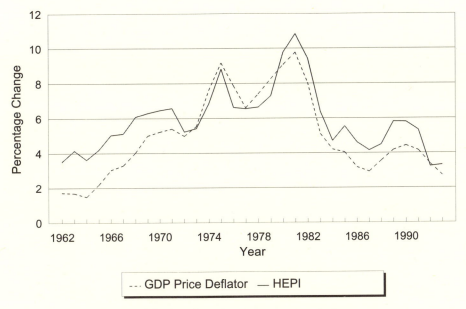

Figure 3.5 Inflation: All Prices and the HEPI.
Source: Data are from Research Associates of Washington (1994).

Trends in Federal Support

Federal programs are a significant source of revenue for higher education in general and for research universities in particular, accounting for about 15 percent of current fund revenue of private colleges and universities in 1991/92 (U.S. Department of Education 1994, Table 318, p. 326). The largest share of these funds supports student financial aid and university research. Figure 3.6 plots the real value of federal expenditures for university research and for other postsecondary programs (the most important of which were the cost of grants and loans to students) from 1965 to 1992. As the graph shows, the most prominent trend in this federal spending was the leveling off that occurred after 1975, following a decade of rapid growth. Between 1975 and 1992, research funding, including that

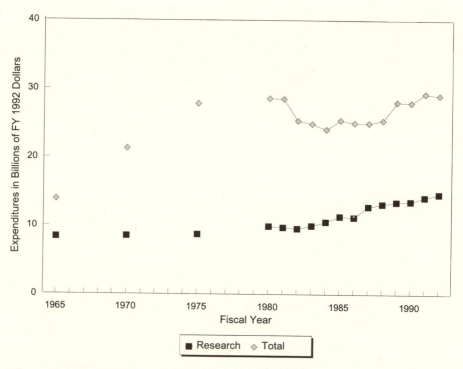

Figure 3.6 Federal Expenditures on Higher Education.

Source: Data are from U.S. Department of Education (1992), Table 345.

Note: Research refers to research at educational institutions. Total includes research as well as on-budget federal support for postsecondary institutions.

sponsored by the National Science Foundation, increased by \$5.9 billion, in constant 1992 dollars, whereas other spending fell by \$4.7 billion. Because it did not grow in real terms, federal funding as a percentage of revenues of private colleges and universities fell during the 1980s, from 18.8 percent in 1980/81 to 15.3 percent in 1991/92 (U.S. Department of Education 1994, Table 318, p. 326).

Two aspects of federal support of research appear to have made it more difficult for the top research universities to receive support for their research projects during this period. First, as Geiger and Feller (1993) have shown, there was a subtle redistribution of research activity among universities, with the premier research universities accounting for a shrinking share of total research expenditures. As an illustration, the share of all academic R&D expenditures accounted for by the top 30 institutions fell from 45.1 percent in 1979/80 to 42.3 percent in 1989/90 (Geiger and Feller 1993, Table 2). Second, equally subtle changes in the awarding of federal grants had the effect of increasing the share of costs borne by institutions. Quite apart from negotiated indirect cost rates, it apparently became much more common for federal granting agencies to ask universities for matching expenditures or cost sharing in the process of awarding grants.[17] Regardless of whether negotiated indirect costs systematically fail to cover the full costs of research, as some have argued,[18] these trends had the effect of reducing the importance of federal support to the top research universities.

As for other federal support, the most prominent shift was away from grants and toward loans as the preferred form of student financial aid. Counting loans at their face value, total federal student financial aid decreased slightly between 1980/81 and 1988/89, from \$20.6 to \$19.9 billion. This 3.7 percent decline was the combination of a 31 percent increase in loans and a 36 percent decrease in grants and college work-study. If the cost of loans was valued at one-half the face value of the loans, then total federal support would have decreased by 14.7 percent (Clotfelter et al. 1991, pp. 99–100).[19] Because econometric studies suggest that financial aid affects the enrollment decisions of college applicants, it is reasonable to believe that these changes had an impact on enrollment patterns.[20]

THE ESCALATION IN TUITIONS AT THE SAMPLE INSTITUTIONS

As we have seen, beginning in the late 1970s the tuition levels charged by private colleges and universities surged, and all four institutions examined in the present study participated in this trend.

For the 1976/77 academic year, Harvard charged $4,100 in tuition and mandatory fees. By 1991/92, the comparable charge had risen to $16,560, a fourfold increase, representing an average annual growth rate of 9.3 percent. Nevertheless, among the four institutions, Harvard's growth was the slowest. Duke's average rate was 10.1 percent, Chicago's was 10.2 percent, and Carleton's was 10.4 percent. Even accounting for the inflation over this period (5.7 percent per year using the GDP price deflator), these increases in tuition represented substantial increases in real dollars. Figure 3.7 plots the rise in the inflation-adjusted levels of tuition and fees for the four institutions over the period 1976/77 to 1992/93 and adds for comparison the average level for all the members of the Consortium on Financing Higher Education (COFHE), a group of private, selective institutions. It is readily apparent not only that the levels marched relentlessly upward, but that they did so in close formation. Except for occasional jumps—such as Harvard's and Carleton's in the academic year ending in 1983, Chicago's in 1987, and Duke's in 1989—the four institutions more or less retained their positions and did not diverge from the general trajectory denoted by the average for all COFHE institutions.

The apparent bunching of tuitions and tuition increases is consistent with the observations of Rothschild and White (1993), who note that colleges and universities are aware of price differences and avoid large divergences from institutions that they view as competing for the same students. In the case of highly selective institutions, such as those studied here, the authors argue that the relevant market of potential students is largely a national one. They further point out that both colleges and universities in a given market are competing for some of the same students; universities are simply "multiproduct enterprises that operate in many markets," one of which is the market for undergraduate education (Rothschild and White 1993, p. 23). Although this portrait of market awareness resonates with most economists, little research on this behavior has been conducted, other than that related to the Justice Department's investigations into the collaboration among institutions over financial aid awards. Moreover, that collaboration applies to the pricing of education for individual students more than it does to the setting of the "sticker price" that is represented by published tuition and fees.

Nevertheless, close observation of individual institutions lends weight to the notion that colleges and universities do pay close attention—both to the prices of their competitors and to how their own price may affect the demand by potential matriculants. Comparisons are feasible because data on the tuitions charged by competing insti-

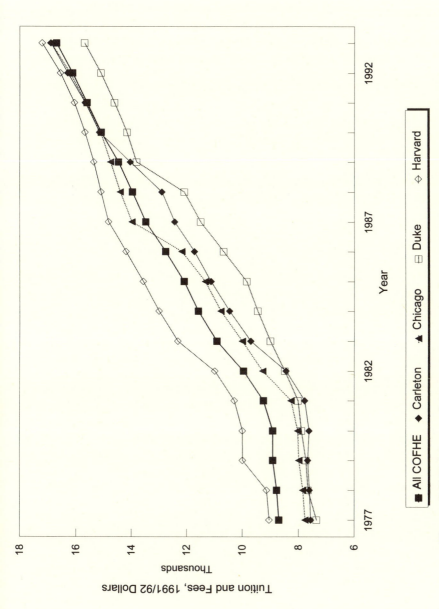

Figure 3.7 Tuition and Fees, Four Institutions and All COFHE Institutions.
Source: Table 3A.5.
Note: The GDP price deflator was used to deflate.

tutions are easily obtained from informal contacts, surveys carried out by such associations as COFHE or published college guides, such as *Peterson's* and *Barron's*. Information on admissions outcomes, measured by numbers of applications, acceptances, and matriculants, is also readily available. Institutions appear to pay close attention to this information and to consider the likely impact of their pricing decisions on their admissions as well as on their budgets.

Carleton College whose budget committee deliberated in recorded sessions about these issues, provides an illuminating example of how one institution viewed itself in this market. The college routinely used three groups of institutions for comparison: (1) a group of Midwestern colleges, (2) a group of highly selective national colleges, and (3) a group of highly selective national universities.[21] Throughout the period covered by this study, Carleton had the highest tuition among the first group but was below the average of each of the other two. In setting its tuition each year, the college appeared to be very aware of its place in these rankings and endeavored not to institute any policy that would change its position dramatically. In one meeting, the college's pricing strategy was described explicitly as one of maintaining a tuition level between those of the Midwestern colleges and the national colleges, a strategy that could be consistent with this balancing of effects.

Not only was Carleton aware of its competitors' prices, the budget committee's deliberations revealed considerable interest and not a little sophistication regarding the effects of tuition increases on ability to attract good applicants. The director of admissions routinely was invited to give advice about the likely effect of contemplated tuition increases. During these sessions, he brought studies that have become a staple for admissions offices in private selective institutions, including "overlap" analyses of the success in attracting students who had been accepted both to Carleton and to similar institutions, as well as surveys of accepted students that asked why they did or did not enroll at Carleton. With respect to the tuition ranges under discussion at Carleton during this time, the prevailing belief appeared to be that tuition increases would not have a serious impact on the number or quality of the students applying to Carleton, but that applicants' perceptions of the quality of the college would have such an impact.[22] In fact, one report presented to the committee in 1980 called for a policy of "aggressive pricing."[23] In 1988, Carleton president Stephen Lewis urged the committee to endorse an extraordinary tuition increase, arguing that it would enable the college to reduce the spending rate on the endowment.[24] In another discussion, administrators expressed confidence that tuition increases could be undertaken without harm, because Carleton's tuition was inexpensive relative to those of national institutions.[25]

To put this line of discussion into the context in which the institutions themselves were operating during this period, it is useful to review some of the basic indicators of success in undergraduate admissions. A fear underlying discussions surrounding the setting of tuition, which is alternately spoken and implicit in the reported meetings of the Carleton budget committee, is that excessive increases will hurt the ability of the admissions office to attract able students. To track admissions strength and comparative selectivity, colleges and universities pay especially close attention to two indicators: (1) the percentage of applicants to which an institution offers admission; and (2) the percentage of accepted applicants who choose to matriculate, the latter being known as the "yield rate." Other measures of the quality of matriculants also are used widely to indicate selectivity, such as average standardized test scores or the percentage of students with high rankings in their high schools.

Table 3.2 presents admissions data for the four institutions over the period of study. By most standards, all four are very selective indeed, with acceptance rates ranging from 57 to 17 percent in 1992, and yield rates from 31 to 74 percent. For all the institutions with the exception of Harvard, these measures show clear trends: acceptance rates declined, suggesting greater selectivity, and yield rates declined as well. The latter trend would seem to indicate decreasing success in attracting matriculants. This interpretation is doubtful, however, given the strong evidence that high school students, especially those applying to selective colleges and universities, were applying to a higher average number of institutions than in previous years. Assuming that this increase in applications was directed at a fairly constant set of institutions and that enrollments did not increase, a fall in yield rates was the inevitable result. Yet, among the four institutions studied here, Harvard seems to have been immune from this particular effect. The third indicator shown in the table, the percentage of students who were in the top 10 percent of their high school classes, suggests an increase in the quality of entering classes at Carleton and Duke and no trend in those of the remaining two universities.

Despite sharp increases in tuition over this 15-year period, therefore, none of the four institutions examined here seems to have experienced any obvious ill effects. What did result, for all four, were increases in the percentage of undergraduates who received need-based financial aid. Because the formula that all the institutions used to calculate financial aid was based on the difference between the

TABLE 3.2
Selected Admissions Indicators for Four Institutions, Four Sample Years

	1976/77	1981/82	1986/87	1991/92
Carleton				
Percentage of applicants accepted	70	51	48	57
Yield rate[a]	50	47	39	33
Percentage of students in top 10% of high school	60	66	76	74
Percentage of students receiving financial aid	45	57	57	58
Chicago				
Percentage of applicants accepted	60	46	44	45
Yield rate[a]	45	39	42	31
Percentage of students in top 10% of high school	NA	69	78	69
Percentage of students receiving financial aid	60	66	67	80
Duke				
Percentage of applicants accepted	39	36	26	29
Yield rate[a]	50	44	47	43
Percentage of students in top 10% of high school	75	73	76	88
Percentage of students receiving financial aid	29	30	37	38
Harvard				
Percentage of applicants accepted	18	16	17	17
Yield rate[a]	76	74	71	74
Percentage of students in top 10% of high school	98	90	95	95
Percentage of students receiving financial aid	66	67	70	74

Source: Peterson's Guide to Four-Year Colleges (Princeton, NJ: Peterson's Guides 1978, 1983, 1988, and 1993).
[a]Matriculants as percentage of accepted applicants.
NA: not available.

costs of attendance (of which tuition is the largest component) and estimates of families' ability to pay, it is not surprising that an increasing proportion of applicants would become eligible for such assistance during a period in which tuitions increased faster than incomes.

LOFTY AMBITIONS IN A TIME OF PLENTY

As the previous chapter suggests, one consequence of the organizational peculiarities of private research universities is an all-encompassing striving for excellence, one that suffuses the culture of the institution, manifests itself in a continually revised list of worthy but unfunded projects, and is restrained only by the limited nature of the available resources. During the 1980s, this insatiable appetite for excellence encountered market forces highly favorable to their satisfaction by means of increases in tuition—the principal source of revenue for virtually all private research universities. Events conspired to make the acceptance to one of the 50 most selective colleges and universities a commodity with few peers—one that was rationed not by price, but by "merit." These institutions, already enrolling a disproportionate share of the nation's high-income students as well as its most able students,[26] found the demand for spots in their entering classes stimulated by good economic times among affluent households and by an apparently heightened appreciation for the type of education that they were offering. The coincidence of these developments is suggested in Figure 3.8, which plots average tuition at private universities and the mean income of the most affluent 20 percent of families. After increasing modestly in real terms during the

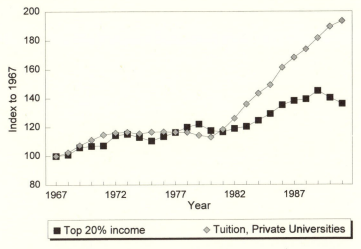

Figure 3.8 Tuition and Top Quintile Average Income.
Source: Table 3A.1: U.S. Department of Education (1992), Table 301.
Note: Indices are relative to 1967 real values.

1970s, both tuition and mean income accelerated after about 1980. These trends do not prove anything about causation, but they do provide one possible explanation for why demand for the limited places at selective institutions increased after 1980.

Although they in no way determined behavior, these circumstances certainly made it easier for private institutions to raise tuitions at rates faster than those which would have been necessary simply to maintain existing levels of quality.[27] Because virtually all the selective institutions individually decided to increase their tuition at similar rates, and all provided similar need-based financial aid to undergraduates, no single institution damaged its ability to attract able students. The result was an increase in tuition-based revenues all around, some of which would be used to make up for shortfalls in federal funding.

If correct, this interpretation of events offers at most a partial explanation for increases in outlays during the 1980s. It may suggest the means by which selective institutions were able to raise tuitions, but it does not explain *why* this happened. It is hoped that a closer examination of a few such institutions will provide a fuller and more satisfying answer to this question.

Appendix 3.1

Supplementary Tables for Chapter 3

TABLE 3A.1

Mean Family Incomes, Selected Percentile Ranges, 1967–1992, in Constant 1992 Dollars

	Mean Family Income, 1992 Dollars		
Year	All	Top 20%	Others
1967	34,859	72,253	25,511
1968	35,983	72,900	26,754
1969	37,674	76,549	27,955
1970	37,728	77,192	27,862
1971	37,705	77,412	27,778
1972	39,894	82,534	29,234
1973	40,491	83,226	29,807
1974	39,768	81,601	29,310
1975	38,810	79,814	28,559
1976	39,846	81,962	29,317
1977	40,545	84,040	29,671
1978	41,760	86,631	30,542
1979	42,310	88,165	30,846
1980	40,869	84,915	29,858
1981	40,234	84,202	29,242
1982	40,198	85,881	28,777
1983	40,597	86,921	29,016
1984	41,931	89,970	29,921
1985	42,956	93,356	30,356
1986	44,707	97,784	31,438
1987	45,553	99,875	31,973
1988	45,788	100,736	32,051
1989	46,962	104,844	32,492
1990	45,785	101,338	31,897
1991	44,539	98,406	31,072
1992	44,483	99,252	30,791

Source: Data are from U.S. Bureau of the Census, *Current Population Reports*, Series P60, No. 184, *Money Income of Households, Families, and Persons in the United States: 1992* (Washington, DC: Government Printing Office, 1993), Table B–7; and author's calculations.

TABLE 3A.2

Comparison of CBO Forecasts with the Actual Rate of Inflation

Two Year Period	CBO Forecast of Two-Year Average Inflation Rate, in CPI	Actual CPI Two-Year Average from CBO	Overestimate	Underestimate
1976–77	7.1	6.1	1.0	—
1977–78	4.9	7.0	—	2.1
1978–79	5.8	9.4	—	3.6
1979–80	8.1	12.4	—	4.3
1980–81	10.1	11.9	—	1.8
1981–82	10.4	8.2	2.2	—
1982–83	7.2	4.6	2.6	—
1983–84	4.7	3.8	0.9	—
1984–85	4.9	3.9	1.0	—
1985–86	4.1	2.7	1.4	—
1986–87	3.8	2.8	1.0	—
1987–88	3.9	3.9	—	—
1988–89	4.7	4.4	0.3	—
1989–90	4.9	5.1	—	0.2
1990–91	4.1	4.8	—	0.7
1991–92	4.2	3.6	0.6	—

Source: Data are from U.S. Congressional Budget Office (1993), Table A–2.

TABLE 3A.3
Annual Increases in Faculty Salaries and Prices

Period	Percentage Change in	
	Faculty Salaries	All Prices (GDP Price Index)
1971/72 to 1972/73	4.1	5.5
1972/73 to 1973/74	5.1	7.6
1973/74 to 1974/75	5.8	9.2
1974/75 to 1975/76	6.0	7.9
1975/76 to 1976/77	4.7	6.6
1976/77 to 1977/78	5.3	7.4
1977/78 to 1978/79	5.8	8.3
1978/79 to 1979/80	7.1	9.1
1979/80 to 1980/81	8.7	9.8
1980/81 to 1981/82	9.0	8.0
1981/82 to 1982/83	6.4	5.1
1982/83 to 1983/84	4.7	4.2
1983/84 to 1984/85	6.6	4.0
1984/85 to 1985/86	6.1	3.2
1985/86 to 1986/87	5.9	2.9
1986/87 to 1987/88	4.9	3.6
1987/88 to 1988/89	5.8	4.2
1988/89 to 1989/90	6.1	4.4
1989/90 to 1990/91	5.4	4.2
1990/91 to 1991/92	3.5	3.2

Source: Data are from *Academe* (March/April 1992), Table 1; and U.S. Council of Economic Advisers (1993), p. 352.

TABLE 3A.4

Average Faculty Salaries, in 1991/92 Dollars

Year	Full Professor	Associate Professor	Assistant Professor	Instructor	All Ranks
1971/72	59,505	44,884	37,016	29,952	43,491
1972/73	58,809	44,742	36,513	29,489	42,900
1973/74	57,489	43,738	35,557	28,690	41,897
1974/75	55,717	42,430	34,429	27,805	40,606
1975/76	54,858	41,658	33,738	27,351	39,904
1976/77	53,880	40,915	33,137	26,863	39,192
1977/78	52,779	40,155	32,491	26,364	38,428
1978/79	51,481	39,242	31,782	25,814	37,554
1979/80	50,744	38,500	31,123	25,183	36,879
1980/81	50,297	38,056	30,849	24,916	36,520
1981/82	50,747	38,325	31,153	24,954	36,847
1982/83	51,325	38,763	31,656	25,333	37,302
1983/84	51,517	38,833	31,896	25,550	37,477
1984/85	52,834	39,714	32,681	26,080	38,399
1985/86	54,328	40,760	33,637	26,767	39,485
1986/87	55,950	41,897	34,543	27,280	40,626
1987/88	56,731	42,401	34,991	27,344	41,153
1988/89	57,619	43,431	35,606	27,641	41,798
1989/90	58,680	44,231	36,262	27,912	42,487
1990/91	59,441	44,719	36,732	28,140	42,997
1991/92	59,428	44,753	36,866	28,270	43,030

Source: Calculations using *AAUP Bulletin 58* (summer 1972), p. 197, Table 13; *Academe* (March/April 1992), p. 8, Table 1; and U.S. Council of Economic Advisers (1993), p. 352.

TABLE 3A.5

Tuition and Fees, Four Sample Institutions and COFHE Average,
1976/77–1993/94

Year	Average Tuition and Fees					Ratio of 1991/92 Prices to Current Prices
	All COFHE	Carleton	Chicago	Duke	Harvard	
1976/77	3,942	3,425	3,517	3,330	4,100	2.21
1977/78	4,275	3,702	3,817	3,725	4,450	2.06
1978/79	4,699	4,037	4,207	4,073	5,265	1.90
1979/80	5,126	4,375	4,612	4,535	5,745	1.74
1980/81	5,834	4,903	5,215	5,055	6,490	1.59
1981/82	6,786	5,755	6,320	5,785	7,490	1.47
1982/83	7,818	6,951	7,164	6,450	8,820	1.40
1983/84	8,644	7,810	8,043	7,059	9,700	1.34
1984/85	9,389	8,640	8,802	7,650	10,540	1.29
1985/86	10,226	9,398	9,756	8,556	11,370	1.25
1986/87	11,115	10,250	11,521	9,485	12,225	1.21
1987/88	11,916	11,015	12,300	10,320	12,890	1.17
1988/89	12,867	12,485	13,125	12,286	13,665	1.12
1989/90	14,009	14,070	14,025	13,143	14,560	1.08
1990/91	15,091	15,160	15,135	14,133	15,530	1.03
1991/92	16,124	16,296	16,212	15,101	16,560	1.00
1992/93	17,149	17,360	17,346	16,121	17,674	0.97
1993/94	18,140	18,405	18,207	17,163	18,745	0.96

Source: Consortium on Financing Higher Education (1994), Appendix A; and Consortium on Financing Higher Education (various years).

Note: Figures refer to tuition and mandatory fees.

CHAPTER 4

Patterns and Trends in Expenditures

*Within wide limits, institutions can adjust to
whatever amount of money they are able to
raise.*
Howard Bowen, 1980[1]

THIS CHAPTER presents information on trends in real expenditures
for the sample institutions. The data were taken from detailed financial information provided by each of four institutions: Duke, Harvard, Chicago and Carleton. Although efforts have been made to
compile this information in comparable forms, the differences among
institutions in mission, organization, and accounting practices make
it inevitable that the presentations will not be uniform. The aim of
the study was to collect data at five-year intervals beginning in 1976/77,
but the lack of machine-readable data for the early part of the study
period made it impossible to collect a detailed, consistent data set for
any institution. However, other data were used in an attempt to vali-
date the trends observed in the detailed data. As noted in chapter 1,
expenditures for professional schools and medical centers were excluded from the analysis, as were the expenditures of auxiliaries.
The present chapter begins by considering the source of funds and
then turns to how expenditure data may be usefully organized and
presented. Tabulations for the sample institutions follow.

WHICH EXPENDITURES ARE WE INTERESTED IN?

In considering the problem of rising outlays, all expenditures are
not of equal importance, and some changes other than in expenditures are as significant as the expenditures themselves. In this section, I make four arguments. First, outlays as reported are not identical to costs, but for the most part, the differences are not crucial.
Second, changes in internally financed expenditures are of more significance to the current concern over rising outlays than are those
financed by grants and contracts. Third, expenditures may rise for
three conceptually different reasons, and each has different implica-

tions for the assessment of the increases. Fourth, some "real" effects that are either a cause or a by-product of rising expenditures are worth special attention.

Costs, Prices, and Outputs

According to the economics textbook theory of the firm, an enterprise is seen as taking inputs, doing something to them, and producing one or more outputs. Both inputs and outputs may be goods or services. The cost of producing is the forgone economic benefit of the resources used, which, under ideal conditions, is equal to the actual outlays of the firm. This textbook equivalence is not a bad starting assumption in the case of higher education. Probably the largest category of economic cost that is not reflected in published records of university expenditures is the opportunity cost of the land on which the campus is located. Although universities own and therefore do not pay rent on campuses, they forgo significant income by using them rather than renting them out. A similar point applies to the physical plant, with the additional cost being the difference between the economic depreciation and the amounts spent to maintain or refurbish that plant. Another element in true economic cost that always is omitted from reported expenditures is the value of time, including the time of students as well as that donated by trustees and other volunteer workers.[2] However, the available expenditure data cover most of the important economic costs of universities.

Source of Funds

For the purpose of considering the causes and implications of the rise in spending by colleges and universities, it is clear that not all expenditures are created equal. They differ in both their financial impact and their interpretation. One of the basic motivations for interest in expenditures is the increase in tuitions that students and their families must pay. Thus, expenditures financed by tuitions will have a very different interpretation than those financed by grants and contracts. In order to assess the importance of revenue sources, it is helpful to consider the four principal sources of college and university funding: (1) unrestricted revenues (tuition, unrestricted annual gifts, and unrestricted investment income); (2) restricted gifts and endowment income; (3) grants and contracts; and (4) fees and charges for specific services. In accordance with the practice of "fund accounting" that is common in private colleges and universities, every expenditure is assigned to revenue of one of these types. Because of this close correspondence between revenues and expenditures, it is useful to use the source of revenue as a guide to categorizing expenditures.

One type of expenditure that quickly may be separated from others is that for auxiliaries, which are a class of activities that are designed to have their own dedicated fees. Examples include bookstores, dormitories, dining halls, and student health services. By convention, these activities normally are excluded or are treated separately in analyses of higher education, largely because their functions are easily distinguished, are not integrally academic, and may differ from institution to institution owing simply to differences in the make-or-buy decision (the degree to which service activities are contracted out or to which the private market is allowed to provide services). It makes sense to follow this conventional approach in the present case.

Among the remaining three categories, the most important distinction lies in the degree of discretion that an institution has over how to use those revenues. In the case of grants and contracts, it has very little. Revenues from these sources cover direct costs and indirect costs (how well actual costs are covered is a different, although related, point), and institutions must record rather explicitly the purposes for which the revenues are spent, both through budget and grant reports and through audits of indirect cost rates. In the present study, the direct expenditures funded by grants and contracts will be referred to as *externally funded* expenditures. This is not to say, however, that no spillover effects exist between externally funded and internally funded spending. Grants and contracts probably are used occasionally to pay for activities that the institution would have financed out of internal funds had the external funds been unavailable. More obviously, external funding also generates administrative and infrastructure costs that are impossible to assign to outside grants. These expenditures are paid for out of general revenue, one source for which is the overhead recovery from all grants and contracts. Therefore, although most administrative costs are identified as unrestricted, a portion of them certainly arises because of externally funded grants and contracts.

The two categories that remain—spending financed by unrestricted revenues and those financed by restricted gifts and endowments—will be referred to together as *internally financed* expenditures, on the theory that institutions exercise considerable discretion over their use. Institutions, by definition, have considerable latitude to decide how to spend unrestricted revenues. Within the limits set by laws and regulations, private institutions are accountable only to their governing boards and to the test of the market as to how they spend unrestricted funds. Institutions have somewhat less discretion in the case of expenditures financed from restricted gifts and endowments. For the purpose of this study, these expenditures are grouped together with those funded by unrestricted funds as *internally financed* expenditures, based on the reasoning that, in practice, they are much more like unrestricted current expenditures than expenditures on grants and contracts. Because endowments grow out of gifts that the institution accepted and usually solicited, it does not seem unreasonable to believe that most of their conditions are consistent with the institution's aims. To be sure, some gifts are accepted reluctantly, and institutional missions do change over time, but in general, however, the income from most endowments is used for purposes that continue to be fully consistent with institutional goals. Another reason why it is sensible to lump unrestricted and endowed expenditures is that one often is a substitute for the other. Unrestricted funds often are needed, for example, to supplement the income of restricted endowments established for endowed chairs; funds from the endowments attached to restricted scholarships typically are used to bolster an institution's commitment to meet the financial need of students.

The Interplay Between Real and Financial Effects

At least as important as the increases in the level of expenditures themselves and shifts in their composition are the accompanying altered nonmonetary quantities. As noted in chapter 2, colleges and universities have considerable latitude to respond to changes in such economic circumstances as increasing costs. They have the option of responding to changes in the relative cost of inputs by adjusting inputs in precisely the way that textbooks describe the behavior of the firm, that is, by economizing on the use of one input by substituting a less expensive one. For example, a university can minimize the need to hire relatively expensive faculty by shifting some tasks traditionally performed by faculty, such as advising or departmental administration, to other employees. Another widespread form of substitution that has occurred in many business operations, including those in universities, is the substitution of computers for clerical employees, a trend examined in chapter 6.

But there are other available avenues of flexibility that are not typical of those in textbook discussions. One alternative—an option open to almost any economic actor—is to save money in the short run by undertaking actions that may well be unwise in the long run. An institution can save money in the near term, for example, by deferring the maintenance of its buildings and other physical assets. Similarly, it can increase its revenues in the short run by raising the spending rate from its endowment and other financial assets. It also may have some flexibility in the extent to which it uses grants and contracts to cover what otherwise might be considered ordinary expenditures, such as faculty salaries. Or it may accept gifts that will generate costs in excess of the additional revenue generated. Another class of response to rising costs is, of course, simply that of allowing quality to be degraded, such as by increasing the size of courses without providing concomitant improvements, by hiring less talented faculty, or by reducing the amount of financial aid awards. In light of these possibilities, it is useful to combine an analysis of changing expenditures with attention to other important changes in the institutions being studied. Thus, to supplement the attention focused on expenditures, chapters 5 through 8 examine in part non-monetary quantities.

SPENDING, BY TYPE AND DEPARTMENTAL GROUP

Basic to any evaluation of rising expenditures is information about which categories have experienced the greatest increases. In this study, the two dimensions of classification used to define categories of expenditures are (1) the organizational entity, which corresponds roughly to function; and (2) the type of expenditure. Although a contemporary university may contain hundreds of separate administrative entities, including academic departments, institutes, programs, centers, service divisions, and the like, I have tried to minimize the number of departmental groups. Academic departments, the entities directly responsible for most teaching and research, are separated from purely administrative entities, and the latter are further divided between academic units, such as those headed by provosts and deans, and other administrative offices. Given the different functions of the various entities within a university and the continuing interest in the allocation of resources between administrative and academic units, this functional classification is essential to any analysis of rising expenditures in universities. An additional advantage of dividing expenditures by entity in this way is that it allows the apportioning of general university expenses. General administrative functions, such as physical plant or personnel, provide services to all parts of a university, so it is reasonable to assign only a portion of these costs to the arts and sciences enterprise that is the subject of this study.[3]

The other dimension of classification is the type of expenditure. Because universities are labor-intensive enterprises, the largest broad category of expense consists of salaries, wages, and related compensation. In all the expenditure tables in this chapter, fringe benefits are added to salaries to yield total compensation.[4] Moreover, because there are several distinct categories of labor in universities, it is useful to divide this compensation further between faculty and several other classes of employees. Most, but not all, faculty are classified as regular faculty, that is, those who have tenure or are on the "tenure track" and who hold the title of professor, associate professor, or assistant professor. In addition to payments to labor, other types of payments that are distinguished include scholarships, purchases of goods and services, general operating costs, and capital expenditures. The figures used for capital expenditures are based on actual capital outlays on structure and equipment. Averages of several years were used, rather than one year's outlay, because of the inherent lumpiness of capital spending.[5] This approach is best illustrated by turning to the sample universities.

PATTERNS AND TRENDS: DUKE

Detailed Expenditures

Table 4.1 presents a tabulation for Duke that uses the described method of categorization. The top section shows the internally financed expenditures for Duke over the period 1983/84 to 1991/92, in constant dollars, with departments divided into 13 groups and expenditures split into 14 different categories, by type.[6] For each departmental group not entirely in arts and sciences, a portion of all of the group's expenditures was allocated to arts and sciences, using estimates provided by administrators at each university. The same proportions for each line of the table were applied to all years.[7] Although the question of allocation of general expenditures is important, the specific formula used is of secondary importance for the purposes at hand. The primary aim in these calculations is to use a rather simple and transparent method for allocation and to make it relatively easy to calculate what difference it would make if other

TABLE 4.1

Expenditures, Levels and Changes, by Departmental Group and Type: Duke
(Internally Financed Funds Only; in Thousands of 1991/92 Dollars)

Type of Expenditure

| | Compensation | | | | | | |
	Regular Faculty	Other Faculty	Administrative Staff	Nonexempt Workers	Students	Professional Services	Contract Work
Humanities	10,090	2,882	1,643	1,313	60	204	108
Social Sciences	8,170	1,034	1,084	1,321	48	104	83
Natural Sciences	9,305	1,331	2,317	2,591	59	68	129
Engineering	4,221	321	469	505	21	19	16
Library	0	0	3,291	2,699	240	226	37
Student Services	0	70	2,563	1,022	93	83	135
Plant	0	0	292	1,220	1	0	110
Admissions and Financial Aid	0	0	861	607	151	1	109
Arts and Sciences Administration	2,049	800	4,318	1,814	269	398	856
Provost	597	89	1,537	231	51	25	91
Alumni Affairs and Development	0	0	2,949	1,196	27	149	624
General Administration	3	35	3,046	5,250	117	40	440
Subtotal	34,435	6,561	24,371	19,769	1,137	1,315	2,738
Athletics	0	0	2,935	456	80	117	163
Total	34,435	6,561	27,306	20,226	1,217	1,433	2,901

Changes in Expenditures 1983/84 to 1991/92
Type of Expenditure

| | Compensation | | | | | | |
	Regular Faculty	Other Faculty	Administrative Staff	Nonexempt Workers	Students	Professional Services	Contract Work
Humanities	3,642	2,099	854	542	29	101	35
Social Sciences	2,437	629	518	372	−50	82	42
Natural Sciences	3,431	804	1,083	632	−90	−7	43
Engineering	1,812	270	206	87	−1	1	11
Library	0	0	740	356	74	70	−1
Student Services	0	65	990	233	63	25	100
Plant	0	0	38	109	−3	−1	23
Admissions and Financial Aid	0	−9	144	303	147	1	85
Arts and Sciences Administration	890	420	2,728	707	76	246	473
Provost	−239	29	906	26	44	−8	77
Alumni Affairs and Development	−8	0	1,244	420	24	4	540
General Administration	−3	33	857	1,549	8	−194	218
Subtotal	11,961	4,339	10,307	5,337	322	320	1,646
Athletics	0	0	1,081	148	13	13	−14
Total	11,961	4,339	11,388	5,485	335	333	1,633

Source: Calculations using unpublished data from Duke University.

TABLE 4.1 (*cont.*)

Computers	Financial Aid	Supplies	General Operating Expenses	Capital	Maintenance	Residual	Total
42	3,513	333	1,250	140	54	7	21,639
86	2,790	304	1,129	1,478	15	4	17,650
253	3,999	943	902	3,894	1	−0	25,794
93	1,477	199	183	184	60	2	7,771
88	12	241	360	3,789	207	6	11,196
407	244	175	112	1,819	60	0	6,785
2	0	118	867	389	1,050	0	4,048
213	16,124	67	686	1	22	1	18,842
405	3,229	518	4,916	804	134	16	20,525
773	41	142	50	54	34	1	3,715
573	1	272	1,587	55	46	1	7,480
−462	27	3,060	−7,635	28	333	−53	4,229
2,471	31,457	6,373	4,409	12,635	2,017	−15	149,673
8	4,052	526	3,566	129	386	2	12,420
2,479	35,508	6,900	7,974	12,764	2,402	−13	162,093

Computers	Financial Aid	Supplies	General Operating Expenses	Capital	Maintenance	Residual	Total
−62	2,233	166	737	−109	26	12	10,306
−4	1,757	116	7	1,404	−10	−3	7,298
123	2,216	173	121	2,957	90	9	11,584
60	729	26	18	−1,348	−36	−16	1,818
−44	11	34	186	1,190	150	1	2,766
78	197	62	−489	985	23	−1	2,331
2	0	−18	−64	77	232	0	395
−280	10,873	50	305	1	20	1	11,640
−528	1,543	168	3,007	494	2	18	10,243
710	−16	111	−361	26	10	1	1,316
393	1	90	236	−10	1	1	2,935
174	20	402	−2,458	−204	26	−36	392
620	19,564	1,379	1,244	5,464	534	−14	63,024
−2	2,114	142	589	−318	214	−496	3,485
618	21,678	1,522	1,833	5,146	747	−510	66,508

reasonable weights were used. In all likelihood, the specific allocation rules will make little difference in any assessment of overall
trends and patterns of expenditures.[8]

As noted in appendix 4.1, this table takes into account inter-
departmental charges, such as a payment by the English department
to the purchasing department for a box of pencils. Consequently,
the totals in the far-right column of the table more nearly reflect
resource use by the divisions of the university than they would if
transfers were not counted.[9] Mindful of these caveats and limitations, one can view the tables as a rough summary of the university's
expenditures for arts and sciences. The top part of the table gives
the breakdown of total spending for the 1991/92 academic year.
Duke spent an estimated $150 million in the arts and sciences and
engineering, and $162 million if athletics is included. (Recall that
professional schools, the medical center, and most auxiliaries are excluded.) By departmental group, the natural sciences accounted for
the largest share, $26 million, or about one-fifth of the total. By type
of expenditure, scholarships and graduate assistance comprised the
largest category, at $36 million (including athletics). Of this figure,
scholarships for undergraduates (excluding athletic scholarships)
roughly corresponds to the entry in that column for admissions and
financial aid, or $16 million, whereas the amounts in the various
departmental groups correspond to graduate assistance.[10] Next in
size was faculty compensation, at $34 million, followed by compensa-
tion for administrative staff and nonexempt (hourly) workers. Spending for computers accounted for $2.5 million, and other capital ex-
penditures totaled $13 million.[11]

The bottom half of Table 4.1 shows the changes in expenditures,
in constant dollars, over the eight-year period between 1983/84 and
1991/92. The subtotal on the far-right column indicates that, excluding athletics, total spending increased $63 million during this period,
an increase of more than 70 percent. What is apparent is that a large
share of the total increase in spending can be attributed to just a few
categories.[12]

To make it easier to examine the broad pattern of changes in expenditures, Table 4.2 presents levels and changes only for the subtotals for the rows and columns in Table 4.1. Thus, total spending is
broken down once by departmental grouping and again by type of
expenditure. For each subtotal, the table shows total spending for
the beginning and ending year of the period and other measures of
share and growth. Columns 3 through 5 give a simple way to show
the relative importance of the various categories in contributing to

the overall increase in spending. The contribution of any category is, by definition, the product of its share of the total, shown in the third column, and its percentage increase, shown in the fourth.[13] Columns 3 through 5 in the bottom part of the table show, for example, that faculty salaries accounted for the largest share of spending in 1992 (23 percent), and that the salaries of nonregular faculty showed the fastest growth (66 percent). The category with the largest contribution, however, was financial aid, contributing 13 percent of the total 42 percent increase, or more than 30 percent of the total growth. None of the departmental groups shown in the top section of the table contributed much to the overall increase. Columns 6 and 7 express these increases in terms of annual growth rates, both nominal and real.

Internally Funded Versus Externally Funded Expenditures

Because the implications of changes in internally funded expenditures may be radically different from those applying to changes in spending from external funds of various types, it is important to investigate the patterns of funding underlying these expenditures. The remaining columns of Table 4.2 focus on differences between internally funded and externally funded expenditures. The eighth column gives, for 1986/87, the percentage of the category funded with external funds. The departmental group most dependent on outside funding is the natural sciences (more than 40 percent external funding). By category, wages paid to students receive the largest share of outside support, reflecting the work-study program that is an important part of the federal role in financial aid, but which is not shown in the financial aid category. The last four columns show in more detail changes over the eight-year period in expenditures, by type. Overall, internally funded spending decelerated slightly between the 1984–87 and 1987–92 periods, while the growth in externally financed spending remained steady.

To examine further the revenue sources for these spending increases, Table 4.3 shows how the distribution of spending by type of funding changed over the eight-year period for which detailed data were available. Although there was a dip in the share of federal funding for arts and sciences at Duke in the first part of the period, the share actually increased from 1987 to 1992.[14] By 1991/92, about one-fifth of arts and sciences spending at Duke was supported by federal funds, 5 percent was based on sponsored research from

TABLE 4.2

Shares of Expenditure Growth, by Departmental Group and Type of Expenditure: Duke
(In Millions of 1991/92 Dollars Unless Otherwise Indicated)

Department Group	Internally Funded Expenditures 1983/84 (1)	1991/92 (2)	Percent Share 1991/92 (3)	Percentage Increase[a] (4)	Contribution[b] (5)	Annual Growth Rate (1983/84 to 1991/92) Real (6)	Nominal (7)	Percentage Externally Funded 1986/87 (8)	Real Annual Growth Rates 1983/84 to 1986/87 Internal (9)	External (10)	1986/87 to 1991/92 Internal (11)	External (12)
Humanities	11.3	21.6	0.14	0.48	0.07	8.1	11.7	8.9	11.7	12.55	5.9	7.61
Social Sciences	10.4	17.7	0.12	0.41	0.05	6.7	10.3	27.4	6.3	20.38	6.9	12.67
Natural Sciences	14.2	25.8	0.17	0.45	0.08	7.5	11.1	41.5	10.3	-1.54	5.8	5.72
Engineering	6.0	7.8	0.05	0.23	0.01	3.3	7.0	28.3	1.2	10.30	4.6	9.09
Library	8.4	11.2	0.07	0.25	0.02	3.5	7.2	1.0	3.9	82.39	3.3	31.99
Student Services	4.5	6.8	0.05	0.34	0.02	5.3	8.9	0.1	-0.6	0.00	8.8	22.07
Plant	3.7	4.0	0.03	0.10	0.00	1.3	4.9	0.0	5.2	0.00	-1.1	0.00
Admissions and Financial Aid	7.2	18.8	0.13	0.62	0.08	12.0	15.7	19.1	15.6	-7.02	9.9	1.70
Arts and Sciences Administration	10.3	20.5	0.14	0.50	0.07	8.6	12.3	26.4	12.1	63.90	6.6	7.66
Provost	2.4	3.7	0.02	0.35	0.01	5.5	9.1	7.0	7.5	14.77	4.2	-3.72
Alumni and Development	4.5	7.5	0.05	0.39	0.02	6.2	9.9	0.0	6.1	0.00	6.3	0.00
General Administration	3.8	4.2	0.03	0.09	0.00	1.2	4.9	0.4	-0.3	-129.96	2.1	-6.52
Total	86.6	149.7	1.00	0.42	0.42	6.8	10.5	21.7	8.2	7.30	6.0	7.46

Type of Expenditure												
Regular Faculty	22.5	34.4	0.23	0.35	0.08	5.3	9.0	18.6	5.5	8.30	5.2	8.65
Other Faculty	2.2	6.6	0.04	0.66	0.03	13.5	17.2	21.4	23.2	2.75	7.7	2.69
Administrative Staff	14.1	24.4	0.16	0.42	0.07	6.9	10.5	10.5	7.5	14.37	6.5	4.11
Nonexempt Workers	14.4	19.8	0.13	0.27	0.04	3.9	7.6	13.0	4.1	1.65	3.8	5.19
Students	0.8	1.1	0.01	0.28	0.00	4.2	7.8	53.9	11.4	−7.24	−0.2	−1.67
Professional Services	1.0	1.3	0.01	0.24	0.00	3.5	7.1	23.2	11.9	16.05	−1.6	12.67
Contract Work	1.1	2.7	0.02	0.60	0.01	11.5	15.2	31.3	8.6	−4.54	13.3	43.23
Computers	1.9	2.5	0.02	0.25	0.00	3.6	7.3	30.2	3.8	1.23	3.5	4.72
Financial Aid	11.9	31.5	0.21	0.62	0.13	12.2	15.8	34.9	15.8	27.74	10.0	−0.68
Supplies	5.0	6.4	0.04	0.22	0.01	3.0	6.7	21.8	6.7	4.51	0.8	4.21
General Operating Expenses	3.2	4.4	0.03	0.28	0.01	4.1	7.8	25.2	15.1	−11.19	−2.4	14.75
Capital	7.2	12.6	0.08	0.43	0.04	7.1	10.7	17.8	1.4	−14.53	10.5	17.38
Maintenance	1.5	2.0	0.01	0.26	0.00	3.8	7.5	24.2	11.5	−15.61	−0.8	−8.70
Total	86.6	149.7	1.00	0.42	0.42	6.8	10.5	21.7	8.2	7.30	6.0	7.46

Source: Calculations using unpublished data from Duke University.
[a]Change as a percentage of 1991/92 level.
[b]Product of the share and the percentage increase.

TABLE 4.3

Expenditures, by Source of Funds: Duke, 1984, 1987, and 1992 Fiscal Years
(Percentage Distribution)

	Federal			Other Sponsored Research			Gifts and Endowment			Other Unrestricted Funds		
	1983/84	1986/87	1991/92	1983/84	1986/87	1991/92	1983/84	1986/87	1991/92	1983/84	1986/87	1991/92
Humanities	4	4	5	5	5	5	7	7	7	84	84	83
Social Sciences	14	12	26	6	16	10	4	5	4	76	67	61
Natural Sciences	41	36	39	11	6	6	4	10	5	44	48	51
Engineering	20	21	23	8	9	10	7	8	4	65	63	63
Library	0	1	2	0	0	2	5	7	8	95	92	88
Student Services	0	0	0	0	0	0	7	6	7	93	94	93
Plant	0	0	0	0	0	0	0	0	1	100	100	99
Admissions and Financial Aid	30	17	12	2	2	2	15	16	19	54	65	68
Arts and Sciences Administration	25	25	23	3	1	4	6	12	12	66	62	61
Provost	0	0	2	6	7	3	45	34	19	49	59	76
Alumni and Development	0	0	0	0	0	0	3	5	10	97	95	90
General Administration	1	0	0	0	0	0	9	11	3	90	89	96
Total	20	17	19	5	5	5	7	10	8	68	68	68

Source: Calculations using unpublished data from Duke University.

other sources, and 8 percent came from gifts and endowment, leaving about two-thirds of spending funded from unrestricted sources, mainly tuition.

PATTERNS AND TRENDS: HARVARD

Detailed Expenditures

Table 4.4 presents similar tabulations of expenditures for Harvard. As in the previous presentation, expenditures have been classified by administrative unit and type of expenditure. Although every reasonable attempt has been made to make the classes comparable among institutions, several important differences remain. The most important of these, one owing to the considerably more decentralized approach to accounting followed at Harvard and, therefore, to the kind of data available in comparable form, is that Harvard's figures generally apply only to its Faculty of Arts and Sciences—which includes Harvard College, the Graduate School of Arts and Sciences, and the major libraries—and to a number of "affiliated departments," such as the museums and the massive Division of Applied Sciences, whose budgets traditionally have been overseen by Arts and Sciences. (Table A4.3, in the appendix of the chapter, lists each administrative unit included in the tables.)

Not only are the professional schools excluded from these tabulations, as they are with the Duke tabulations, so, too, are most of the central administrative units that serve the entire university, covering such functions as accounting, personnel, campus security, and the office of the president. As a result of this accounting structure, the data for Harvard show both fewer university-produced services and fewer internal "sales" of services than is the case with Duke. The virtue of using this more restricted accounting base is that it greatly reduces the necessity of relying on arbitrary rules for allocating general expenditures to arts and sciences. It does, however, add one more difference between the data sets for Duke and Harvard. Although intra-institutional purchases of services should appear in either case as expenditures by academic departments, they will appear as internal transactions in the Duke data but will be indistinguishable from purchases of outside services in the Harvard data. Other significant differences between the data for the two institutions include marked differences in the list of departments and different classification systems used to classify expenditures by type. These differences in organization and accounting practices are only the most

TABLE 4.4
Expenditures, Levels and Changes, by Departmental Group and Type: Harvard
(Internally Financed Funds Only; in Thousands of 1991/92 Dollars)
Type of Expenditure

	Compensation					
	Regular Faculty	*Other Faculty*	*Administrative Staff*	*Students*	*Support*	*Extra Comp*
General Academic	2,164	271	4,368	6,619	1,469	−11
Humanities	19,944	5,384	5,491	3,746	2,641	−36
Social Sciences	12,122	1,366	2,141	2,955	1,974	−7
Natural Sciences	16,757	1,073	8,200	4,535	6,656	−34
Museums	1,078	6	1,990	197	1,109	
Library	2,357	3	6,535	1,708	7,448	1
Student Services	621	268	4,490	935	1,962	−1
Admissions and Financial Aid	225	0	2,042	502	694	1
Administration	3,292	263	4,258	67	1,201	87
Plant	14	0	3	35	6	
Athletics	496	225	2,667	860	395	
Total	59,070	8,857	42,185	22,160	25,554	1

Changes in Expenditures, 1981/82 to 1991/92
Type of Expenditure

	Compensation					
	Regular Faculty	*Other Faculty*	*Administrative Staff*	*Students*	*Support*	*Extra Comp*
General Academic	1,669	−409	3,413	3,545	964	4
Humanities	6,791	2,543	2,500	1,052	557	2,19
Social Sciences	5,071	576	1,225	809	550	1,17
Natural Sciences	4,862	342	4,703	1,424	1,264	1,60
Museums	−126	6	1,225	−44	27	
Library	−539	3	3,926	679	2,147	1
Student Services	372	113	2,746	390	272	37
Admissions and Financial Aid	−77	0	1,197	246	45	30
Administration	1,235	−95	2,938	542	387	−5,64
Plant	14	0	3	35	6	
Athletics	−92	−98	1,259	257	4	
Total	19,181	2,979	25,135	8,935	6,224	7

Source: Calculations using unpublished data from Harvard University.

TABLE 4.4 (*cont.*)

Operating Expenses	Capital	Supplies	Professional Services	Maintenance	Financial Aid	Computers	Total
6,474	39	246	1,452	171	740	625	24,526
3,861	1,612	790	799	0	5,804	294	50,006
2,905	2,024	539	388	0	4,490	392	31,217
7,134	8,062	5,406	1,616	1,798	6,944	1,963	69,803
3,044	3,164	518	758	584	18	155	12,626
3,772	713	7,201	2,368	1,707	98	314	34,237
10,583	1,082	1,168	2,048	11,545	435	130	35,253
1,988	7	86	103	0	29,128	139	34,929
30,260	9,944	262	6,712	143	199	198	57,675
6,781	720	218	755	8,152	2	3	16,689
3,598	176	988	1,119	1,230	17	15	11,791
80,402	27,543	17,421	18,118	25,329	47,874	4,228	378,752

Operating Expenses	Capital	Supplies	Professional Services	Maintenance	Financial Aid	Computers	Total
2,521	−83	94	826	−62	391	585	13,499
1,840	1,248	95	234	0	2,515	274	21,846
1,460	1,821	278	−124	0	1,962	294	15,097
2,681	1,227	1,258	83	641	2,593	1,932	24,609
1,317	649	−30	86	39	−5	140	3,288
1,503	250	2,048	1,156	29	98	152	11,465
4,360	822	169	1,500	3,667	431	−2	15,213
1,372	3	−25	71	0	13,750	75	16,963
15,360	6,106	50	6,447	143	172	97	27,740
1,456	−1,517	214	445	1,827	2	3	2,489
1,133	−94	−104	285	245	17	14	2,827
35,003	10,432	4,048	11,009	6,527	21,927	3,563	155,036

obvious reasons to re-emphasize the significant sources of noncomparability of figures for different institutions. Equally important are the myriad differences in history, mission, and, indeed, quality, among institutions.

The resulting tabulations for Harvard contain 11 departmental groupings and 13 expenditure types.[15] The time period covered by detailed financial records in electronic form, which extends back to the 1981/82 academic year, is two years longer than for Duke. The top section of the table presents total expenditures for the 1991/92 academic year, expressed in thousands of dollars. For all of arts and sciences, broadly construed to include the affiliated departments listed, total expenditures were some $379 million. The largest share of this total, roughly $70 million, is attributed to natural sciences, which, at Harvard, includes the Division of Applied Science. Administration accounted for the second largest share—$58 million. Humanities was next, at $50 million, followed by student services, admissions and financial aid, the library, and social sciences. By type of expenditure, the broad category of general operating expenses was the largest, totaling $80 million in 1991/92. This category owes its large size relative to that in the Duke tabulation to the exclusion from the Harvard data of most central university support functions. Consequently, many purchases of university-produced services appear as operating expenses, rather than as expenditures for the labor and other inputs used to produce those services. Much the same can be said for the larger size of Harvard's maintenance and professional services relative to those of Duke. The next largest category was compensation for regular faculty (faculty with appointments lasting longer than one year), at $59 million, followed by compensation for staff, at $42 million.[16]

The bottom part of the table shows changes over the decade, by category. Of the 143 cells shown, the largest increase at $15 million, was registered by general operating expenditures in administrative units. The only other item that increased by more than $10 million was the financial aid category of the admissions and financial aid line, which corresponds roughly to undergraduate financial aid, at $14 million. This item also registered the largest gain at Duke over the comparable eight-year period.

Internally Financed and Externally Financed Expenditures

Table 4.5 presents figures for Harvard, comparable to those in Table 4.2, for the 10-year period covered by the detailed financial data. As in the comparable table for Duke, figures are given for the subtotals for departmental groups and types of expenditures. The table's sixth column shows the average annual real growth rate in total expenditures. For all of arts and sciences, real expenditures grew at an average annual rate of 5.3 percent, a rate that would imply a doubling of spending every 13 years. Comparing departmental groups, the table reveals considerable similarity in overall growth rates. With the exception of plant, athletics, and museums, the rates of growth in spending in the remainder of the groups were clustered between 4.1 and 8.0 percent. By contrast, rates of growth among the various types of expenditures showed much larger differences. The most rapidly growing item, perhaps not surprisingly, was computers, which grew from a modest base almost sixfold. Next came professional services, at 9.4 percent, and compensation for professional staff, at 9.1 percent. The extent to which the latter increase can be ascribed to the unionization of Harvard's clerical workers is uncertain; the increase appears to be spread rather evenly between the first and second halves of the period. The only other above-average rate of increase was in financial aid.

The eighth column of the table shows that the sources of funding differ markedly, especially among the departmental groups. The percentage of funds from external funds (grants and contracts) ranged from a low of zero for plant to a high of 49 percent in the natural science units. The share of external funding varied much less by type of expenditure. For Harvard as a whole, about 20 percent of all arts and sciences spending in 1987 was funded by external sources.

The last four columns of the table show how the growth rates of spending differed by period and type of funding. Overall, spending from internal sources exceeded that from external sources during both periods, the difference narrowing considerably during the latter period. Focusing on the four academic departmental groups shows a decline in the growth in internally financed spending in every case. By contrast, external funding accelerated in the humanities and social sciences. However, the natural sciences, the academic division most dependent on outside funding, did not follow this pattern, but instead saw a slowing in the rate of spending supported by external funds.

The patterns of growth by type of expenditure show considerable variation. Double-digit growth rates were recorded in six instances (excluding extra compensation, a small residual category), and not one of the six was compensation for employees. During the first half of the period, there were large increases in internally funded spending for capital and computers. During the second half, expenditures for both computers and for professional services grew very rapidly, and these increases drew from both internal funds and external funds.

TABLE 4.5

Shares of Expenditure Growth, by Departmental Group and Type of Expenditure: Harvard
(In Millions of 1991/92 Dollars Unless Otherwise Indicated)

Departmental Group	Internally Funded Expenditures 1981/82 (1)	Internally Funded Expenditures 1991/92 (2)	Percent Share 1991/92 (3)	Percentage Increase[a] (4)	Contribution[b] (5)	Annual Growth Rate 1981/82 to 1991/92 Real (6)	Annual Growth Rate 1981/82 to 1991/92 Nominal (7)	Percentage Externally Funded 1986/87 (8)	Real Annual Growth Rates 1981/82 to 1986/87 Internal (9)	Real Annual Growth Rates 1981/82 to 1986/87 External (10)	Real Annual Growth Rates 1986/87 to 1991/92 Internal (11)	Real Annual Growth Rates 1986/87 to 1991/92 External (12)
General Academic	11.0	24.5	0.06	0.55	0.04	8.0	11.8	4.4	13.0	3.8	3.0	-17.9
Humanities	28.2	50.0	0.13	0.44	0.06	5.7	9.6	6.4	7.6	-8.5	3.8	16.3
Social Sciences	16.1	31.2	0.08	0.48	0.04	6.6	10.5	21.0	7.2	8.5	6.0	6.6
Natural Sciences	45.2	69.8	0.18	0.35	0.06	4.3	8.2	49.0	5.4	5.5	3.3	3.9
Museums	9.3	12.6	0.03	0.26	0.01	3.0	6.9	22.4	1.3	-8.8	4.7	-11.2
Library	22.8	34.2	0.09	0.33	0.03	4.1	7.9	1.5	3.8	1.9	4.4	5.7
Student Services	20.0	35.3	0.09	0.43	0.04	5.6	9.5	1.6	3.4	1.2	7.9	2.5
Admissions and Financial Aid	18.0	34.9	0.09	0.49	0.04	6.6	10.5	7.4	7.8	0.8	5.5	-0.2
Administration	29.9	57.7	0.15	0.48	0.07	6.6	10.4	1.6	7.0	-3.8	6.1	-1.9
Plant	14.2	16.7	0.04	0.15	0.01	1.6	5.5	0.0	-0.4	0.0	3.7	0.0
Athletics	9.0	11.8	0.03	0.24	0.01	2.7	6.6	0.7	3.6	-13.1	1.8	-12.5
Total	223.7	378.8	1.00	0.41	0.41	5.3	9.1	19.7	5.8	3.8	4.7	4.1

Expenditure Type												
Regular Faculty	39.9	59.1	0.16	0.32	0.05	3.9	7.8	2.7	4.2	−2.1	3.6	6.0
Other Faculty	5.9	8.9	0.02	0.34	0.01	4.1	8.0	33.3	2.8	1.9	5.4	2.5
Professional Staff	17.0	42.2	0.11	0.60	0.07	9.1	12.9	25.1	10.0	3.5	8.1	6.8
Students	13.2	22.2	0.06	0.40	0.02	5.2	9.0	23.7	9.2	3.7	1.2	3.8
Support Staff	19.3	25.6	0.07	0.24	0.02	2.8	6.6	15.4	3.2	0.1	2.3	1.6
Extra Compensation	−0.1	0.0	0.00	6.32	0.00	0.0	0.0	34.2	23.4	38.6	0.0	−2.2
Operating Expenses	45.4	80.4	0.21	0.44	0.09	5.7	9.6	26.0	7.5	5.0	3.9	3.2
Capital	17.1	27.5	0.07	0.38	0.03	4.8	8.6	24.3	3.2	9.5	6.3	−5.4
Supplies	13.4	17.4	0.05	0.23	0.01	2.6	6.5	23.4	4.3	1.4	1.0	3.5
Professional Services	7.1	18.1	0.05	0.61	0.03	9.4	13.2	23.7	6.5	−6.9	12.2	15.2
Maintenance	18.8	25.3	0.07	0.26	0.02	3.0	6.8	0.0	2.3	0.0	3.6	0.0
Financial Aid	25.9	47.9	0.13	0.46	0.06	6.1	10.0	21.8	7.1	7.4	5.2	3.1
Computers	0.7	4.2	0.01	0.84	0.01	18.5	22.4	29.8	13.7	9.9	23.4	22.1
Total	223.7	378.8	1.00	0.41	0.41	5.3	9.1	19.7	5.8	3.8	4.7	4.1

Source: Calculations using unpublished data from Harvard University.
[a]Change as a percentage of 1991/92 level.
[b]Product of the share and the percentage increase.

TABLE 4.6

Expenditures, by Source of Funds: Harvard, 1984, 1987, and 1992 Fiscal Years
(Percentage Distribution)

	Federal			Other Sponsored Research			Gifts and Endowment			Other Unrestricted Funds		
	1981/82	1986/87	1991/92	1981/82	1986/87	1991/92	1981/82	1986/87	1991/92	1981/82	1986/87	1991/92
General Academic	7	4	2	0	0	0	10	4	6	83	91	92
Humanities	7	5	4	6	2	7	38	35	33	49	59	55
Social Sciences	19	14	12	1	7	10	35	27	29	45	52	49
Natural Sciences	51	47	43	1	4	9	26	27	28	22	21	21
Museums	31	24	11	8	3	3	37	47	61	24	26	25
Library	2	2	1	0	0	1	25	26	22	74	72	76
Student Services	2	2	0	0	0	1	9	11	13	90	87	86
Admissions and Financial Aid	10	6	5	0	1	0	56	48	49	34	45	45
Administration	3	2	1	0	0	0	13	20	21	84	79	78
Plant	0	0	0	0	0	0	18	19	16	82	81	84
Athletics	2	1	0	0	0	0	10	15	20	88	85	80
Total	21	18	15	2	2	5	26	26	27	51	53	53

Source: Calculations using unpublished data from Harvard University.

Changes in the sources of funding are shown in more detail in Table 4.6, which gives the percentage distribution of expenditures by type of funding for the beginning, middle, and end of the period under study. The table clearly reveals two striking facts. First, it shows the heavy reliance on federal support in the natural sciences. About one-half of all spending in the natural sciences used federal support, whereas no other group depended on that source for as much as one-fifth of its spending. The second striking fact is the across-the-board decrease in the importance of federal funding. For the university as a whole, the share of total spending supported by federal funds fell from 21 to 15 percent. A slight offset to that decline was the growing importance of nonfederal sponsored research, mainly foundations, which was especially evident in the social sciences. With gifts and endowment remaining steady at about one-fourth of the total, the net decline in outside support resulted in an increase in the share of unrestricted spending from 51 percent in 1982 to 53 percent a decade later. Thus, unrestricted revenue, of which tuition is a major component, came to have a larger importance in funding the rising arts and sciences expenditures.

PATTERNS AND TRENDS: CHICAGO

Detailed Expenditures

The basic expenditure summary for the University of Chicago is presented in Table 4.7. For the most part, the departmental groups and expenditure classifications are similar to those used for Duke and Harvard, with one difference: the classification of payments to students is combined with nonexempt compensation. Because administrative and service components from the entire university were used in making the table, the interpretation of the columns for service-related functions, namely maintenance, professional services, and general operating expenses, is closer to the Duke case than to the Harvard case.

For all of Chicago's arts and sciences in 1991/92, estimated expenditures were roughly $247 million, standing between Duke's $162 million and Harvard's $379 million. As in the comparable case of Duke, Chicago's largest single category of expenditure was financial aid, at $54 million, followed by compensation for regular faculty, at $51 million. Of the departmental groups, admissions and financial aid represented the largest expenditure, $51 million, followed by general administration, at $49 million, and natural sciences, at $48

TABLE 4.7
Expenditures, Levels and Changes, by Departmental Group and Type: Chicago
(Internally Financed Funds Only; in Thousands of 1991/92 Dollars)
Type of Expenditure

| | Compensation | | | | | |
	Regular Faculty	Other Faculty	Administrative Staff	Nonexempt Workers	Professional Services	Contract Work
Humanities	11,398	1,416	962	398	530	34
Social Sciences	11,194	809	784	626	265	0
Natural Sciences	17,144	2,040	3,762	2,135	1,056	0
Library	0	1,935	1,280	2,407	622	0
Student Services	0	0	646	375	86	0
Plant	0	0	1,770	4,602	5,215	0
Admissions and Financial Aid	0	33	810	493	408	0
Provost	488	65	356	101	173	0
Alumni and Development	9	0	4,355	1,054	2,235	0
Arts and Sciences Administration	6,118	881	3,550	1,897	1,970	0
General Administration	3,129	242	13,557	10,592	3,875	0
Other	1,062	676	1,244	1,058	1,307	0
Total	50,543	8,096	33,076	25,737	17,743	34

Changes in Expenditures, 1983/84 to 1991/92
Type of Expenditure

| | Compensation | | | | | |
	Regular Faculty	Other Faculty	Administrative Staff	Nonexempt Workers	Professional Services	Contract Work
Humanities	1,498	561	562	−217	129	34
Social Sciences	2,731	276	267	−183	83	0
Natural Sciences	3,003	1,155	1,791	−554	213	0
Library	0	1,935	−930	108	−630	0
Student Services	−120	−1	185	−39	−18	0
Plant	−79	0	943	3,570	5,024	0
Admissions and Financial Aid	−38	22	249	−26	−186	0
Provost	381	55	140	50	94	0
Alumni and Development	7	0	1,877	−28	−468	0
Arts and Sciences Administration	2,552	535	1,769	−117	1,031	0
General Administration	900	−97	3,331	−915	−777	0
Other	517	427	442	256	637	0
Total	11,354	4,868	10,626	1,906	5,133	34

Source: Calculations using unpublished data from the University of Chicago.

TABLE 4.7 (*cont.*)

Computers	Financial Aid	Supplies	General Operating Expenses	Capital	Maintenance	Residuals	Total
110	375	385	825	626	38	−41	17,055
109	324	151	467	95	21	−164	14,682
617	2,266	1,915	1,595	15,502	242	42	48,315
268	1	3,575	216	30	53	62	10,449
22	26	69	27	321	7	16	1,595
37	0	1,486	3,083	24	1,288	196	17,701
19	48,906	98	429	8	14	24	51,242
44	5	25	271	21	8	3	1,559
75	47	210	920	75	21	151	9,151
514	1,953	838	921	198	515	−1	19,353
2,022	−2	2,464	9,017	2,077	1,437	408	48,819
26	57	595	689	87	51	−141	6,710
3,862	53,958	11,809	18,460	19,064	3,694	556	246,632

Computers	Financial Aid	Supplies	General Operating Expenses	Capital	Maintenance	Residuals	Total
92	219	214	425	543	21	−19	4,063
−92	75	61	151	−45	3	−108	3,217
−45	393	481	1,324	10,401	−179	16	17,997
242	1	1,459	349	−5,640	−21	62	−3,066
11	−25	23	79	321	2	10	430
35	0	693	−149	−37	1,281	165	11,446
−14	30,438	29	933	8	5	14	31,434
43	−144	21	241	17	4	−2	900
−53	−161	15	615	66	−1	84	1,952
270	1,452	523	1,514	−5	316	36	9,877
907	−43	−953	8,384	579	366	−1	11,681
17	56	242	1,967	11	36	−102	4,506
1,413	32,260	2,808	15,831	6,217	1,832	155	94,436

million. By far the largest of the individual cells in the table for 1991/92 expenditures was the cell for financial aid at the admissions and financial line, a figure corresponding roughly to aid for undergraduates.

The bottom part of the table shows the changes in expenditures, in 1991/92 dollars, over the eight years beginning with the 1983/84 academic year. During this period, the largest increase, representing an astounding one-third of the total increase in spending, was in undergraduate financial aid. No other item of increase comes anywhere near that figure in magnitude.

Internally Financed and Externally Financed Expenditures

Table 4.8 presents summary measures for the column and row totals. Overall, internally financed spending at Chicago rose at an annual rate of 6.0 percent, which stands between Harvard's 5.3 percent rate and Duke's 6.8 percent rate. As in the comparable tables for Duke and Harvard, column (5) shows the contribution of each category to the total percentage increase of 38 percent over the period. Not surprisingly, of the departmental groups, admissions and financial aid was the largest contributor to this increase, representing by itself a 13 percent increase in total spending, or one-third of the total. Large percentage increases occurred in several groups, including plant, admissions and financial aid, and the provost's areas of administration. However, the large share of total spending accounted for by admissions and financial aid, combined with the rapid increase, was responsible for that group's major impact on total spending. With respect to types of expenditures, the most rapid growth was recorded for general operating expenses, financial aid, and nonregular faculty.

Regarding the importance of external funding, the third entry in column (8) shows the importance of federal support in the natural sciences. Over the period, externally financed spending slowed between the 1984–87 period and the 1987–91 period, while the rate of growth of internal funding increased. As with Duke and Harvard, the rates of growth in internal and external funding for the various groups over these two time periods varied greatly, looming quite large in cases in which the base amounts were small.

The changes in the sources of funding at Chicago are summarized in Table 4.9. The importance of federal funding decreased, as it did at Harvard. At Chicago, this funding source fell from 22 percent of

TABLE 4.8

Shares of Expenditure Growth, by Departmental Group and Type of Expenditure: Chicago
(In Millions of 1991/92 Dollars)

Departmental Group	Internally Funded Expenditures 1983/84 (1)	Internally Funded Expenditures 1991/92 (2)	Percent Share 1991/92 (3)	Percentage Increase^a (4)	Contribution^b (5)	Annual Growth Rate 1983/84 to 1991/92 Real (6)	Annual Growth Rate 1983/84 to 1991/92 Nominal (7)	Percentage Externally Funded 1986/87 (8)	Real Annual Growth Rates 1983/84 to 1986/87 Internal (9)	1983/84 to 1986/87 External (10)	1986/87 to 1991/92 Internal (11)	1986/87 to 1991/92 External (12)
Humanities	13.0	17.1	0.07	0.24	0.02	3.4	7.1	8.9	4.3	−9.0	2.8	9.8
Social Sciences	11.5	14.7	0.06	0.22	0.01	3.1	6.7	37.1	−0.5	20.3	5.3	−5.0
Natural Sciences	30.3	48.3	0.20	0.37	0.07	5.8	9.5	64.2	1.9	1.5	8.2	2.4
Libraries	13.5	10.4	0.04	−0.29	−0.01	−3.2	0.4	3.8	−12.0	7.1	2.1	0.6
Student Services	1.2	1.6	0.01	0.27	0.00	3.9	7.6	0.0	−0.3	0.0	6.5	0.0
Plant	6.3	17.7	0.07	0.65	0.05	13.0	16.7	0.0	33.3	0.0	0.8	0.0
Admissions and Financial Aid	19.8	51.2	0.21	0.61	0.13	11.9	15.5	13.7	15.5	0.6	9.7	11.7
Provost	0.7	1.6	0.01	0.58	0.00	10.8	14.4	23.4	20.7	175.0	4.8	−2.8
Alumni Affairs and Development	7.2	9.2	0.04	0.21	0.01	3.0	6.7	0.3	−4.8	81.4	7.7	0.0
Academic Administration	9.5	19.4	0.08	0.51	0.04	8.9	12.6	16.5	10.4	9.6	8.0	16.0
General Administration	37.1	48.8	0.20	0.24	0.05	3.4	7.1	4.6	−6.9	−10.2	9.6	−7.8
Other	2.2	6.7	0.03	0.67	0.02	13.9	17.6	3.8	8.4	−2.1	17.2	9.6
Total	152.2	246.6	1.00	0.38	0.38	6.0	9.7	29.3	3.8	2.8	7.4	3.4

Type of Expenditure												
Faculty	39.2	50.5	0.20	0.22	0.05	3.2	6.8	12.4	2.9	2.3	3.4	0.6
Nonfaculty	3.2	8.1	0.03	0.60	0.02	11.5	15.2	62.9	3.5	5.0	16.3	8.2
Administrative Staff	22.5	33.1	0.13	0.32	0.04	4.8	8.5	12.9	3.7	-0.7	5.5	9.5
Nonexempt Staff	23.8	25.7	0.10	0.07	0.01	1.0	4.6	16.4	7.4	-1.1	-2.9	-7.2
Professional Services	12.6	17.7	0.07	0.29	0.02	4.3	7.9	17.4	7.1	0.1	2.5	0.7
Subcontracts	0.0	0.0	0.00	1.00	0.00	0.0	0.0	—	0.0	18.9	0.0	14.7
Computers	2.4	3.9	0.02	0.37	0.01	5.7	9.4	35.7	3.5	27.6	7.0	6.7
Financial Aid	21.7	54.0	0.22	0.60	0.13	11.4	15.0	25.5	14.6	8.0	9.4	10.1
Supplies	9.0	11.8	0.05	0.24	0.01	3.4	7.1	23.2	14.2	7.5	-3.1	-2.1
General Operating Expenses	2.6	18.5	0.07	0.86	0.06	24.4	28.0	—	0.0	1.1	0.0	-1.1
Capital	12.8	19.1	0.08	0.33	0.03	4.9	8.6	84.8	-17.0	-6.5	18.1	2.6
Maintenance	1.9	3.7	0.01	0.50	0.01	8.6	12.2	19.0	12.3	7.2	6.3	-4.8
Residual	0.4	0.6	0.00	0.28	0.00	4.1	7.7	—	7.2	7.4	2.2	5.2
Total	152.2	246.6	1.00	0.38	0.38	6.0	9.7	29.3	3.8	2.8	7.4	3.4

Source: Calculations using unpublished data from the University of Chicago.

[a] Change as a percentage of 1991/92 level.

[b] Product of the share and the percentage increase.

— Percentage not meaningful due to transfers and negative accounting entries.

TABLE 4.9

Expenditures, by Source of Funds: Chicago, 1984, 1987, and 1992 Fiscal Years
(Percentage Distribution)

	Federal			Other Sponsored Research			Gifts and Endowment			Other Unrestricted Funds		
	1983/84	1986/87	1991/92	1983/84	1986/87	1991/92	1983/84	1986/87	1991/92	1983/84	1986/87	1991/92
Humanities	10	6	6	3	3	6	8	9	13	79	82	75
Social Sciences	15	14	10	9	24	16	8	4	4	68	59	70
Natural Sciences	58	58	48	3	4	6	2	3	3	36	35	43
Library	0	2	3	2	2	0	7	4	3	91	92	93
Student Services	0	0	0	0	0	0	7	9	2	93	91	98
Plant	0	0	0	0	0	0	0	0	0	100	100	100
Admissions and Financial Aid	20	12	10	0	2	5	19	12	7	62	75	78
Provost	0	1	0	0	22	17	6	9	20	94	67	63
Alumni and Development	0	0	0	0	0	0	1	3	0	99	97	100
Arts and Sciences Administration	12	6	10	5	11	13	29	24	23	54	59	54
General Administration	3	7	−2	−1	2	3	1	10	1	97	81	97
Other	2	1	0	3	3	2	16	2	1	78	94	97
Total	22	26	19	2	5	6	6	7	5	71	62	70

Source: Calculations using unpublished data from the University of Chicago.

total arts and sciences funding in 1983/84 to 19 percent by 1991/92. Federal funding was of greatest importance in the natural science departments. At the same time that federal funding was becoming less important, sponsored research from other sources increased in importance. Reflecting the trends in the other universities, there was an increase over the period in the percentage of expenditures supported by other unrestricted funds.

PATTERNS AND TRENDS: CARLETON

Detailed Expenditures

Not only is Carleton College quite different from the three research universities covered in this study, the financial information available for it was distinctive as well, in that detailed disaggregated data were not available in machine-readable form even for the last 5 years of the period of study. The next best alternative was to use tabular summaries of expenditures contained in annual financial reports published by the college. Although these reports offer the advantage of consistent coverage for the entire 15-year period of the study, they present breakdowns only for six categories of expenditures, two of which (student work and travel) are quite small. Moreover, these data do not permit the separation of internally funded and externally funded expenditures. The classification by departments was considerably more detailed than in the three sample universities. Therefore, the departmental groups could be rearranged to be somewhat comparable to the presentations for the research universities. The components included in the departmental groups listed are noted in appendix Table 4A.5. It also was possible to add two additional "departmental" categories that actually reflect different types of expenditures or sources of funding. The category for scholarships in effect adds one important additional expenditure type, and the organized research category can be viewed as largely comprising outside grant and contract funding.

Table 4.10 presents the division of expenditures for Carleton in 1991/92. Out of a total of $43 million spent during that year (which includes externally financed expenditures), fully one-half was accounted for by the nearly all-inclusive compensation category. Of the 98 individual cells in the table, the largest category of spending was for scholarships, at $7.4 million, very much in line with the high cost of undergraduate aid in the research universities. The bottom section of the table shows changes in real spending for all the categories over the decade 1982–1992. Here again, financial aid is the largest single category, with an increase of $4 million, or about one-fifth of the total increase.

Table 4.11 summarizes the changes in spending for Carleton over the entire 15-year period in a form similar to that used for the research universities. Overall spending doubled over this period, for an average annual growth rate in real terms of 4.7 percent. For the decade 1982–1992, the annual rate was 5.7 percent, which compares with 6.8 percent for internally funded spending at Duke, 5.3 percent at Harvard, and 6.0 percent at Chicago. The departmental groups showing the most rapid growth over the decade were computing and organized research, but the line with the largest contribution was scholarships, owing to the relative importance of this item (17 percent of all spending) and to its strong rate of growth (7.9 percent). Variation in growth rates among the types of expenditures showed much less variation; equipment expenditures rose the fastest during the 1982–1992 period.

SUMMARY

This chapter presents data on expenditures for the four sample institutions. It focuses on internally financed expenditures, that is, spending that is not specifically tied to outside grants and contracts. For each institution, expenditures are divided by type and departmental group and are compared over time to determine both the distribution of spending of different types and the growth in that spending. In line with the aggregate trends noted in chapter 1, expenditures at the sample institutions grew rapidly in real terms from the early 1980s to 1991/92. The annual growth rates in total spending were: Duke, 6.8 percent; Harvard, 5.3 percent; Chicago, 6.0 percent; and Carleton, 5.7 percent. Among the components of this overall increase, financial aid was conspicuous for its growth; all the institutions experienced rapid growth in this category. Another regularity among the three universities was a decline over the period in the importance of federally supported expenditures. It is worth noting a proviso stated earlier. Despite the attempts made to arrange the expenditure data in comparable ways for all four institutions, the differences among institutions in organizational structure, accounting conventions, and functions mean that comparisons among institutions inevitably will be problematic. For this reason, the present

TABLE 4.10
Expenditures, Levels and Changes, by Departmental Group and Type:
Carleton (In Thousands of 1991/92 Dollars)
Type of Expenditure

	Compensation	Student Work	Supplies
Humanities	5,664	133	127
Natural Sciences	3,136	157	151
Social Sciences	1,898	27	59
General, Other Academic Departments	1,386	81	66
Organized Research	589	16	94
Library	784	167	28
Academic Administration	435	50	83
Computing	565	76	298
Student Services	1,534	343	235
Admissions and Financial Aid	777	26	286
Scholarships	0	0	0
General Administration	1,914	83	182
Alumni, Development, Public Relations	1,720	49	879
Plant	1,242	50	56
Total	21,645	1,258	2,545

Changes in Expenditures, 1981/82 to 1991/92
Type of Expenditure

	Compensation	Student Work	Supplies
Humanities	2,189	72	36
Natural Sciences	1,215	21	44
Social Sciences	590	10	31
General, Other Academic Departments	576	20	22
Organized Research	462	13	41
Library	267	11	1
Academic Administration	210	39	45
Computing	329	45	268
Student Services	617	107	104
Admissions and Financial Aid	274	11	77
Scholarships	0	0	0
General Administration	849	39	109
Alumni, Development, Public Relations	784	23	422
Plant	336	0	3
Total	8,699	411	1,204

Source: Calculations using data in Carleton College, *Report of the Treasurer*, 1976/77, 1981/82, 1986/87, and 1991/92.

TABLE 4.10 (*cont.*)

Equipment	Travel	Other Expenses	Total
49	13	111	6,097
165	12	48	3,670
10	2	29	2,025
16	116	1,837	3,503
355	103	162	1,319
808	10	59	1,856
52	70	398	1,089
690	18	24	1,671
96	274	759	3,240
6	136	56	1,288
0	0	7,394	7,394
32	160	1,036	3,407
36	218	328	3,231
79	4	2,158	3,589
2,394	1,136	14,400	43,378

Equipment	Travel	Other Expenses	Total
−59	−16	79	2,302
125	−74	1	1,332
7	−1	−12	625
1	63	785	1,468
313	59	27	916
266	1	−1	545
38	2	275	610
538	13	15	1,208
70	140	380	1,419
−4	65	16	439
0	0	4,023	4,023
10	78	629	1,714
−38	72	20	1,283
−3	−1	621	955
1,263	401	6,859	18,837

TABLE 4.11

Shares of Expenditure Growth, Growth Rates, by Departmental Group and Type of Expenditure: Carleton

Departmental Group	Expenditures ($1000)				Share 1991/92	Percentage Increase	Contribution	Real Growth Rates		Nominal Growth Rate
	1976/77	1981/82	1986/87	1991/92				1981/82 to 1991/92	1976/77 to 1991/92	1981/82 to 1991/92
Humanities	3,746	3,795	5,129	6,097	0.14	0.38	0.05	4.7	3.2	6.6
Natural Sciences	2,138	2,338	3,389	3,670	0.08	0.36	0.03	4.5	3.6	6.4
Social Sciences	1,223	1,401	1,857	2,025	0.05	0.31	0.01	3.7	3.4	5.6
General, Other Academic Departments	1,389	2,035	2,470	3,503	0.08	0.42	0.03	5.4	6.2	7.3
Organized Research	462	403	1,423	1,319	0.03	0.69	0.02	11.9	7.0	13.8
Library	1,272	1,311	1,692	1,856	0.04	0.29	0.01	3.5	2.5	5.4
Academic Administration	462	479	695	1,089	0.03	0.56	0.01	8.2	5.7	10.1
Computing	461	463	1,354	1,671	0.04	0.72	0.03	12.8	8.6	14.7
Student Services	1,598	1,822	2,395	3,240	0.07	0.44	0.03	5.8	4.7	7.7

	1	2	3	4	5	6	7	8	9	10
Admissions and Financial Aid	621	849	1,104	1,288	0.03	0.34	0.01	4.2	4.9	6.1
Scholarships	2,428	3,370	4,912	7,394	0.17	0.54	0.09	7.9	7.4	9.8
General Administration	1,532	1,692	2,465	3,407	0.08	0.50	0.04	7.0	5.3	8.9
Alumni, Development, Public Relations	1,215	1,948	2,160	3,231	0.07	0.40	0.03	5.1	6.5	7.0
Plant	2,787	2,635	3,136	3,589	0.08	0.27	0.02	3.1	1.7	5.0
Total	21,334	24,541	34,181	43,378	1.00	0.43	0.43	5.7	4.7	7.6
Type of Expenditure										
Compensation	11,793	12,946	17,481	21,645	0.50	0.40	0.20	5.1	4.0	7.0
Student Work	625	847	1,083	1,258	0.03	0.33	0.01	4.0	4.7	5.9
Supplies	1,023	1,341	1,980	2,545	0.06	0.47	0.03	6.4	6.1	8.3
Equipment	1,182	1,132	3,014	2,394	0.06	0.53	0.03	7.5	4.7	9.4
Travel	521	735	765	1,136	0.03	0.35	0.01	4.4	5.2	6.3
Other Expenses	6,189	7,541	9,857	14,400	0.33	0.48	0.16	6.5	5.6	8.4
Total	21,334	24,541	34,181	43,378	1.00	0.43	0.43	5.7	4.7	7.6

Source: Calculations using data in Carleton College, *Report of the Treasurer,* 1976/77, 1981/82, 1986/87, and 1991/92.

study focuses on *changes* in spending over time for the same institution. One cannot expect to discover, for example, which institution spends the highest percentage on natural sciences or administration. In the next chapter, these expenditure data are combined with other observable quantities in an effort to find explanations for the spending increases.

Dealing with Interdepartmental
Transfers and Recharges

THE KIND of fund code accounting practiced by the universities studied here involves a significant amount of internal transfers and recharges. The first aim in dealing with these transfers and recharges is to avoid double counting. Beyond that, however, the way these are dealt with will have implications for the kind of information that can be gathered. Consider, for example, a simple kind of recharge whereby one unit of the university (let us say, the copy center) performs a service for another (in this case, the physics department). The copy center purchases inputs and "sells" the output to the academic department. Suppose that, during a year, it buys $500 worth of paper, pays $250 for machine rental, and pays workers $250 to photocopy material for the physics department. The end-of-year ledger will show expenditures for these items under the copy center (general administration); a recharge receipt of −$1,000, also under the copy center; and a recharge expenditure of $1,000, under the physics department. If all recharges are ignored, the university's expenditures are reflected correctly, but the portion accounted for by physics is understated and the portion accounted for by general administration is overstated. Stated another way, the summary table for the university would look different if physics had purchased the photocopying service directly from an outside vendor. If the recharges are counted, as they are in the chapter, it is possible to reflect both the university's expenditures on inputs and the use of the resulting goods and services within the university. However, this approach necessitates the inclusion of the recharges, which appear as a negative entry in the general operating columns of the origin-destination expenditure tables.

It is useful to illustrate the approach taken with a simple example. Table 4A.1 shows the categorization of expenditures for a hypothetical university having three departmental groups (all arts and science departments, a professional school, and general administration) and three types of expenditures (salaries, services provided by one unit for another, and other operating expenses). Many services are provided by one unit for another—for example, security, housekeeping,

TABLE 4A.1
Accounting for Shared Costs and Internally Provided Services:
A Simple Example

Departmental Group	Type of Expenditure			
	Salaries	Services Provided Internally	Other Operating Expenses	Total
Entire University				
Arts and Sciences Departments	60	10	20	90
Professional School[a]	50	20	30	100
General Administration	40	−30	100	110
Total	150	0	150	300
Arts and Sciences Only—Allocating 50% of General Administration to Arts and Sciences, Counting Internal Transactions				
Arts and Sciences Departments	60	10	20	90
General Administration[b]	20	−15	50	55
Total	80	−5	70	145
Arts and Sciences Only—Allocating 50% of General Administration to Arts and Sciences, Ignoring Internal Transactions				
Arts and Sciences Departments	60	—	20	30
General Administration[b]	20	—	50	70
Total	80	—	70	150

[a]Omitted below.

[b]Expenditures for arts and sciences assumed to be 50 percent of actual levels shown in the top section.

repairs, and photocopying. Although practices differ, institutions typically make accounting entries for services that are easily attributable; these services are the ones measured in the second column. The top part of the table presents expenditures for the university as a whole. It shows that the units of the general administration spent a total of $140 on salaries and other operating expenses but "sold" $30 worth of services to academic units. Including the column for internal transfers makes it possible to attribute all identifiable expenditures to the units that are the ultimate beneficiaries. Thus, the $30 worth of services provided by the general administration appropriately is assigned to the arts and sciences departments and to the professional school. These services are counted toward the ultimate user in the same way as if they had been purchased outside the university.

A problem arises, however, in allocating services that are not re-

corded by means of internal transfers of this sort. General operations, ranging from groundskeepers and road repair to the president's office, are not easily allocated. In the present study, which
examines only arts and sciences, a portion of these general functions
is attributed to arts and sciences, where the specific proportions are
based on the rough estimates and educated guesses of administrators at each institution. In the example shown in Table 4A.1, that
proportion is 50 percent. The middle section of Table 4A.1 shows
the resulting summary of expenditures for the arts and sciences portion of the university only: the line for the professional school is
omitted, and only 50 percent of each entry for general administration is included. The problem is that, after some entities have been
omitted and a proportion applied to general administrative expenditures, the internal transfer column no longer necessarily sums to
zero—it may be positive or, as it is in this case, negative. One approach that avoids this ambiguity is to ignore internal transfers altogether, as is done in the third section of Table 4A.1. By ignoring
internally provided services, however, this approach overstates the
portion of the university's total expenditures accounted by general
administration. Furthermore, to the degree that various components
of the academic division use differing amounts of such services, the
approach illustrated in the table's third section would misstate their
relative sizes as well. Thus, the approach taken in the present study
is that illustrated by the second section: a portion of general administrative units is assigned to arts and sciences, and internally provided services are recorded where possible. In practice, these transfers usually will come close to netting out. The gain in reflecting the
relative size of departmental groups appears to be worth the loss in
accounting tidiness.

To summarize, the approach taken here implies that the costs of
some activities that are performed by a service unit in the university
(such as photocopying) will be reflected in three places. The total
cost will show up as a general operating cost under the department
that ordered it; the cost of inputs will show up in the appropriate
columns in general administration; and a negative entry (the recharge) will appear in the general operating column for administration. As a consequence, the arts and sciences totals along the bottom
of the table will reflect the actual use of resources, and the totals
along the right-hand side will reflect total spending by the divisions
of the university.[17] As noted in the text, the accounting data for
Duke and Chicago include the expenditures of general administration units. Thus this approach will make the most pronounced difference in tabulations for those institutions.

A related issue arises in measuring expenditures for purchases of capital, which includes such items as computers and scientific equipment. At most institutions, data on operating expenses in the general ledger do not include expenditures for construction or for some major capital expenditures. At Duke, these capital items are paid for out of separate plant accounts. Those accounts receive their funds either by way of transfers from operating accounts, which are readily monitored, or by way of borrowing. In the case of debt finance, similar transfers from operating accounts are used to retire the debt. At Duke, the funding of capital expenditures is treated differently in administrative units and academic units. Administrative units employ depreciation ("betterments") codes, wherein current funds are transferred into plant accounts, from which expenditures for such items as computers, renovation, and furniture are made. Academic expenditures for these items are often made from current accounts, however, and are designated here as computers or capital expenditures. Thus, although I ignore most transfers, I include transfers to plant accounts for academic units because they reflect capital expenditures that have taken place or that will take place.

Appendix 4.2

Categories Used to Create Expenditure Tables

To EXAMINE IN some detail changes in expenditures over time for individual universities, it was convenient to categorize expenditures by departmental group and by type of expenditure. These categories are only approximately comparable among institutions, however, in part because the available data differ in a variety of ways. The data from Harvard, which are from the Faculty of Arts and Sciences, provide virtually no detail on a number of nonacademic departments. In contrast, the information for Duke and Chicago covers all departments in the university with equal detail. Another reason why the categories are not strictly comparable is simply the difference in the functions that each institution carries out: one university may offer programs that are simply not found in another university. Thus, "natural sciences" represents an amalgamation of departments and other administrative entities that has a different weighting of disciplines, not to mention individuals, from one institution to the next.

The categories used in this study are summarized in this appendix in some detail for each of the institutions examined. In most cases, it seems fairly clear how to categorize a program or a type of expenditure, although some choices may be debatable. For the most part, "area studies" programs were placed under humanities, although there is undeniably a social science element in much that goes on in such programs. Another ambiguous discipline is history, which I also grouped with humanities.[18]

Tables 4A.2 through 4A.5 give detailed descriptions of the entities and types of expenditures used in defining the departmental groupings and types of expenditures in the tables presented in the chapter.

TABLE 4A.2

Detailed Expenditure Categories, Duke

Rows (Departmental Groupings) Line Name	Number	Primary-Component Code	Description
Humanities	1	22010, 22170, 22340, 22420, 22460, 22540, 22580, 22780, 22900, 22475, 23030, 23200, 23233, 23280, 23351, 23352, 23356, 23357, 23358, 23820, 23960, 22820, 23010, 23020, 23035, 23070, 23100, 23110, 23120, 23150, 23180, 23231, 23233, 23332, 23350, 23810, 23945, 23025, 23960, 22820, 23238, 23033, 23236	Art and Art History, Classical Studies, English, Germanic Language and Literature, History, Music, Philosophy, Religion, Slavic Language and Literature, Literature, Program in Literature, Judaic Studies, Interdepartmental Communication on Linguistics, Humanities Computing Program, Asian and African Language and Literature, Asian/Pacific Language and Literature, Canadian Studies, Islamic Studies, Latin American Studies, Language Lab, Soviet and Eastern European Studies, Romance Studies, Art Museum, Carlyle Letters, Science, Technology and Human Values, Women's Studies, Documentary Studies, Duke Caroale, Institute of the Arts, Drama, Dance, 20th Century American Program, Committee on Linguistics, Focus, International Studies, Film and Video, Medieval Studies, Office of the Editor of Journal of American Speech, Schondorf Exchange, Romance Studies, Graduate Program in Literature, University Writing Program
Social Sciences	2	22020, 22040, 22210, 22250, 22700, 22740, 22745, 22800–222806, 22940, 22090, 23060, 23232, 23234, 23355, 23940, 23995, 23205	Biological and Cultural Anthropology, Economics, Education, Political Science, Psychology, Public Policy, International Development Research, Sociology, Management Sciences, Environmental Center, Human Development, Marxism and Society, Center for East-West Trade, Demographic Studies, Psychology Clinic, Fast Track Program
Natural Sciences	3	22050, 22130, 22180, 22380, 22500, 22660, 22661, 22980, 23040, 23090, 23235, 23260, 23261, 23990, 29661, 29663, 23980–23986, 23989, 23330, 29662, 29180	Botany, Chemistry, Computer Science, Geology, Mathematics, Physics, Zoology, Communication on Cellular and Molecular Biology, Program in Genetics, Program in Neurosciences, Biology, Primate Facility, Physics Instrument Shop, Cryogenics, Marine Lab, Statistics and Decision Sciences, Liquid Air Department, Computer Science Lab

Category	No.	Account Numbers	Description
Engineering	4	22301–22304, 23065, 23303	Civil, Electrical, Mechanical, and Biomedical Engineering; Center for Biochemical Engineering
Libraries	5	51000–59000	All library administration, collections, public services, and technical services
Student Services	6	11301–11320, 11350–11352, 11370–11380, 98312, 98313	Office of Vice President Student Affairs, Registrar, Arts and Sciences Special Programs, International Office, Career Development Office, Counseling and Psychological Services, Sexual Assault Program
Plant	7	13300–13410, 23050	Physical Plant, Chief Engineer, Duke Gardens
Admissions and Financial Aid	8	11330–11349, 11390, 11360, 36913	Office of Admissions, Office of Financial Aid, Undesignated Student Financial Assistance, A.B. Duke Regional Prize Office
Arts and Sciences Administration	9	21007–21940, 22861–22863, 22951–22958, 22990, 23080, 23190–23195, 23300, 23400–23621, 23740, 23075	Arts and Sciences Administration, ROTC, Study Abroad, Unallocated Budget, Special Programs and Short Courses, Phi Beta Kappa, Continuing Education, Talent Identification, Health & Physical Education, Intramurals, Club Sports, String School, Locker and Towel Service, Preschool Laboratory, Arts and Sciences Roundtable on Science and Public Affairs
Provost	10	11100–11255, 22350	General Administration, Academic Administration
Alumni Affairs and Development	11	14000–14805	Vice President Alumni Affairs and Development, Director—University Development, Alumni Affairs, Office of Development, Office of Vice President for Alumni Affairs and Development, Office of Public Relations, Gift Records Office, Office of University Publications
General Administration	12	10000–10501, 13000–13224, 13500–13999, 18000–18500	General Activity, Office of the President, Office of University Counsel, Office of Executive Vice President—Asset Management, Office of Executive Vice President for Administration (Accounting, Business & Finance, Materials Management, Public Safety, Human Resources, Vice President for Planning and Treasury, Service Components), General Administrative Expense

TABLE 4A.2 (*cont.*)

Columns (Expenditure Types)[a]			
Type	Description	Object Codes	Description
1	Compensation: Regular Faculty	6001, 6013, 6003, 6004	Administrative effort supporting instruction, instruction, cost sharing—training, cost sharing—sponsored research
2	Compensation: Other Faculty	6015, 6350–6371	Compensation for nonfaculty instructors, postdoctoral stipends and awards
3	Compensation: Administrative Staff	6019, 6098, 6000	Other professional staff, allocated vacancy allowance, staff, administrative effort supporting general services
4	Compensation: Nonexempt	6051, 6052, 6056, 6055, 6061, 6062, 6065, 6066, 6071, 6072, 6075, 6076, 6090, 6099, 6190, 6064, 6073, 6074	(Clerical, technical, service, skilled crafts) effort supporting general departmental operations, instruction/training/departmental research, exceptional performance awards, allocated vacancy allowance—biweekly
5	Compensation: Students	6057, 6067, 6077–6079, 6205, 6084–6087, 6093–6096, 6210, 6097, 6380–6399, 6010, 6017, 6069, 6070, 6088	Students (undergraduates, graduates, house counselors) payments to professional students, subspecialty fellows
6	Professional Services	6220, 6221, 6225, 6228–6229, 6921, 6922	Other professional services, experimental subjects, consultants, trust beneficiary distribution, data processing service, other computing services
7	Contract Work	6916, 6927, 6971, 7151, 7152, 7991	Contract work, subcontracts, student labor recharge, student labor resale recharge, temporary service recharge
8	Computers	6672, 6674, 6676, 6774, 6776, 7180, 7994, 7321–7335, 6874, 6672	Microcomputers, mini-mainframe computers, software, computer recharges, computer maintenance and repair, machinery and equipment
9	Financial Aid	6012, 6014, 6058, 6068, 6094, 6095, 6311–6327, 6330–6349, 6069	Salaries for graduate student research, instruction and support, graduate stipends and awards, undergraduate stipends, awards and scholarships
10	Supplies and Materials	6440–6469, 6471–6499, 6702, 6710, 6720, 6725, 6727, 6730, 6740, 6747, 6750, 6757, 6771, 6772, 6761, 6763, 7141, 7144, 7565	Supplies and materials, minor acquisitions of land, buildings, utilities and building appurtenances, ships and vessels, automotive equipment, furniture, library materials, recharges for copy equipment rentals, midrange copier, office products
11	Other General Operating Expenses	6470, 6535, 6936, 6980, 6981, 6982, 6983, 6986–6989, 6914, 6938, 6954, 6994, 6500–6534, 6546–6599, 6536–	Printing and publication, freight and mail, telephone services, travel, direct utility charges, university subsidies, cost of food items sold, cost of other goods sold, collection agency fees, training expenses, contributions, dormi-

		Codes
	tory charges/housing/board—outside Duke, interview expense, relocation expense, entry fees, public relations and social expense, equipment rentals, groundskeeping, housekeeping, insurance and interest expense, laundry, losses, damages and other write-offs, maintenance non-billable payroll cost, business-related meals meetings and symposiums, moving and assembly, valet parking, royalties, space rentals, services purchased (not under contract), student damage, taxes and licenses, landfill tipping fee, transportation (of persons), business travel and living expenses, university copy center recharge, printing services recharge, mail room recharge, recharges for accounting, university functions, investment and management, benefits and records office, child care, job training, health care plan manager, workers' compensation administration, audiovisual education, student labor technical recharge, conference services recharge, moving services recharge, recharges for transit, motor pool, vehicle repair, fuel service, liquid air recharges, various credits for services rendered, office machines and products recharge, Searle Center recharges, nuclear magnetic resonance support recharge, university photographer recharge, Crystal Structure Center recharge, operating expenses nonresearch grants, hospitalization (workers' compensation), operating expenses research grants, credit for third-party sale of equipment, pediatric metabolic recharge (Chemistry Department), Physics Instrument Shop recharge	6544, 6915, 6901–6912, 6917–6920, 6926, 6928–6934, 6940, 6944, 6969, 6947–6952, 6956–6964, 6965, 6970, 6972–6977, 6984, 6988, 6990–6993, 6999, 7100, 7120, 7140, 7145, 7146, 7149, 7166, 7153–7165, 7175, 7185–7188, 7440, 7450, 7510–7549, 7560, 7565, 7850, 7851, 7860, 7992, 7993, 7995, 6967, 6968, 7508, 6942, 7241, 7610
12	Capital	
	Capital (minus computers), credit for transfers of equipment; acquisition to be capitalized—land, buildings, utilities, and building appurtenances, ships and vessels, automotive equipment, library materials, furniture, construction/renovation materials, plant and equipment, Duke communications systems	6600, 6627, 6675, 6681–6697, 6634, 6639–6671, 7509
13	Maintenance and Repair	
	Maintenance and repair, physics instrument shop recharge—capital equipment fabrication	6802–6816, 6820–6899, 7611
14	Residual	

Source: Unpublished data from Duke.

aObject code 6016 (sponsored research—faculty and staff) has been allocated to the faculty salaries and staff salaries expenditures types. Ninety percent of code 6016 was placed in faculty salaries and ten percent went to staff salaries. This 90:10 ratio was estimated by Tom Davis, Director of Sponsored Programs.

TABLE 4A.3

Detailed Expenditure Categories, Harvard

Rows (Departmental Groupings)			
Line Name	Number	Code	Description
General Academic	1	Megasub M13 Megasub 153 (except subdept 349) Megasub 040, 480 Depts 17, 34	Core Curriculum, Freshman Seminar, House Seminars, General Education, Society of Fellows, Danforth Teaching Lab, Derek Bok Center, University Extension, Continuing Education
Humanities	2	Groupcode HU Megasubs 167, 320, 325 Groupcode IC (except megasub M04) Groupcode OC (except megasub M08) Megasubs 097, 100, 103, 109, 116, 086, 159, 221, 232, 285, 370, 372, 400, 448, M11, 095, 101, 102, 123 Subdepts 098, 380 in megasub M16 Subdepts 449, 467 in megasub 001	Celtic Language and Literature, Canadian Studies, Classics, Comparative Literature, Erasmus Lectureship, Linguistics, English-American Language and Literature, Fine Arts, Germanic Language and Literature, Sanskrit and Indian, Music, Philosophy, Poetry, Romance Language and Literature, Near East Language and Civilization, Center for Jewish Studies, Slavic Language and Literature, East Asian Language and Literature, Visual and Environmental Studies, Carpenter Center Courses, Film Committee, Department of History, History of Science, Afro-American Studies, Center for Middle Eastern Studies, Aga Kahn Program, Russian Research Center, Ukrainian Studies, Civilization of France, Japan Institute Council of East Asian Studies, Chinese Studies, Korean Studies, Vietnamese Studies, National Resources Center, Afro American DuBois Endowment, Collection of Historical Scientific Instruments, Charles Warren Center, Degrees in American Civilization, Committee on History and Literature, Regional Studies of East Asia, Latin American Studies, Committee on African Studies, Modern Greek Studies, Literature Concentration, Folklore and Mythology, Medieval Studies, Coolidge Hall Operations, Committee on Women's Studies, Committee on the Study of Religion Ex-

Social Sciences	3	Groupcode SS (except megasubs 167, 320, 325) Megasubs M04, 130, 131	cliffe Professor, Charles Warren Fund, Latin American Scholarship Program, Far East Studies, East Asian Studies Anthropology, Biological Anthropology, Archeological Anthropology, Behavioral Science Center, Psychology Department, Laboratory General Psychology, Study of Black Politics, Department of Government, Government Department Data Center, American Center, Political Economy Program, Economics 10 Course, Department of Economics, Harvard Institute of Economic Research, Quarterly Journal of Economics, Harvard Institute of Social Research, Center for International Affairs, Social Studies—Teaching & Research, Degrees in Social Studies
Natural Sciences	4	Groupcodes NS, AS Megasubs M08, 135, 250, 349 Subdept 349 in megasub 153 Megasubs M07, 438, M20 Depts 44, 49, 52, 66 Subdepts 831 in megasub 001	Astronomy, Animal Care Facilities, Mathematics, Dept of Statistics, Biology Labs, Biology Undergraduate Tutorial, Biochemistry General 10, Biochemistry Lab, Biochemistry Program, Biochemistry & Molecular Biology, Teaching and Research Grants—Biochemistry, Biology Prather Lecture, Biology Teaching and Administrative Cost, Biology Cellular and Developmental Biology, Chemistry Dept, Chemistry Labs, X-ray Facility, FTIR Room, Vax Room, Mass Spectrometry, Nuclear Magnetic Resonance Room, Glass Shop, Earth and Planetary Science, Physics Dept, Physics Lab, Jefferson Laboratories Machine Shop, Physics NSF Supplement, Cyclotron Development and Operations, Oceanography, Committee Biophysics Studies, Quantitative Reasoning, Math Core Computer Instruction, Computer Technical Services, Computer Operations General, Course Computer Expenses, Computer Based Lab, Science Center, Science Center Stock Room, Division of Applied Sciences, Organismic and Evolutionary Biology/Research, Harvard Forest, Observatory Biomedical Annex
Museums	5	Depts 63, 69, 74	Museum of Comparative Zoology, Peabody Museum, Semitic Museum
Library	6	Dept 58	College Library
Student Services	7	Megasub 016 Subdepts 067, 068, 069, 071, 614, 755 in megasub M15	Graduate School of Arts & Sciences, Harvard Review—GSAS, Student Affairs GSAS, Grad Soc GSAS Operations, Phillips Brooks House, Graduate Dormitories, Houses and College Dorms, Allston

TABLE 4A.3 *(cont.)*

Rows (Departmental Groupings) Line Name	*Number*	*Code*	*Description*
		Depts 22, 78, 91 Subdepts 021, 023, 025, 060, 061, 048, 140 in megasub D91	Burr Senior Tutors, Registrar's Office Computers, Registrar Harvard College, Freshman Dean's Office Unrestricted, Freshman Dean's Office Restricted, Career Services, Bureau of Study Counsel
Admissions and Financial Aid	8	Groupcodes GS, UA Megasubs M22, 041 Subdepts 066, 070 in megasub M15	Committee Administrative Scholar Undergraduate, Dean Admissions & Financial Aid, Faculty Aide Prog, University Financial Aid, Prize Office, Admissions GSAS, GSAS Admissions & Financial Aid
Administration	9	Groupcode CA, GE Megasubs 480, 035, 040, 045, 050 Subdept 065 in megasub M15 Subdepts 007, 125 in megasub M16 Subdepts 018, 020, 046 in megasub D91	Administration, Academic Planning, Finance, Administrative Computing Systems, Administrative Salaries, Dean Faculty A&S, Secretary, FAS—Personnel Services, Administration General, Audio Visual Service, Dept of Media Services, Overhead on Government Contracts, Administrative Special, FAS—Recruitment & Relocation, Associate Dean GSAS, Institutional Research and Evaluation, Associate Dean Undergraduate Education, Sourcebook Publication, Harvard Foundation, Dean of Harvard College, Associate Dean Special
Plant	10	Group PR Subdepts 800–899 Subdepts 487, 488 in megasub 001	Buildings Administration, Pooled Reserve Building Maintenance
Athletics	11	Dept 85	Athletics

Columns (Expenditure Types) Description	*Number*	*Code*	*Description*
Compensation—Regular Faculty	1	Class 01, 02	Compensation for tenured faculty and faculty with appointments more than one year
Compensa-	2	Class 03	Compensation for faculty with appointments one year or less

		Class	Description
	tion—Professional Staff		empt from overtime
4	Compensation—Students	Class 05, 07, 23	Wages to Harvard or Radcliffe students, wages to non-Harvard or non-Radcliffe students, Payments to exempt employees enrolled as students
5	Compensation—Nonexempt	Class 06, 08	Compensation to support staff, not exempt from overtime, Non-exempt support staff in service departments
6	Extra Compensation	Class 10	Unallocated costs of fringe benefits, extra compensation and over-time
7	Operating Expenses	Class 15, 16, 19, 20, 33, 34, 35, 39, 11, 17, 18, 22, 24, 25, 28	Cost of binding books and publications, design and layout of printed mat, telephone, postage, express and freight, heating, ventilation and AC, water, light and power, gas, rubbish removal, vine trimmings, insurance, items charged to grants that do not earn overhead, travel, foreign travel, subscriptions and books, share of university expenses, transfers, miscellaneous
8	Capital	Class 12, 31, 27	Cost of equipment, building improvements and alterations, payment of debt service
9	Supplies	Class 13	Cost of supplies and equipment with unit value less than $100
10	Professional Services	Class 26	University Police Service
11	Maintenance	Class 29, 30, 32, 36, 37, 38	Maintenance expenses, building maintenance including painting, roofing, minor repairs, custodial- and maintenance-related expenses for buildings. Mechanical maintenance, care of fire protection equipment, elevators and HVAC operations, grounds maintenance and snow removal
12	Financial Aid	Class 40, 41, 42, 43, 44, 45 46, 49	Fellowships and scholarships, tuition scholarships, beneficiary aid, prizes, dependency allowance as part of govt grants or contracts, research fellow stipends
13	Computers	Class 14	Charges for Office of Information Technology and outside computer services

Abbreviations: *FAS Faculty of Arts and Sciences*
                  GSAS Graduate School of Arts and Sciences

TABLE 4A.4

Detailed Expenditure Categories, Chicago

Rows (Departmental Groupings) Line Name	Number	Code	Description
Humanities	1	Exec 21 (except 200), 41 Dept 303, 308, 403, 458	Art, English, Committee on Social Thought, Classical Languages and Literature, East Asian Languages and Literature, Germanic Languages and Literature, Linguistics, Music, Near Eastern Languages and Civilizations, Philosophy, Romance Languages and Literature, Slavic Languages and Literature, South Asian Languages and Literature, History, New Testament and Early Christian Literature, Committee on Art and Design, Language Laboratory, Center for International Language Studies, Humanities Collegiate Division, Oriental Institute
Social Sciences	2	Exec 23 (except Dept 300, 302, 303, 308) Dept 404	Psychology, Anthropology, Economics, Social Sciences Collegiate Division, Education, Committee on Geographic Studies, Political Science, Sociology
Natural Sciences	3	Exec 22 (except Dept 250, 257, 258, 263, 264) Dept 402 Dept 141, 142, 144, 146, 401	Astronomy and Astrophysics, Chemistry, Ben May Institute, Mathematics, Geophysical Sciences, Statistics, James Franck Institute, Enrico Fermi Institute, Computer Science, Center for Advanced Radiation Resources, Physical Sciences Collegiate Division, Biochemistry, Biophysics and Theoretical Biology, Ecology and Evolution, Biochemistry/Molecular Biology, Biological Sciences Collegiate Division
Library	4	Dept 470	Library
Student Services	5	Exec 43 Dept 660, 661, 665–669	International House, International Student Services, Office of the Dean of Students, Career and Placement Services, Mandel Hall, Student Activities Office, Ida Noyes Clubhouse, Reynolds Club
Plant	6	Dept 649, 652 (until 1988/89) 655, 657, 702, 703, 706, 710, 742, 744	Office of Energy Management Conservation and Safety, Facilities Planning and Management, Utilities, Physical Plant and Construction (until 1988/89), Energy Management and Conservation, Safety Coordinator, Office of Hazardous Waste Disposal, Office of Radiation Safety

Admissions and Financial Aid	7	Dept 415, 615, 616, 662, 663	College Admissions and Financial Aid, Central Unrestricted Student Aid, Graduate Admissions and Aid, Office of Student Loan Counseling, Graduate Student Aid
Provost	8	Dept 610, 611, 651, 652 (since 1988–89)	Office of the Provost, Academic Contingency, Office of Research Administration, Office of Director of Special Projects
Alumni Affairs and Development	9	Exec 60 Dept 673, 674, 680	Office of the Vice President for Development, Development Office, Office of Alumni Affairs, Alumni Magazine, Office of the Vice President for University News and Community Affairs
Arts and Sciences Administration	10	Dept 405, 200, 250, 264, 300, 400, 664, 302, 100, 104, 105	Humanities Divisional Administration, Social Science Divisional Administration, College Administration, New Collegiate Division, Physical Sciences Division (PSD) Administration, PSD Graduate Dean of Students, Registrar/SIS, Social Science Divisional Administration—Credit, New Collegiate Division Biological Sciences Division (BSD) Academic Administration, BSD Facilities Management, BSD Introduction and Research Services
General Administration	11	Exec 50, 65, 75, 70 (except Dept 680, 717, 718) Dept 405, 406, 640–648, 650, 653, 690–694, 622, 671, 716, 746, 750, 705, 707, 711, 713, 106–108, 257, 258, 471, 263, 450–455	College Summer Programs, Employee Relations, University Computing General Management, University Computing Finance and Administration, Administration and Library Information Systems, Academic and Public Computing, Networking and Large Scale Computing, Planning and Vendor Relations, Office of the President, Dean and Directors, Office of Investments, Office of Legal Counsel, Secretary of the Faculties, Secretary of the Board of Trustees, Office of the Vice President for Business and Finances, Office of Financial Planning and Budget, Information Systems Group, Office of the Comptroller, Office of Internal Audit, Professional Accounting Expense, Operations Office, Auxiliary Services (became Operations Office in 1984/85), Purchasing Office, Risk Management Office, Faculty Exchange, Office of Official Publications, Office of University News and Information, Office of Special Events, Security Department, University Publications, Central Debt Service, Insurance and Rent, Business Administration Credits, Centrally Budgeted Restricted Funds, Affirmative Action Office, University Human Resources Management, Printing Department, Consolidated Budget Administration, Biological Sciences Division Audio Visual Service, BSD Animal Resources Center, BSD Lab Materials Management, Physical Sciences Division Glass Shop, Central Shop, Library Photoduplication, Research Institute—Graphic Arts, Office of the Vice President for Research
Other	12	Dept 672, 740 Exec 46	Physical Education and Athletics, Smart Museum, Office of Continuing Education

TABLE 4A.4 *(cont.)*

Columns (Expenditure Types)		
Description	Number	Code	Description

Description	Number	Code	Description
Compensation—Regular Faculty	1	Subaccount 1000–1099	Salaries and wages: faculty, faculty extra service, faculty three-quarter salary accrual
Compensation—Other Faculty	2	Subaccount 1100–1199, 8370–8399	Salaries and wages: other academic, stipends—postdoctoral fellowships
Compensation—Professional Staff	3	Subaccount 1200–1399	Salaries and wages: professional, supervisory/managerial/administrative
Compensation—Nonexempt Staff	4	Subaccount 1400–1799	Salaries and wages: technical, services/trades, clerical—nonunion, clerical—union
Professional Services	5	Subaccount 2100–2999, 3100–3199, 4100–4199, 4300–4599, 4900–4999	Services: audiovisual, animal care, central shop charges—PSD, computing—Computation center, computing—other University computers, computing—Non-university computers, consultants and professional fees, departmental service unit charges, duplicating/printing, human subjects/volunteer expense, radiation protection, temporary agency help, transportation services/livery services, all other services
Subcontracts	6	Subaccount 8600–8699, 9103–9107	Subcontracts, indirect costs—subcontracts
Computers	7	Subaccount 6300–6399, 5800–5999, 7800–7899	Computing equipment, computer software, lease/rental: computing/word processing equipment
Financial Aid	8	Subaccount 1800, 1801, 8310–8399, 1804–1899, 1802	Research assistants (Ph.D.), research assistant tuition aid, student aid—graduate students, stipend aid—graduate student dependents, tuition aid, student prizes, fee aid, institutional/supply allowance—graduate students, research and course assistants, all other RAs/TAs, salaries and wages: writing lectors, course assistants, writing interns, laboratory course assistants, College Fellows

Supplies	9	Subaccount 5100–5799, 5900–5999, 6500–6599, 8500–8599	Animal purchase/supplies, food supplies, hospital/clinical supplies, laboratory supplies, office and educational supplies, shop supplies, wearing apparel, printing supplies, recreational supplies, all other supplies (except computer software), furniture and fixtures, library materials acquisitions, art acquisitions
General Operating Expenses	10	Subaccount 0991–0998, 3700–3798, 3200–3299, 4200–4299, 4600–4699, 3800–4099, 7100–7599, 7900–8199, 8905–8985, 9100–9102, 9108–9179, 9800–9829, 9840–9899, 9901–9907, 9909–9911, 9004, 9009	Electricity recharges, metropolitan sanitary district recharges, gasoline purchases, water recharges, city sewer recharges, steam recharges, gas fuel recharges, postage/mailing/shipping charges, profession developmental charges and fees, staff benefit expenses, relocation expenses, equipment lease/rental charges (except on computer equipment), credit transfers, publication costs, utilities/electricity/water/steam/fuel/oil/sewer/property tax payments, advertising, selling and marketing costs, automobile use costs, fines and penalties, housing and personal living expenses, donations and contributions, membership costs, noncash gifts, pension costs, trustee expenses, procurement card charges, insurance, telephone/telegraph/telex, subscriptions, domestic travel—faculty/staff/students, foreign travel—other, foreign travel—faculty/staff/students, foreign travel—other, cost of goods sold, credit subaccounts, unallowable cost subaccounts, interest expenses, indirect costs (except for subaccounts 9103–9107), physical plant department services, office of facilities, planning and management—fixed services
Capital	11	Subaccount 6100–6299, 6400–6499, 6600–6999, 8700–8899	Scientific and technical equipment, shop machinery and tools, vehicles, all other equipment, construction/property acquisition, purchase of land and buildings, renovation and alteration, general purpose office equipment (includes typewriters, copiers, audiovisual equipment, and duplicating equipment)
Maintenance	12	Subaccount 00–99, 3300–3399	Maintenance/repair costs
Residuals	13	Subaccount 1901–1909	

TABLE 4A.5
Expenditure Categories, Carleton

Departmental Group	
Humanities	American Studies, Archaeology, Art and Art History, Arts Studies, Asian Languages and Literature, Asian Studies, African/African-American Studies, Classical Languages, Cognitive Studies, English, Media Studies, German and Russian Languages, History, Judaic Studies, Latin American Studies, Linguistics, Music, Philosophy, Religion, Romance Languages, Russian Studies, Women's Studies, Colloquia Performance Progam
Natural Sciences	Biology, Chemistry, Geology, Mathematics and Computer Science, Physics and Astronomy
Social Sciences	Economics, Educational Studies, Political Science, Psychology, Sociology and Anthropology, Urban Studies
General, Other Academic Departments	Integrated General Studies, Physical Education, Studies in Technology and Public Policy, Learning Disabilities Program, Science and Ethics, Other Educational Programs
Organized Research	
Library	
Academic Administration	Instructional support, less computer center; registrar
Computing	Computer center; data processing
Student Services	Student services, less admissions, financial aid, registrar
Admissions and Financial Aid	Financial aid; admissions and minority admissions; student financial services in 1992
Scholarships	Student aid, less faculty and staff scholarships
General Administration	Administration; general institutional, less data processing
Alumni, Development, Public Relations	Public services and information (1977); development (other years)
Plant	

Type of Expenditure	
Compensation	Salaries plus staff benefits allocated in proportion to salaries; for faculty, also includes furloughs and faculty-staff financial aid
Student Work	
Supplies	
Equipment	Includes maintenance and new equipment
Travel	
Other Expenses	

Source: Carleton College, *Report of the Treasurer*, Schedule B–2, "Detail of Current Expenditures," 1976/77, 1981/82, 1986/87, and 1991/92.

Appendix 4.3

Trends in Duke Expenditures from 1976/77 to 1983/84

As NOTED IN chapter 4, machine-readable financial data were not available for Duke or Chicago before 1983/84 or for Harvard before 1981/82, making it impossible to conduct a full analysis of trends in spending at any of the three universities over the entire 15-year study period. Almost no machine-readable accounting data for Carleton were available, but consistent tabular information covering the entire 15-year period had been published. As a partial remedy for this deficiency (mainly as a check on the representativeness of the most recent period), accounting records for Duke extending back to 1976/77, stored as microfiche, were examined. Because it was impractical to undertake the kind of full examination of expenditures by unit and type made possible by computers, aggregated data in the form of fund codes were collected for a selected number of departmental units. In order to use these data to get an idea of trends in the earlier period, two questions were posed: First, using the fund code data, how did the growth in spending in the earlier period compare with that in the period 1984–1992? Second, how do the two types of data compare for the period for which detailed information exists? If both types of data yield similar results for the more recent period, then one can more confidently rely on the fund code information for the earlier period.

Fund codes are the basic accounting unit used in most private colleges and universities. In the case of academic departments at Duke, a single fund code often covered an entire department over the entire 15-year period in question; this comparability allows at least a gross analysis of trends in spending over time. On the administrative side, however, fund codes appear to have proliferated in accordance with changes in organizational changes, making it necessary in most cases to add together a number of individual fund codes to approximate the total expenditure for any one administrative area.[19]

Table 4A.6 presents a comparison between fund code data and detailed accounting data (for unrestricted expenditures only) for selected academic department groupings and administrative areas.[20] The first two columns compare the 1992 dollar amounts of expenditures, giving some idea of how closely the total from the selected

TABLE 4A.6
Growth in Real Expenditures, Selected Duke Fund Codes

	Comparable Amounts, 1991/92 ($M)		Annual Growth Rates, by Fiscal Year		
	Fund Codes	Total Unrestricted	1976/77–1983/84 Fund Codes	1983/84–1991/92 Fund Codes	1983/84–1991/92 Total Unrestricted
Academic Departmental Groups (Excluding Graduate Aid)					
Natural Sciences	$13.4	$14.5	0.7	5.6	4.7
Humanities	12.0	14.1	0.3	6.1	6.6
Social Sciences	12.2	11.0	0.6	3.1	3.9
Engineering	5.8	5.5	3.8	6.4	5.9
Selected Departments					
Library	14.7	11.4	3.0	3.7	3.4
Student Services	3.9	3.3	4.5	1.7	2.4
University Counsel	1.6	1.0	14.2	8.1	3.4
Provost	6.7	8.7	-0.3	4.6	5.4
Accounting	8.9	8.7	5.0	4.5	7.4
Alumni and Development	9.4	5.6	1.7	5.4	5.9
Human Resources	3.5	3.4	12.1	1.7	2.0
Selected Financial Aid Categories					
Undergraduate Awards	8.8	12.1	2.5	14.4	14.5
Graduate Awards					
Natural Sciences	2.0	3.6	3.0	5.9	10.1
Humanities	0.8	2.6	-3.3	17.1	10.2
Social Sciences	0.6	2.3	-0.4	12.9	11.9
Engineering	0.3	1.3	6.8	3.0	10.4

Source: Unpublished accounting data for 1976/77, 1983/84, and 1991/92; and tabulations by Duke Planning Office.

Note: Selected departments included the following fund codes: library, 1540100–1541090; student services, 1551000–1552811, 1554000, 1559600, 1809033, and 1809037; university counsel, 1570400–1570415; provost, 1571100–1571550; accounting, 1573100–1573180; alumni and development, 1574800, 1574805, and 1574000–1574500; human resources, 1573500–1573513; undergraduate awards, 1680102 and 1681110; and graduate awards: natural sciences, 1681423, 1681426, 1681428, 1681441, 1681447, and 1681459; humanities, 1681435 and 1681439; social sciences, 1681429 and 1681448; and engineering, 1681432 and 1681433.

fund codes approximates the total unrestricted spending as calculated using the detailed financial data.[21] Comparisons are made for academic departmental groupings (the same ones used in Table 4.2, specific administrative areas, and several categories of financial aid. In general, the amounts shown in the first two columns are similar in magnitude. The similarity suggests that, in most cases, the fund codes chosen provide reasonably similar coverage to the tabulations based on the detailed financial data. The largest differences are in the financial aid categories. Other than simply providing less coverage, one reason why the total based on fund codes is smaller is the omission of salaries to graduate student instructors, which are added to financial aid in the total unrestricted numbers. However, there are other categories in which the differences in totals suggest that the two sets of data are not comparable.

Turning to the growth rates for these categories of spending, it is instructive to begin by comparing the last two columns, in order to assess the similarity of growth rates calculated for the period 1984–1992 using the two methods of measuring expenditures. In a majority of categories, the two growth rates calculated for the period are within one percentage point. Where the rates diverge significantly, it is for a category in which the two measures differ in coverage. In summary, even if two different bases are used to collect data, the growth rates for the 1984–1992 period appear to be fairly comparable in most cases. This comparability gives us some confidence that using the fund code information to detect trends over a longer period will provide useful supplemental information on rates of growth in expenditures.

With this background, it is now possible to compare the growth in expenditures based on fund codes. Was the period 1977–1984 one of slower or faster growth compared to the 1984–92 period for which detailed data are available? Looking first at the four major departmental groups, there is little doubt as to the answer: real expenditures accelerated rapidly in each division after 1984. Engineering led the way in both periods. Marked by the hiring of a number of prominent professors beginning in 1983, the humanities division showed the most dramatic jump in its rate of spending increase. The administrative units shown in the next section of the table generally exhibited faster rates of growth, especially in the earlier period. Whereas three of the four academic groups had growth rates of less than 1 percent from 1977 to 1984, only one among the selected administrative units did. But these rates of growth generally subsided during the second half of the period, falling from an average of 5.7 to 4.2. The unit displaying the most rapid increase over the entire period is the university counsel.[22] There was a similar racheting-up of spending in the selected financial aid categories. No doubt the item with the largest impact was undergraduate financial aid. (Recall that these expenditures are taken from unrestricted funds and thus do not include endowed scholarships or government-financed aid.) After growing at "only" 2.5 percent per year in real terms before 1984, this item exploded after 1984, growing at a 14.4 percent rate. Moreover, although the magnitudes are smaller, there were similar jumps in three of the four categories of graduate aid, with the largest increase recorded for humanities, perhaps indicating the degree to which support for graduate students is considered a necessary ingredient to improvement in academic departments. Overall, these comparisons suggest that the growth in administrative expenditures slowed after 1984 (although continuing to increase in real terms), whereas academic budgets generally grew significantly only during the later period.

CHAPTER 5

The Sources of Rising Expenditures

Universities cannot keep up with the growth
of expenses associated with their entire enterprise, and they have to come to terms with
the overextension and underinvestment that
affect them.

Hanna Holborn Gray, 1992[1]

As SHOULD be clear from chapter 4, expenditures increased significantly in many different categories in the sample institutions. In
seeking to explain this escalation, the current chapter attempts to
attribute portions of these increases to specific factors. This attribu-
tion is made on the basis of simple accounting identities. Thus, the
decompositions that are presented should be thought of as categorization, rather than as behavioral explanation. The first section of
this chapter discusses the contributions of several major items, including faculty compensation, other factor prices, financial aid, and
administration. The second section presents a decomposition of the
spending increases at the sample institutions in order to obtain an
idea of the relative importance of these factors. After attributing to
various factors some portions of the increase, a sizable unexplained
residual remains. The third section offers several additional possibilities for explaining this residual, including new programs, the cost
of scientific equipment, and the slowdown in the growth of federal
funding.

KEEPING UP WITH THE MARKET

A search for the sources of rising expenditures in any organization
logically begins by focusing on outside forces, particularly the market prices for inputs and other costly activities induced by competition. In the case of universities, the dominant outside influences are
faculty compensation and financial aid. This section also addresses
the roles of other factor prices and administrative growth.

Payments to Labor: Faculty and Other Employees

Like many other service industries, higher education is quite labor intensive. Given their prominence and unusually high degree of autonomy, faculty undoubtedly comprise the most distinctive class of worker in colleges and universities. Because they also constitute a large share of the workforce, payments to them loom large in the overall financial landscape of higher education. The growth in real faculty salaries during the 1980s further heightens the importance of this factor. It is therefore important to pay special attention to this category of spending.

Trends in Faculty Salaries

Figure 5.1 presents data based on the annual survey of faculty salaries conducted by the AAUP. The figure shows average salaries over the sample period for full professors and assistant professors at the four sample institutions; salaries are expressed in 1991/92 dollars, using the GDP price deflator. An important proviso is that these data include faculty in professional schools as well as in arts and sciences, which certainly affects the average salaries, if not the patterns of growth.

Several features of the figure stand out. First, the average salaries at the three sample universities are higher than those at Carleton. This contrast reflects the difference in general between private colleges and universities and, in particular, the higher salaries that faculty in professional schools receive. A second feature is the pattern of changes over time. For each institution, the first four years of the period, up to 1980/81, were ones of declining real salaries. As noted in chapter 3, the decrease in real faculty salaries during the 1970s was the result of high nominal raises being overwhelmed by even faster price inflation. From 1976/77 to 1981/82, nominal salary increases averaged 7.8 percent per year at private, doctoral-level universities surveyed by the AAUP, whereas price inflation averaged 8.2 percent. During the next 10 years, faculty salaries in nominal terms actually increased at a slower pace, 6.5 percent, but the markedly reduced inflation rate (3.9 percent) meant that real salaries increased over the decade at an impressive 2.6 percent rate.[2] For this 10-year period, the average full professor's salary at Chicago increased by 3.9 percent per year, compared with 3.5 percent at Duke, 2.6 percent at Harvard, and 2.0 percent at Carleton.

What explains the heady increases in real salaries at the sample

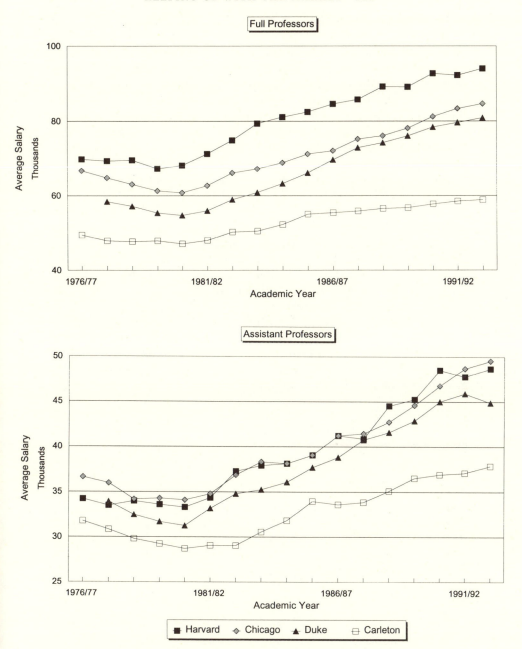

Figure 5.1 Real Salaries, Full and Assistant Professors, Sample Institutions.
Source: Academe, Annual Reports on the Economic Status of the Profession, 1977–1992.

universities during the 1980s? As noted in chapter 3, the earnings of professionals and other highly educated workers rose in relative terms during that decade. Regardless of whether the real increases in faculty salaries were viewed as "catch-up" from the previous decade, during which significant nominal salary increases had been outweighed by rapid inflation, the increases recorded by university faculty as a whole were by no means out of line with increases enjoyed by workers in comparable occupations. The question then turns to why salaries at these institutions did better than the average. One possibility would be changes in the composition of the faculty. If the percentage of the faculty in the sample institutions with tenure and more experience had increased over time, then the normal forces of tradition and the market would be expected to have pushed up real salaries there. Table 5.1 shows the percentage of faculty at the sample institutions who were tenured and the percentage who were full professors, based on AAUP data covering all faculty in its survey. It is evident that no dramatic changes occurred in these percentages. Chicago was the only one of the four institutions at which both of these reported percentages increased over the period; however, Chicago also was the institution showing the most growth in salaries at the full professor level.

To what extent was an institution itself—as opposed to the anonymous forces of the market—responsible for the increase in the salaries that it paid to faculty? Certainly it is part of the job description

TABLE 5.1
Percentage of Faculty with Tenure, with Rank of Full Professor

	1976/77[a]	1981/82	1986/87	1991/92
Percentage with Tenure				
Duke	78	79	74	72
Harvard	59	49	53	60
Carleton	65	71	62	60
Chicago	68	70	73	71
Weighted average	68	64	65	66
Percentage Full Professors				
Duke	49	52	52	51
Harvard	63	55	54	60
Carleton	42	51	51	45
Chicago	50	53	56	58
Weighted average	54	54	54	57

Source: Data are from *Academe* (August) 1977; (July/August) 1982; (March/April) 1987 and 1992.

[a]For Duke, figures refer to 1977/78.

of deans and provosts to search for the best possible candidates to fill faculty vacancies created by retirements and departures. Over time, however, this process should produce salary increases in line with market averages, as long as the average quality of the institution's faculty did not change. If, an institution set out to upgrade the quality of its research and teaching by hiring scholars of higher quality than its existing faculty, then its average salary would be expected to rise faster than the market average. To this extent, therefore, higher expenditures would be the result of deliberate policy, not of externally generated market forces.

During the sample period, all three universities participated actively in the national market for scholars, a market that increasingly featured highly paid "stars." At least one, Duke, made it a deliberate policy to increase the quality of its faculty by extending outside offers to senior faculty. The behavior of other universities, Chicago and Harvard among them, was not dissimilar in many respects. Although it was not possible to obtain data on individual faculty for this study, published information could be used to indicate the effect of this policy at Duke. The annual AAUP survey of institutions collects data on average salary increases for continuing faculty; of the sample institutions, only Duke and Carleton provided this information. By comparing these increases for continuing faculty with the overall percentage increase in salaries, it is possible to make a rough inference about the salaries of faculty hired from the outside and the salaries of continuing faculty. Consider only faculty at the level of full professor. In a steady state, in which retirees continuously are replaced by new faculty, the percentage increase in salaries for continuing faculty would be expected to be greater than the overall increase in salaries, because the salaries of the replacements would be lower than those of the retirees.[3] The overall increase could exceed the increase for continuing faculty only if an institution had begun the practice of hiring faculty from outside at above-average salaries.

Figure 5.2 shows the differential in salary increases for full professors between continuing faculty and all faculty for the years 1978 to 1994 for Carleton, Duke, and all institutions. As shown by the bars for all institutions, the usual pattern is one in which the increase for continuing faculty is higher than that for all faculty. This pattern also characterizes Carleton. For Duke, however, the pattern is reversed in nine of the years shown, suggesting the effect of outside hires at the full-professor level. Interestingly, in the last four years, the pattern at Duke reversed, indicating that the salaries of departing full professors exceeded those of newly appointed ones. Another indication of this pattern of faculty hiring at Duke emerged in a

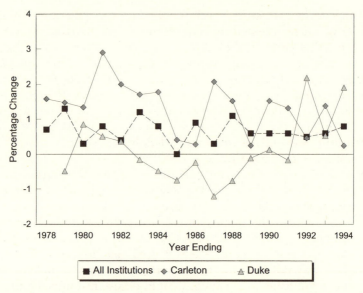

Figure 5.2 Percentage Change in Full Professor Salaries:
Continuing Full Professors Minus All Full Professors.
Source: Table 5A.2.

study of faculty salaries in 1993, which found that salaries were related systematically to the number of years spent at Duke[4]; the survey showed the average salary falling by about $1,000 for each year
at the university, holding constant highest degree, age, and number
of years of experience.

Fringe Benefits

Fringe benefits—encompassing health, retirement, and other non-
wage benefits—have grown relatively faster than salaries in higher
education, as they have virtually everywhere in the United States in
recent decades. Table 5.2 shows, for the sample institutions, the average fringe benefit rates reported on the annual AAUP surveys of
faculty compensation. In each case, the rate inches inexorably upward over the period, with the weighted average for the sample institutions increasing from 18 percent in 1976/77 to 23 percent in
1991/92. It seems unlikely that these reported rates are strictly comparable across institutions, and they may not be comparable over
time for the same institution, but the general upward trend corresponds to everything else that is known about fringe benefits as a

TABLE 5.2
Fringe Benefit Rates for Faculty

	1976/77[a]	*1981/82*	*1986/87*	*1991/92*
Duke	16	22	22	22
Harvard	20	20	21	23
Carleton	17	19	18	25
Chicago	17	21	22	23
Weighted average	18	21	21	23

Source: Data are from *Academe* (August) 1977; (July/August) 1982; (March/April) 1987 and 1992.

[a]For Duke, figures refer to 1977/78.

broad topic. To illustrate what goes into fringe benefits and into their rise, Table 5.3 details the components of the fringe benefit pool for faculty and staff at Duke for the sample period. Over this 15-year period, fringe benefits increased as a percentage of salaries from 15.3 to 22.7 percent, figures that are close, but not identical, to the comparable AAUP percentages. Duke's overall increase was caused largely by a tripling of the percentage for health insurance and by sizable increases for social security and retirement contributions.[5] By itself, this increase in the fringe benefit rate is responsible for a 0.4 percent average annual growth in faculty and staff compensation.[6]

Other Prices

In the same way that universities were subject to the rigors of market forces in the labor market, they also faced changing prices in other factor markets. Often using the rapid rise in the HEPI as evidence, some defenders of university costs pointed to extraordinary inflation in the cost of important inputs purchased by colleges and universities, including faculty. Just as rapidly increasing utility prices affected the cost structure of universities during the 1970s, the real cost of other items rose during the 1980s. For example, spurred by dramatic hikes in the cost of books and journals, the inflation-adjusted cost of library acquisitions increased 35 percent from 1981/82 to 1991/92.[7] On the other hand, the increase in the price of some items was less than the overall rate of inflation.[8] Because institutions had little choice but to pay the market price of goods and services that they purchased, it is essential in evaluating the escalation in costs to account for the change in these prices.

TABLE 5.3
Faculty and Staff Benefits per $100 of Salaries, by Type of Benefit: Duke

| | Fiscal Year | | | |
Benefit Category	1976/77	1981/82	1986/87	1991/92
Retirement				
Pensions	6.76	7.23	7.59	8.23
Social Security	4.27	5.80	6.15	6.46
Medical Care	1.53	2.63	3.37	4.90
Educational Assistance	1.57	1.43	1.75	1.55
Group Insurance and				
Survivors Benefits	0.75	1.03	0.20	0.57
Benefits Administra-				
tion	—	—	0.18	0.23
Health and Recreation				
Programs and Sub-				
sidies	0.23	0.29	0.36	0.35
Housing Subsidies	—	0.01	0.04	0.03
Child Care Subsidy	—	—	—	0.06
Parking Allowance	—	—	—	0.06
Workman's Compensa-				
tion	0.10	0.07	0.15	0.15
Other	0.08	0.05	0.10	0.09
Total	15.28	18.53	19.87	22.69

Source: Calculations using unpublished data from the Duke University Accounting Department.
— Benefit not offered or not separately recorded.

Student Financial Aid

Much has been written about the spiraling cost of financial aid at private colleges and universities. Most of the concern has been directed toward need-based aid given to undergraduates. Increases in this item have been presented as reasons why some private institutions have abandoned the policy of "need-blind" admissions policies. Less has been written about the cost of graduate aid, which generally is not based on need, although this support is acknowledged to be a central element in the functioning of graduate training.[9]

As shown in the tables of expenditure changes in chapter 4, financial aid to undergraduates grew faster than any other category of spending, and its increase was on the same order of magnitude as the total increase in faculty compensation. To be sure, some commentators tend to dismiss this category of spending, preferring to think about financial aid merely as a discount on the "sticker price" of published tuition rates. Certainly, financial aid is a different kind of expenditure than, say, salaries or utility costs, in that almost no aid is "paid out," but rather, is credited against certain revenue streams. The opposing argument is at least as strong, however. In the present environment, particularly among private selective institutions, financial aid is simply one cost of doing business. Its impact on the financial well-being of institutions is much the same as those of other expenditure categories. Moreover, to the extent that the national concern about rising costs has been spurred by the increase in "sticker" tuition rates, it is necessary to pay attention to financial aid as one category of expenditure.

Administrative Services

Another shift that may or may not have been spurred by market forces is the alleged increase in administrative spending. Although some critics, noted in chapter 2, pointed to such increases as evidence of "bloat," the expansion of services, especially student services, that colleges and universities routinely offered over this period suggests that institutions were competing by enhancing the services they provided. One very simple way of assessing the likely importance of growth in administrative expenditures is to focus on the change in the proportion of total spending that is accounted for by administrative functions. In the context of the kind of information presented in chapter 4, this reasoning translates quite directly to measuring the share of spending accounted for by the lines in the tables referring to various administrative units, including arts and sciences administration, admissions and financial aid, alumni and development, general administration, and plant.[10]

DECOMPOSING THE INCREASE

In assessing the various explanations for rising costs, it is useful to step back and attempt to attach an order of magnitude to each possible source of cost increase. This section attempts to break out the effects of four sets of changes, using simple calculations for the sample institutions. The calculations do not analyze behavior or the reasons for the increases, but rather, associate parts of the increases with changes in quantities or shares. The components identified here are based on simple calculations taken one at a time, with interactions ignored. The portion of expenditures that cannot be attributed to one of the changes remains "unexplained" (as will be seen, this portion is large), but it would be incorrect to say that the attributed portions have been "explained" in anything more than an accounting sense. The calculations, summarized in Table 5.4, examine four sets of factors: (1) market prices of factors, (2) institution-specific changes in faculty compensation, (3) financial aid, and (4) administrative costs.

The first generic reason why any entity's expenditure might increase is that the real cost of its purchased inputs might have risen. Using price indices for major components of university purchases, I calculated the increase in expenditures that would have been ex-

TABLE 5.4

Decomposition of Expenditure Increases

	Duke	Harvard	Chicago	Carleton
Base Year	1983/84	1981/82	1983/84	1981/82
Ending Year	1991/92	1991/92	1991/92	1991/92
1 Percentage Change in Real Expenditures	73%	69%	62%	77%
2 Average Annual Growth Rate	6.8%	5.3%	6.0%	5.7%
Proportion of Increased Spending due to				
3 Market prices	0.122	0.122	0.144	0.141
Regular faculty				
4 Growth	0.047	0.063	0.010	0.078
5 Over-market salary increases	0.035	−0.024	0.017	−0.002
6 Over-market increase in fringe benefits	0.002	0.002	−0.007	0.004
7 Nonregular faculty	0.063	0.013	0.046	0.000
Financial aid				
8 Number of students	0.051	0.033	0.049	−0.003
9 Aid per student	0.259	0.108	0.293	0.217
10 Increased administrative spending	0.046	0.049	0.052	0.008
11 Residual	0.376	0.635	0.398	0.557
12 Total	1.000	1.000	1.000	1.000

Source: Calculations using unpublished data from the sample institutions; Research Associates of Washington (1994); *Academe* (July/August) 1982, p. 17; *Academe* (July/August) 1984, pp. 11, 15; *Academe* (March/April) 1987, p. 9; *Academe* (March/April) 1992, p. 19.

pected on the basis of rising factor prices alone. Data on factor prices were taken from the HEPI and from the AAUP's annual survey of faculty compensation. The index for faculty compensation used for the three universities is a fixed-weight average of salaries plus fringe benefits at three ranks for private independent doctoral institutions; for Carleton, it is a comparable index using private independent four-year colleges.[11] The average nominal faculty salary at private independent doctoral institutions rose 33 percent in real terms and 96 percent in nominal terms between 1981/82 and 1991/92.[12] Thus, an increase of 33 percent of an institution's 1981/82 faculty compensation (expressed in 1991/92 dollars) can be "attributed" to the increase in the market price of faculty, in the sense that an institution's outlay for faculty would have to have increased by that much in the absence of any adjustments in faculty size, just so that the institution could retain faculty of comparable quality.

Similar calculations were made for nine other categories of expenditures, applying in each case the appropriate price index for the period corresponding to the data for each institution. Line 3 in Table 5.4 summarizes all the calculations for each institution, expressing the total of the hypothetical increases due to the price alone as a percentage of the total increase in spending for the institution. What can be seen clearly is that these increases in factor prices do not explain much of the overall increases; in no case do they explain more than 15 percent of the total increase.

Lines 4–6 of the table attribute spending increases to changes in the institution's regular-rank faculty and its compensation, other than increases in line with the marketwide growth in salary and fringes already included in line 3. The first component, shown on line 4, is the increase simply due to growth in numbers.[13] The number of regular faculty increased at all four of the sample institutions over the period of study, ranging from a 3 percent increase at Chicago (over 8 years) to increases of more than 20 percent at Harvard and Carleton (over 10 years).[14] Yet, as the figures in the table show, increases even as large as those at Harvard and Carleton account for less than one-tenth of the total increase in arts and sciences spending. Lines 5 and 6 measure the effects of increases in salaries and fringe benefit rates in excess of the average rates in the market; positive numbers refer to increases above the market increases and negative numbers (representing reductions in expenditures) refer to increases below the market average.[15] Differentials in fringe benefits have little effect, but extraordinary increases in salaries at Duke account for 3.5 percent of the university's total increase.

The next component of increased spending is that attributable to the increasing use of nonregular faculty, that is, the adjunct professors, lecturers, and other instructors who are neither permanent faculty or graduate students and who have shouldered an increasing share of teaching in American higher education. The figures shown on line 7 refer to the increase in spending on nonregular faculty that is not explained by the increase in real salary rates (which is included in line 3 with the figures on market prices). Separate data on payrolls for nonregular faculty were not available for Carleton. The line shows that the otherwise unexplained increase in spending for nonregular faculty was relatively large at Duke and Chicago, representing 6 and 5 percent of the total increases in spending, respectively.

The fourth component examined in the decomposition, financial aid, accounts for a much larger share of the total increase than does any other. Some of this increase at the three universities is due to the number of students; this is shown on line 8. Because undergraduate enrollments did not increase significantly, virtually all of this increase can be laid to the growth in graduate enrollments.[16] The residual increase in aid is shown in line 9. This component is the largest single attributed element in the table, accounting for 30 percent of the total at Chicago, one-fourth of the total at Duke, and more than one-fifth of the total at Carleton. Increases in the average award to graduate students reflect a strengthening of overall graduate financial support. For undergraduates, the increase in average aid was due largely to the interaction between disproportionate tuition increases and the formula underlying the need-based aid. When tuition increases faster than income and most other items in the standard financial aid formula, both the percentage of students eligible for aid and the percentage of aid in the form of grants (as opposed to loans and self-help) increase, causing a more-than-proportional increase in grants to those receiving aid.[17]

The last item in the decomposition is administrative expenditures, shown on line 10. A way to assess the contribution of administration is suggested by the fact that the percentage of total arts and sciences spending devoted to administration at all four institutions increased over the study period. To determine the portion of the overall increase that one might attribute to the increase in administration, I calculated how much higher administrative spending in the base year would have been if the 1991/92 percentage of total spending on administration had applied rather than the actual percentage. For the three universities, at which the administrative shares increased noticeably, the portions of the total increase so attributed were almost 5 percent each.[18] For Carleton, the portion was less than 1 percent.

The literal bottom line of this decomposition shows a substantial unexplained residual, ranging from 38 to 64 percent of the total increase in arts and sciences spending. In other words, after attributing all of the increases to changes in other known quantities or shares, a large portion of the growth remains unexplained. The unavoidable conclusion is that a sizable portion of the increase is due to higher quality or new functions, or to increased waste. One of these possibilities can be explored further. The next section discusses that possibility and suggests two additional explanations for the residual.

SOME EXPLANATIONS OF THE RESIDUAL

Three explanations that have been offered for rising expenditures in higher education are worth considering at greater length. They are: (1) universities have added new programs; (2) the cost of science has escalated dramatically; and (3) the federal government has scaled back its support of universities, forcing institutions to take up the slack.

New Programs

To what extent are rising expenditures due simply to an increase in the number of things that universities are doing? We know that knowledge grows, probably at an accelerating rate. We also know that the universities in our sample have added academic programs faster than they have eliminated them. Therefore, one simple way of thinking about increasing expenditures is to focus on the impact of new programs, or to separate the increase that arises from any excess of new programs over discontinued programs.

By definition, the increase in spending in any component of the university can be written in terms of the following identity:

> Expenditures in newly established programs
> − Expenditures in discontinued programs
> + Changes in expenditures in continuing programs
> = Change in total expenditures

Within limits, this kind of decomposition of the overall increase can indicate the relative contribution of new activities. One must recognize, however, that this division depends on someone's determination of what constitutes a "program"—the unit of accounting—which muddies the interpretation of any empirical application of this decomposition. Continuing programs may institute new activities, and new programs may well be composed largely of previously existing parts.

With this inherent drawback in mind, I applied this reasoning to the detailed expenditure data for Duke, allowing the accountants' definition of a fund code to determine what constitutes a "program." Fund codes differ enormously in size, from academic departments with budgets in the hundreds of thousands of dollars to individual faculty members with very small amounts of research funds, measured in the hundreds of dollars. They are good indicators of continuity, however, because they tend to remain on the books as long as an activity continues to exist and because they have money to spend or receive. Fund codes with expenditures of at least $100 in absolute value in constant dollars were taken to signify existing programs; those existing in both years were counted as continuing programs.[19]

For each of the four major academic departmental groupings, the components of the change in spending shown in the identity above were calculated. In the case of Duke, the beginning year was 1983/84, the first year for which detailed financial information was available. Table 5.5 shows this decomposition separately for internally funded and externally funded expenditures. Among the internally funded programs, the growth in continuing programs was far more important than new programs in explaining expenditure growth. The difference between new and discontinued programs, $7.4 million, accounted for only about one-fifth of the total $38.8 million increase in spending. During this period, the three largest new programs were new departments; two of the three (the Institute of Statistics and Decision Sciences and Asian and African Languages and Literature) were created out of whole cloth, albeit using some faculty who previously had been members of other departments. The third was merely the result of splitting a large department (Psychology) into two parts. As these examples illustrate, it is uncommon to find large, internally financed, genuinely "new" programs.

Not surprisingly, the story was quite different for externally financed expenditures, for which continuing programs had virtually no importance. By their nature, individual grants and contracts do not have long lives. All the growth in external funding can be attributed to the difference between new and discontinued fund codes.

Science Costs

One hypothesis that has been offered for the rapid increases in expenditures in research universities is the escalating cost of scientific

TABLE 5.5

The Importance of New Programs in Explaining Growth in Expenditures
(In Millions of 1991/92 Dollars)

	Departmental Groups				
	Humanities	Social Sciences	Natural Sciences	Engineering	Total
Internally Financed					
New accounts, 1991/92	2.6	2.9	3.8	1.1	10.3
− Discontinued accounts, 1983/84	0.8	0.3	1.4	0.3	2.9
Continuing accounts					
+ 1991/92	18.2	13.4	18.8	6.7	57.1
− 1983/84	10.3	10.1	1.2	4.1	25.7
= Change in expenditures	9.7	6.0	19.9	3.3	38.8
Externally Financed	0.0	0.0	0.0	0.0	0.0
New accounts, 1991/92	2.3	8.9	18.1	3.8	33.2
− Discontinued accounts, 1983/84	1.1	2.6	14.3	1.8	19.7
Continuing accounts					
+ 1991/92	0.0	0.0	0.1	0.0	0.1
− 1983/84	0.0	0.0	0.1	0.0	0.1
= Change in expenditures	1.2	6.3	3.9	2.0	13.5

Source: Calculations using unpublished data from Duke.

Note: Figures give expenditures in new, discontinued, and continuing accounts, using data from the 1983/84 and 1991/92 academic years.

research. In principle, the components of the HEPI should reflect these increases. However, the special scientific requirements of research universities, especially the need for new and expensive equipment, may not be reflected fully in those indices. Although the operating costs of science may be a major source of rising costs, it seems more likely that people have capital costs in mind when they cite the high cost of science. It is certainly worth looking at both costs. Symbolic of the capital costs of science are the large commitments in start-up costs that have become a routine part of recruiting new faculty in the sciences. These start-up costs typically cover such items as scientific equipment, computers, and the renovation of laboratories and are negotiated as a part of financial packages for newly hired faculty.

At Duke, a calculation for 36 appointments in the early 1980s showed an average commitment of $149,000 for appointments in botany, chemistry, geology, physics, and zoology, and an average commitment of $50,000 for appointments in biological anthropology, mathematics, and psychology.[20] Are costs such as these a major factor in the rise in total spending by research universities? The tabulations in chapter 4 on expenditures at Duke suggest that increases in capital spending for research were dwarfed by changes in salaries and other spending. Although the accounting system used at Duke does not lend itself to the identification of such costs, most capital spending for scientific research is reflected in the two columns in Table 4.1 corresponding to computers and capital expenditures. The breakdown by department group gives an indication of the relative importance of capital costs at Duke in 1991/92. Relative to the overall size of each departmental grouping, the natural sciences far outspent the humanities and social sciences in both computers and capital expenditures. The natural sciences accounted for some 40 percent of all internally funded expenditures for computers and other capital.

Harvard's accounting structure makes it simpler to track start-up costs, and the story that the numbers tell is one of rapid increases during the 1980s. As at Duke, these costs almost always arise from commitments made to newly hired faculty to be used at the faculty member's discretion for such items as computers, laboratory renovation, or laboratory equipment. At Harvard, the practice was to establish a fund at the time of the appointment, out of which subsequent expenditures would be made. Table 5.6 presents a summary of start-up costs at Harvard, covering the three major divisions of arts and sciences plus two additional categories. Although the figures are reasonably comparable, they differ in the matter of timing. The totals listed in the three columns of the table for the three academic divisions and administration represent expenditures made during the designated years from the start-up accounts, many of which were established in previous years. In contrast, the general expense category is the sum of allocations made in those years to academic units

TABLE 5.6
Research Start-Up Costs: Harvard Arts and Sciences, 1982, 1987, and 1992
(In Thousands of 1991/92 Dollars)

	_1981/82_	_1986/87_	_1991/92_
General Expenses[a]	172.9	96.4	258.3
Humanities	10.8	205.9	300.7
Natural Sciences	27.3	1,468.6	1,476.5
Social Sciences	27.1	200.1	906.4
Administration	0.0	97.4	92.6
Total	238.1	2,068.4	3,034.5

Source: Calculations based on unpublished data from Harvard.
[a]Transfers out of Faculty of Arts and Sciences and unspecified.

outside the Faculty of Arts and Sciences but within our definition of "arts and sciences."[21] If these aggregates are taken as a rough indication of total start-up spending, it is clear that this category of expenditure has risen markedly over the period 1982–1992. Because most of the general expense costs probably were directed to an affiliate unit that we classify as natural sciences, Table 5.6 strongly suggests that, despite rapid growth in start-up costs in the social sciences during this period, the bulk of the start-up costs was directed toward the natural sciences.

Stagnant Federal Funding

Federal support for research increased modestly in real terms during the 1980s, but its share of total university support for research declined.[22] This trend is evident among the three universities studied here as well; as a percentage of total arts and sciences expenditures, federally funded spending fell from 21 to 15 percent at Harvard, from 20 to 19 percent at Duke, and from 27 to 19 percent at Chicago. The important question in this study is, How did this changing pattern affect universities' internally funded spending? Because virtually all federal support was tied to specific expenditures, in principle, any decline in support could have been matched by corresponding spending cuts. However, universities could have continued some of these programs, choosing to replace lost federal support with their own institutional funds. This choice is most explicit when funding agencies ask institutions to bear a larger share of the cost of sponsored grants and contracts. By means of matching and other cost-sharing requirements, this shifting of the burden onto institutions appears to have become more common during the 1980s.[23]

It is impossible to determine the precise impact of these changes in funding, as doing so would require knowledge of what would have happened if no change had occurred. However, it is both possible and helpful to make some assessment of that impact through the use of a counterfactual calculation giving a "what-if" level of federal support. The calculation represents what might have occurred if the relative importance of federal support had not decreased and allows comparison of the actual and hypothetical patterns, to give one measure of the possible impact. One reasonable benchmark is the amount of federal support that universities would have received had federal support remained a fixed percentage of total expenditures. If universities used internal funds to make up the difference between this hypothetical amount and what they actually received in federal support, then the additional expenditure of internal funds can be calculated.

Tables 5.7 and 5.8 show these calculations for Duke and Harvard, respectively. The first two columns show the percentage of total arts and sciences spending funded by federal grants and contracts, by departmental group. To illustrate the calculation, consider the largest item in Table 5.8, on the line for natural sciences. If federal funds had continued to account for the 47 percent of natural sciences spending in 1991/92 that it had 10 years earlier, Harvard would have received some $8 million more in federal support than it actually did. If Harvard had used internal funds to make up this shortfall, the impact on internal funds clearly would be $8 million, or about 12 percent of all the internally funded spending in the natural sciences. To commit this amount without reducing other

TABLE 5.7
Hypothetical Impact of Decline in Federal Share of Expenditures: Duke

Departmental Group	Federal Grants as Percentage of Total Expenditures		Hypothetical Loss (Gain) in Federal Funding^a ($ Thousands)	As Percentage of Internally Funded Spending	Required Growth in Internally Funded Spending
	1983/84	1991/92			
Humanities	4	5	(239)	−1.1	−0.1
Social Sciences	14	26	(3,187)	−18.1	−2.5
Natural Sciences	41	39	880	3.4	0.4
Engineering	20	23	(348)	−4.5	−0.6
Library	0	2	(234)	−2.1	−0.3
Student Services	0	0	0	0.0	0.0
Plant	0	0	0	0.0	0.0
Admissions and Financial Aid	30	12	3,923	20.8	2.4
Arts and Sciences Administration	25	23	566	2.8	0.3
Provost	0	2	(78)	−2.1	−0.3
Alumni and Development	0	0	0	0.0	0.0
General Administration	1	0	1,282	30.3	3.3
Total	20	19	2,565	1.7	0.2

Source: Calculations using unpublished data from Duke.

^aDifference between hypothetical federally funded expenditures and actual federally funded expenditures, where the hypothetical is calculated as the percentage of total expenditures that was federally financed in the initial year multiplied by actual total expenditures in 1991/92.

TABLE 5.8
Hypothetical Impact of Decline in Federal Share of Expenditures: Harvard

Departmental Group	Federal Grants as Percentage of Total Expenditures		Hypothetical Loss (Gain) in Federal Funding[a] ($ Thousands)	As Percentage of Internally Funded Spending	Required Growth in Internally Funded Spending
	1981/82	1991/92			
General Academic	1	7	(1,496)	−6.1	−0.6
Humanities	7	4	1,690	3.4	0.3
Social Sciences	16	10	2,387	7.6	0.7
Natural Sciences	47	41	8,344	12.0	1.1
Museums	31	11	2,853	22.6	2.0
Library	2	1	348	1.0	0.1
Student Services	2	0	714	2.0	0.2
Admissions and Financial Aid	10	5	1,851	5.3	0.5
Administration	4	1	1,749	3.0	0.3
Plant	0	0	0	0.0	0.0
Athletics	2	0	237	2.0	0.2
Total	21	15	18,675	4.9	0.5

Source: Calculations using unpublished data from Harvard.
[a]Difference between hypothetical federally funded expenditures and actual federally funded expenditures, where the hypothetical is calculated as the percentage of total expenditures that was federally financed in the initial year multipled by actual total expenditures in 1991/92.

spending would have required a real growth rate in internal funds of 1.1 percent per year. For the university's total arts and sciences operation, this calculation suggests that the burden of sluggish growth in federal funding could have accounted for more than $18 million in internally funded spending in 1991/92. For Duke, the implied burden is less, owing to the more modest decline in the share of its arts and sciences spending supported by federal funds.

Although these calculations are suggestive, they are by no means definitive. In fact, they would appear to represent an upper bound to the impact of the slowdown in the growth of federal funding. These calculations would represent the true cost of the change in funding patterns only if universities had decided to continue all the projects and expenditures that formerly had been supported by federal money. Universities could have avoided at least some portion of this burden by deciding not to undertake certain activities. However, to the extent that the federal government's cuts occurred in categories that universities felt were central, such as the support of graduate students, or in expenditures for infrastructure deemed essential to the projects themselves, a certain shifting of the burden from federal to institutional funds was inevitable.

CONCLUSION

The aim of this chapter is to seek reasonable explanations for the increases in expenditures documented in chapter 4. When the increases are decomposed into identifiable components associated with other documented changes or trends, roughly half the total increases can be "explained." The largest of these identifiable components are increases associated with financial aid per student, rising real factor prices (including faculty compensation), and growth in faculty size. Some increase also can be attributed to growth in the number of graduate students and in the portion of the arts and sciences budget taken up by administration. At the end of the exercise, however, there remains a sizable share of the increase that cannot be attributed to any of these factors. It seems most likely that the bulk of this residual reflects attempts to provide higher-quality service or to undertake new activities, all within existing departmental and administrative structures. Another strong possibility, especially for the research universities, is that part of the increase represents the institutions taking responsibility for some kinds of expenditures that might formerly have been covered by federal grants and contracts, some of which is in the form of start-up costs for newly hired faculty.

Appendix 5

Supplementary Tables for Chapter 5

TABLE 5A.1
Average Faculty Salaries, by Rank, 1991/92 Dollars

	1976/77	1981/82	1986/87	1991/92	Growth Rate 1982–92
Duke[a]					
Professor	58,504	56,007	69,454	79,600	3.5
Associate professor	42,024	40,866	48,642	56,000	
Assistant professor	33,990	33,222	38,720	45,900	
Instructor	—	—	38,357	—	
All	47,929	47,040	57,112	65,700	3.3
Harvard					
Professor	69,836	71,295	84,337	92,200	2.6
Associate professor	43,979	39,690	44,649	52,000	
Assistant professor	34,255	34,398	41,140	47,800	
Instructor	—	—	23,958	46,600	
All	57,681	55,566	63,283	71,400	2.5
Carleton					
Professor	49,504	48,069	55,297	58,500	2.0
Associate professor	37,349	35,574	44,286	45,500	
Assistant professor	31,824	29,106	33,517	37,100	
Instructor	28,288	23,961	28,556	—	
All	40,210	39,837	45,738	48,100	1.9
Chicago					
Professor	66,742	62,769	71,874	83,300	2.8
Associate professor	45,747	41,454	47,190	54,400	
Assistant professor	36,686	34,839	41,140	48,700	
Instructor	31,161	26,754	29,645	34,800	
All	53,587	50,715	59,169	69,000	3.1
Private Independent, Doctoral Level[b]					
Professor	61,460	59,123	68,849	76,890	2.6
Associate professor	42,764	41,072	46,972	51,700	
Assistant professor	34,189	33,075	38,768	43,630	
Instructor	27,647	26,901	30,117	33,220	
Lecturer	—	26,078	32,247	34,090	

TABLE 5A.1 (*cont.*)

	1976/77	*1981/82*	*1986/87*	*1991/92*	*Growth Rate* *1982–92*
No rank	—	—	—	37,480	
All	47,073	46,246	53,990	60,260	2.6
All Faculty (Doctoral Level)					
Professor	56,731	53,655	61,105	65,190	1.9
Associate professor	41,747	39,264	43,814	46,290	
Assistant professor	34,034	32,208	36,736	39,120	
Instructor	26,852	24,431	26,777	27,670	
Lecturer	—	28,209	31,569	32,510	
No rank	—	—	—	33,150	
All	43,382	41,924	48,158	51,080	2.0
All Faculty[c]					
Professor	52,885	49,216	55,091	58,220	1.7
Associate professor	40,001	37,059	40,922	43,260	
Assistant professor	32,752	30,326	33,783	36,060	
Lecturer	26,343	23,976	25,809	27,170	
No rank	—	27,239	30,165	30,470	
Instructor	—	—	—	33,560	
All	39,625	37,853	42,919	45,360	1.8

Source: Data are from *Academe* (August) 1977, Table 3, p. 154; (July/August) 1982, Table 6, p. 18; (March/April) 1987, Table 3, p. 9; (March/April) 1992, Table 4, p. 19.

Note: The GDP price deflator was used to convert to constant dollars.

— No data available owing to small number of observations.

[a]Figures are for 1977/78; 1976/77 not published.

[b]Category I, covering institutions conferring an average of 15 or more doctorates in a minimum of three nonrelated disciplines.

[c]All four-year and two-year institutions, with ranks.

TABLE 5A.2

Percentage Change in Full Professor Salaries: Continuing Full Professors
Minus All Full Professors, All Institutions, Carleton, and Duke

Year	All	Carleton	Duke
1977/78	0.7	1.6	—
1978/79	1.3	1.5	−0.5
1979/80	0.3	1.3	0.9
1980/81	0.8	2.9	0.5
1981/82	0.4	2.0	0.4
1982/83	1.2	1.7	−0.2
1983/84	0.8	1.8	−0.5
1984/85	0.0	0.4	−0.7
1985/86	0.9	0.3	−0.2
1986/87	0.3	2.1	−1.2
1987/88	1.1	1.5	−0.8
1988/89	0.6	0.2	−0.1
1989/90	0.6	1.5	0.1
1990/91	0.6	1.3	−0.2
1991/92	0.5	0.5	2.2
1992/93	0.6	1.4	0.5
1993/94	0.8	0.2	1.9

Source: Academe (March/April), 1978–1994.

Note: Numbers are the difference between the percentage change in the average
salary of full professors who continued to work at the same institution and the percentage change in the average salary of all full professors.

— No information reported.

CHAPTER 6

Administrative Functions

It is also very likely that some of the increases
in real costs in higher education are ascribable
to inefficiency, i.e., poor management. Education is extremely labor-intensive—nearly twice
as labor-intensive as the average in private
business. Research and development expenditures are tiny, compared to the private sector.
'Capital per worker' is abysmally low.
Henry Rosovsky, 1992[1]

THE NEXT THREE chapters examine some of the observable changes
that have accompanied the expenditure trends noted in the previous
chapters. Considering these changes should aid our understanding
of the increases in spending, suggesting explanations and consequences for them. This chapter focuses on administration in the university, including the everyday office functions that are carried out
in academic departments. The first section discusses administrative
functions generally, and the second section examines data from
some of the sample institutions on actual staffing patterns.

THE TASKS AND TECHNOLOGY OF THE ADMINISTRATIVE SIDE

Setting aside for the moment the university's central functions referred to in chapter 2—research, teaching, service, and patient
care—what is left bears a close resemblance, and in some cases is
virtually identical, to any number of other large business or government bureaucracies. Supporting activities include such functions as
strategic planning, purchasing, maintenance, personnel, payroll, and
accounting. In contrast to the latitude accorded to faculty members
in their research, teaching, and service, the units that provide most
of these support functions operate within a decidedly hierarchical
organizational setting. The business of these units is, in a word, business.

Yet these functions have been cited as one of the culprits in the rising cost in universities. The president of the AAUP stated, "Undetected, unprotested, and unchecked, the excessive growth of administrative expenditures has done a lot of damage to life and learning on our campuses" (Bergmann 1991, p. 12). In particular, these administrative functions have been named in two indictments about cost escalation: (1) growth in number of functions, and (2) inefficiency of operation. Commentators have noted the efforts of colleges and universities to provide new services and "amenities," from manicured lawns, shuttle buses, and telephones in dorm rooms to glossy informational brochures, new recreation programs, and career counseling.[2] Whatever one may think of the need for these features, it seems reasonable to view them as a direct result of the competition among colleges and universities to attract desirable students.[3] Universities themselves frequently point to another example of increased administrative activity—the need to respond to a growing number of government regulations in such areas as occupational and environmental safety, grants and contracts, student records, and financial aid.[4]

A less sympathetic explanation for administrative growth in universities is a version of the age-old tendency for bureaucracies to grow. Analyzed by scores of social scientists and popularized by Parkinson (1957), this growth force has been identified in higher education most recently by Massy and Wilger (1992). They argue that the university's consensual approach to collective decisions, noted in chapter 2, and an increasing timidity in the face of hard decisions, have fed the demand for more administrators.[5] In some publicized cases, high executive salaries and lavish items have aroused critics to denounce expenditures as excessive.

An alternative view is that much of the growth in administrative functions represents a rational substitution designed to economize on the use of faculty time. In the same way that nonfaculty employees may be taking on more of the advising function, administrators increasingly may be assuming some of the consensus-building functions traditionally held by faculty, leaving the latter more time for research. At the same time, the opposite case seems just as likely, namely, that the same forces pushing for more administrators also may have led to the growth of committees.

A second broad explanation for excessive cost in university administration is inefficiency, which corresponds to one of the three generic causes of high or rising costs noted in the introductory chapter.[6] This explanation goes beyond the "cost disease" argument, which states that the lack of technological progress causes productivity to be stagnant, and that stagnant productivity, combined with rising real wages, increases real costs. As it is used here in the context of administrative work, inefficiency can be seen as waste. When managers do not use "best-practice" techniques to accomplish a job, or when workers are untrained or simply do not perform to their potential, less is accomplished per dollar of expenditure than could be accomplished under ideal circumstances.[7] Rosovsky's (1992) criticism of the inadequate training and the "abysmally low" capital-labor ratio in universities speaks to this concern. So, too, do the current efforts in universities to apply management-improvement techniques in order to reduce staffs and improve service.

Yet, over the period covered by this study, the administrative workplace changed dramatically. Like the rest of the business world, universities were engulfed in a wave of new technology, most prominently in computing and communications. Consider what the office of 1976 did not have that, by the early 1990s, was taken for granted: touch-tone phones, voice mail, overnight package delivery, FAX machines, electronic mail, and, most important, personal computers.[8] To suggest the growing importance of this type of equipment, Table 6.1 gives the total expenditures on computers and office machines for Duke's four sample academic departments and for a group of administrative units.[9] Reflecting the overall growth in spending on computers discussed in chapter 4, outlays for these units grew rapidly. The spending by the academic departments reflects the purchase of expensive minicomputers, used in research. Perhaps the

TABLE 6.1

Purchases of Computers and Other Office Machines, Selected Academic and Administrative Departments: Duke

	1981/82	1986/87	1991/92
Expenditures on Office Machines, Computers, and Software (Thousands of 1991/92 Constant Dollars)			
Four academic departments	$205	$654	$586
Selected administrative units[a]	$27	$36	$56
Number Purchased by Four Academic Departments, Selected Equipment			
Typewriters	3	2	0
Minicomputers (multi-user)	3	6	15
Personal computers	7	32	51

Source: Data are from unpublished tabulations, Duke University.

[a]University Counsel, Office of Research Support, Student Activities Office, Registrar, Accounting, General Services, Cost Accounting, and Sponsored Programs (component codes 10400, 11254, 11317, 11320, 13128, 13143, and 13180).

most striking aspect of this table is the rapid increase in the number of personal computers, from 7 to 51, standing in contrast to the virtual disappearance of the typewriter.

As striking as these numbers are, the astounding aspect of this change is the increase in the power and capacity of the machines. Table 6.2 illustrates this improvement by presenting data on three computers actually purchased by one of Duke's academic departments during this period. Although the real prices for listed machines increased only modestly, all their important operational attributes improved dramatically. From the first to the third machine, the computational speed increased by a factor of 10, memory (RAM) increased by a factor of 60, and storage capacity increased by a factor of 500. Surely, one would think, changes such as these must have had a large impact on the nature of costs in universities, as in business more generally. Studies of insurance and other service industries indicate that these innovations have indeed had an impact, but not necessarily what would have been predicted. The typical pattern appears to be that the initial impact of computers and other innovations is simply to increase costs.[10] Although their introduction was accompanied by little or no reduction in staff, a shift in staff composition from clerical workers to professional workers occurred. Only after computers become a part of the business routine were service firms able to achieve significant restructuring of work routines or reductions in workforce.[11]

In universities, computers were welcomed warmly. But rather

TABLE 6.2

Progress in Personal Computers: Three IBM-Compatible Computers Purchased by a Duke Academic Department

| | Year Purchased | | |
	1983	1986	1992
Machine	IBM PC	IBM AT	Gateway 2000
Price (1992 Dollars)	3,854	5,535	4,129
Random Access Memory (in Thousands of Bytes)[a]	128	512	8,000
Speed (MHz)	4.77	8	50
Storage Capacity (in Thousands of Bytes)	360	30,000	200,000

Source: Data are from purchase orders, Plant Accounting Department, Duke University.

[a]Includes enhancements in the original purchase.

than using them to save costs, the faculty, libraries, and administrative units that purchased them used these machines to increase output, for example, by increasing the number of statistical tests in research projects, reducing the time needed to retrieve information, or increasing the amount and complexity of the data that could be stored in administrative databases.[12]

STAFFING PATTERNS

With these advances in technology as backdrop, how did staffing patterns change during this period? A useful starting point in examining changes in staffing patterns is to consider the evidence on expenditures presented in the two previous chapters. Table 6.3 shows how the composition of compensation at Duke, Harvard, and Chicago changed over the periods for which detailed information was available for each institution. For Duke and Harvard, compensation for nonfaculty workers is divided among students (but does not count payments to graduate students for teaching and research assistance), administrative and professional staff, and nonexempt workers. The latter are workers who are subject to the provisions of the Fair Labor Standards Act, which requires supervised employees to be paid overtime. In each case, payments to faculty constituted the largest category of compensation but grew more slowly than did all compensation. By contrast, payments to administrative and professional staff at all three universities grew more rapidly than did all compensation and compensation for nonexempt employees. These patterns are consistent with an increase in the professionalization of the university workforce.

The aggregate evidence on employment in higher education also is consistent with this trend. Table 6.4 presents data on full-time staff in universities, based on reports to the Equal Employment Opportunity Commission (EEOC). The commission uses standardized job categories, which are briefly described and illustrated by specific jobs in Table 6.5. Over the 16-year period covered by Table 6.4, the number of full-time faculty grew at an average rate of 1 percent per year. By contrast, the number of administrators increased almost twice as fast, at a rate of 1.8 percent per year. However, the greatest growth was in the "other professionals" category—an average rate of 4.8 percent per year. These aggregate trends in growth and professionalization clearly are consistent with the models of bureaucratic growth noted in chapter 2, although they also might be explained by an increase in the complexity of the functions performed. In order to obtain a better idea of the forces behind these changes in staff

TABLE 6.3

Share and Growth of Payments to Labor, Arts and Sciences:
Duke, Harvard, and Chicago

Category of Labor	Beginning year[a] Amount	Beginning year[a] Share	1991/92 Amount	1991/92 Share	Growth Rate
Duke					
Regular faculty	22,474	40.0	34,435	38.4	5.3
Other faculty	2,222	4.0	6,561	7.3	13.5
Administrative and professional staff	15,918	28.3	27,306	30.4	6.7
Nonexempt	14,741	26.2	20,226	22.5	4.0
Students	882	1.6	1,217	1.4	4.0
Total	56,237	100.0	89,745	100.0	5.8
Harvard					
Regular faculty	39,889	41.8	59,070	37.4	3.9
Other faculty	5,878	6.2	8,857	5.6	4.1
Administrative and professional staff	17,050	17.9	42,185	26.7	9.1
Nonexempt	13,225	13.9	22,160	14.0	5.2
Students[b]	19,330	20.3	25,554	16.2	2.8
Total	95,372	100.0	157,826	100.0	5.0
Chicago					
Regular faculty	39,189	44.2	50,543	43.0	3.2
Other faculty	3,228	3.6	8,096	6.9	11.5
Administrative and professional staff	22,450	25.3	33,076	28.2	4.8
Nonexempt[c]	23,831	26.9	25,737	21.9	1.0
Total	88,698	100.0	117,452	100.0	3.5

Expenditures (In Thousands of 1991/92 Dollars) and Share

Source: Tables 4.1, 4.4, and 4.7.

Note: Figures for Duke and Chicago include prorated amounts from central administration and service components; Harvard compensation includes only Arts and Sciences.
[a]The beginning year was 1983/84 for Duke and Chicago and 1981/82 for Harvard.
[b]Includes exempt staff enrolled as students and payments to non-Harvard students.
[c]Includes students.

composition, it is useful to take a closer look at staffs and the functions they perform.

Approach

Information on staffing in several specific academic and administrative areas in the sample institutions was studied in order to examine

TABLE 6.4

Full-Time Employees of Higher Education Institutions,
by Occupational Group, 1975 and 1991

	Number of Full-Time Employees			
			Annual	Median
			Growth	Salary,
Category	1975	1991	Rate	1991[a]
Executive, Administrative, and				
Managerial Employees	102,465	136,908	1.8	47,319
Full-Time Faculty Members	446,830	520,551	1.0	40,971
Other Professionals	166,487	359,322	4.8	31,849
Secretarial, Clerical Employees	302,216	365,332	1.2	19,140
Technical, Paraprofessional				
Staff	113,248	146,267	1.6	23,413
Skilled Crafts Workers	51,370	62,052	1.2	25,502
Service, Maintenance				
Personnel	205,790	196,137	−0.3	17,389
Total	1,388,406	1,786,569	1.6	—

Source: Data are from Kirshstein et al. (1990, p. 68) and unpublished tabulations produced by the Equal Employment Opportunity Commission (EEOC). In 1991, 3,285 institutions reported data to the EEOC.

[a]The faculty figure is the median for those with 9- to 10-month contracts, who constitute 70.5 percent of all full-time faculty.

staffing at the level of individual jobs. This level of detail made it advisable to limit the scope of the investigation, as examining an entire institution very likely would generate an overwhelming amount of detail, which would be virtually impossible to digest. The academic departments chosen were the same as those discussed in chapters 7 and 8. As explained there, three academic departments were chosen to represent different divisions of the arts and science enterprise: (1) natural sciences, (2) social sciences, and (3) humanities. At Duke, an engineering department was included as well because that university's arts and sciences included an engineering school. The departments differ not only by subject matter but also by research style, with the natural science department using laboratories and the humanities department using very little technical equipment other than word processors.

The choice of administrative areas is less simple. Virtually any area one chooses to examine is unlikely to be representative of overall patterns of change. For this reason, after consulting with several close students of universities, four areas were selected that either had been pointed to as examples of areas of growing administrative

TABLE 6.5
Occupational Groups Based on EEOC Categories

Group	Description and Examples
Executive, Administrative, and Managerial Employees	President, vice president, dean, director
Full-Time Faculty Members	Tenure-track faculty, adjunct instructors, emeritus professors (except graduate student instructors)
Other Professionals	Support services usually requiring college degree; research associate, administrative assistant, career counselor, psychiatric social worker
Secretarial, Clerical Employees	Secretary, receptionist, staff assistant, clerk-typist, accounting clerk
Technical, Paraprofessional Staff	Positions requiring specialized knowledge; computer programmer, staff specialist, laboratory technician
Skilled Craft Workers	Positions requiring special manual skills; laboratory mechanic
Service, Maintenance Personnel	Positions requiring limited, previously acquired skills; maintenance, laboratory assistant
Graduate Student Instructors	—
Other Student Employment	—

responsibilities or were otherwise thought to represent pressure points in universities' attempts to deal with new functions or demands. Thus, the rates of growth of these areas should not be taken to be representative of administrative units in general. Overall growth rates for administration can be inferred from budget information expenditure data such as that presented in chapter 4. What is of greater interest is the nature and composition of the staff changes that have taken place. In contrast to the academic departments, the sample administrative areas underwent varying degrees of reorganization over the period of study. In collecting this information, therefore, every effort was made to include all the administrative units conducting a given activity. Because the focus of this section is on administrative staffing, I made no effort to separate the portion of these units whose efforts related to arts and sciences activities from the portion related to professional schools, medical centers, or auxiliary enterprises, unless separate offices existed. The four administrative areas chosen were (1) university counsel, (2) sponsored research, (3) student services, and (4) personnel/human relations.

University Counsel

Theories of the increasingly litigious nature of society find a hospitable context in discussions of the growth in university administration, especially to the extent that they feature outside regulations as a cause of the growth of administrative staffs. Typically, at least part of the legal work of a university is performed by a separate office of university counsel, which acts as the university's in-house law firm. Outside law firms also may be hired to perform legal work. At Duke, a sizable portion of the activity of the counsel's office relates to the university's medical center.[13]

Sponsored Research

The term "sponsored research" refers to research that is funded, through grants and contracts, by government agencies, private foundations, or businesses. As this method of funding university research has grown in importance, so, too, has the administrative effort that universities expend to solicit and account for such support. The administrative effort with respect to sponsored research has three main functions: (1) helping faculty find out about and apply for funding, (2) accounting for the money spent, and (3) dealing with patents that might arise from such research.[14] At both Duke and Harvard, the last 15 years has seen considerable change in the number, names, and organization of the offices carrying out these functions.

Student Services

Colleges and universities provide a raft of services to students outside the classroom, ranging from psychological and career counseling to special resources for minority students or foreign students to volunteer opportunities. The extent of these services appears to have grown during the last decade, with some commentators speculating that this trend demonstrates how institutions are becoming increasingly sensitive to consumer demand. The wide variety of services makes it necessary to draw some arbitrary lines. For the purpose of this analysis, I included all parts of student affairs offices dealing with student orientation, counseling, discipline, special programs for the disabled, minority students, and international stu-

dents, and extracurricular programs. Where they are grouped together, religious and cultural organizations, academic advising,
housing, dining, athletics, and student physical health were excluded.[15]

Personnel/Human Relations

The traditional functions of personnel offices are to interview job
applicants, train employees when necessary, and handle the paper-
work associated with employee benefits and, sometimes, pay. This
area, now commonly known as human resources, has witnessed considerable growth, which has been fueled by the variety of new employee benefits, attention to issues of fairness in hiring and supervision, and related government regulation. The functional areas covered
by personnel are wage and salary administration (including job and
pay classification), employee records, fringe benefit administration,
training, labor relations, worker's compensation, and temporary employment.[16] At Duke, the large medical center is the dominant force
behind the size and growth in the human resources area. With a
total workforce of some 21,000 in 1991, the university as a whole
had twice as many employees as students; most of the employees
worked in the medical center. At Chicago, the distinction between
the medical center and the rest of the university was sharper, allowing the nonmedical portion to be identified separately.

The data available from the three universities to conduct an analysis of staffing trends differed markedly. Duke was the only sample
university with computer-readable data from 1981 covering the
number of workers by occupation. Harvard provided data on the
number of FTE workers by unit, but without a detailed breakdown
on occupational classification. At Chicago, the most that could be
obtained was a listing of staff and short job titles taken from the
university's telephone directory, which made either FTE calculations
or classifications by occupation impossible; however, the period for
which this information could be collected was longer than those for
Duke and Harvard. In compiling the tabulations for each university,
every effort was made to include all the relevant organizational units
performing a set of functions over the time period. Nevertheless,
because the importance of functions that had been performed outside these entities could have grown over time, the functions may
have been consolidated into currently organized units, thus leading
to the overstatement of the growth in these functions. Discussions
with administrators who know the areas, however, suggested that
this problem was not significant in the areas examined.

Trends at the Three Universities

Chicago

Table 6.6 presents a summary of the data on staffing in the seven departments at the University of Chicago, excluding faculty, with the three academic departments combined. The totals are simply the number of staff listed in the university directory; no consistent data were available that would allow calculations of FTEs. With one ex-

TABLE 6.6
Staff Positions in Seven Units: Chicago, Selected Years

Administrative Unit or Group	1976/77	1981/82	1986/87	1991/92	Average Growth Rate
Three Academic Departments	24	24	25	22	−0.6
Human Resources					
General	6	6	7	7	
Wage and salary administration	5	4	7	5	
Employment	5	4	5	4	
Benefits[a]	2	1	5	9	
Employee/labor relations	0	0	0	3	
Other[b]	1	1	2	2	
Total, excluding benefits	17	15	21	21	1.4
Legal Counsel	8	7	7	8	0.0
Sponsored Programs	8	5	10	14	3.7
Student Services[c]					
Dean of Students	7	8	10	10	
Single student housing/ house system	2	3	4	4	
Career counseling and placement	5	6	8	6	
Student activities office	3	4	4	12	
International affairs	2	0	0	2	
Total	19	21	26	34	3.9

Source: Data are tabulations from University of Chicago *Directory,* various years.

Notes: Staff counts exclude faculty except those employed as full-time administrators. Functions directly supporting professional schools or the medical center were omitted.

[a]Part of function resided in payroll department before 1986/87.

[b]Includes training, human resources systems, workman's compensation, and employee records.

[c]Excludes the following offices that were part of Student Affairs at the University of Chicago: physical education, registrar, graduate affairs, admissions and financial aid, and residence halls and commons.

ception, the activities covered in each row appear to be consistent over time and are not affected by reorganizations. The exception is the benefits area, part of which was transferred from payroll to human relations between the second and third years shown. The table shows that staff size in the academic departments and in the counsel's office did not grow, but that staff size in the other three areas did. In human resources, the total staff size, excluding benefits, increased from 17 to 21, at an annual rate of 1.4 percent; because of that exclusion, this rate clearly is an understatement of total growth. Over the last five-year period, after benefits were fully included, the implied growth rate was 2.9 percent. In sponsored programs, growth through the period was uninterrupted, with an average annual rate of 3.7 percent. Student services also grew markedly, especially in the student activities office, confirming that the growth in this area noted by Rosovsky was not confined to Harvard.[17]

Harvard and Duke

Table 6.7 compares the staffing and growth for the three of the four administrative areas at Duke and Harvard covering the decade 1981 to 1991. Comparable data on student services at Harvard were unavailable. Employees are counted in terms of FTE workers.[18] They are further divided according to whether they are exempt from overtime pay. Because exempt workers would tend to include most professional workers, it is possible to infer from these data whether the level of professionalization in the staffs carrying out these activities was increasing.

The figures suggest that the most rapid growth in staff size at both institutions occurred in the sponsored research area, with annual rates of 5.4 and 4.5 percent for Harvard and Duke, respectively, which is certainly consistent with the data obtained from Chicago. The only other clean comparison is in the counsel's office, where respective growth rates of 4.9 and 1.9 percent compare with no growth at Chicago. Because the practice of farming out significant legal work to outside firms is common, however, the increase in the number of staff may not be an especially accurate indicator of total activity. In this context, it is interesting to contrast the modest increase in staff in the counsel's office at Duke with the office's rapid rise in expenditures; over the period 1984 to 1992, its spending increased at a real rate of 8.1 percent.[19] For a majority of cases shown in Table 6.7, exempt employment increased at faster rates than did nonexempt employment, suggesting an increase in the level of professionalization in the sample units.

TABLE 6.7

Staff Size in Four Administrative Areas: Harvard and Duke, Selected Years
(FTE Positions)

	1981/82	1986/87	1991/92	Growth Rate
Sponsored Research				
Harvard				
Exempt	17.0	20.6	33.0	6.6
Nonexempt	27.3	25.6	42.7	4.5
Total	44.3	46.2	75.7	5.4
Duke				
Exempt	10.0	16.8	20.8	7.3
Nonexempt	16.4	12.4	20.4	2.2
Total	26.4	29.2	41.2	4.5
Student Services				
Duke				
Exempt	23.7	28.9	38.7	4.9
Nonexempt	27.5	36.0	41.8	4.2
Total	51.2	64.9	80.5	4.5
Legal Counsel				
Harvard				
Exempt	8.0	11.0	11.0	3.2
Nonexempt	3.0	5.0	7.0	8.5
Total	11.0	16.0	18.0	4.9
Duke				
Exempt	7.0	9.0	8.0	1.3
Nonexempt	5.6	6.6	7.3	2.7
Total	12.6	15.6	15.3	1.9

Source: Unpublished tabulations from Harvard; calculations based on unpublished data from Duke.

Duke

Considerably more-detailed information on the number and job titles of employees allowed for the classification of employees according to occupation. Data on nonfaculty employees were obtained from payroll records for December in selected years (1981, 1986, and 1991—years for which machine-readable information was available). The records include information on whether a person was on the payroll at any time during the calendar year and on the job type and level. Jobs were divided according to the EEOC classification scheme presented in Table 6.5. This classification has the virtue of distinguishing between faculty and administrators and makes it pos-

sible to look for the hypothesized increase in professional employment. In contrast to the tabulations for Chicago, figures for the
Duke academic departments include faculty.

Table 6.8 shows the composition of the staffs for the four academic departments added together. Overall, the FTE employment
in these departments increased by 44 percent over the decade covered, for a 3.6 percent annual rate of growth. Not surprisingly, the
category with the largest share of employment for these four academic departments is faculty, a category that includes non-regular-
rank instructors, such as lecturers, adjunct professors, and emeritus
faculty. In contrast to the 1.0 percent rate of growth for faculty in all
universities shown in Table 6.4, the number of faculty in these four

TABLE 6.8

Staff Composition in Four Academic Departments: Duke, Selected Years
(FTE Positions)

| Occupational Group[a] | Year | | | Average Annual Growth Rate, 1981–1991 |
	1981	1986	1991	
Executive, Administrative, and Managerial Employees	0.0	0.0	0.0	—
Full-Time Faculty Members	104.3	114.4	131.3	2.3
Other Professionals	30.0	54.0	47.7	4.6
Clerical and Secretarial Employees	29.4	28.2	30.0	2.0
Technical, Paraprofessional Staff	11.8	22.6	15.7	2.9
Skilled Craft Workers	0.0	0.0	1.0	—
Service, Maintenance Personnel	0.0	0.0	0.5	—
Graduate Student Instructors	16.1	19.2	29.6	6.1
Other Students	21.4	37.9	50.4	8.6
Total	213.0	276.3	306.2	3.6
Detail: Instructional Staff				
Tenure-Track Faculty	88.0	92.0	99.0	1.2
Nonregular Faculty	16.3	22.4	32.3	6.8
Graduate Student Instructors	16.1	19.2	29.6	6.1
Total	120.4	133.6	160.9	2.9

Source: Data for tenure-track faculty are from the provost's office; for all others,
calculations using unpublished payroll data from Duke.

Note: For the purpose of this table, an employee's FTE value was defined as the
product of (1) his or her normal work week as a proportion of 40 hours, and (2) the
number of weeks worked per year as a proportion of 52 weeks.

[a]Occupational groups are defined in Table 6.5.

— No calculation could be made.

departments grew at a 2.3 percent rate, corresponding to the more rapid growth in the arts and sciences faculty at Duke during this period.[20] At the other extreme, there were no administrators (departmental chairs are counted as faculty), skilled crafts workers, or service/maintenance workers in these departments. University employees in the latter two groups normally would be assigned to service units. In light of the possible impact of computers on the university workplace, it is especially interesting that the growth in clerical and secretarial employment was the slowest of any group.

The section at the bottom of the table attempts to distinguish among types of instructors. From a separate source, slightly noncomparable information on the number of full-time faculty in the four departments is shown (the number of full-time not adjusted for leaves of absence or for administrative effort) with the excess of FTE total faculty being designated as nonregular faculty. To these lines are added the FTE totals for graduate student instructors and teaching assistants, whose duties might include grading and assisting during labs as well as teaching sections of larger courses. This breakdown shows that the number of tenure-track faculty in the four departments grew at only about one-sixth the rate for the two other categories of instructors.[21]

Table 6.9 gives similar information for the four administrative

TABLE 6.9

Staff Composition in Four Administrative Areas: Duke, Selected Years (FTE Positions)

	Year			Average Annual Growth Rate,
Occupational Group	*1981*	*1986*	*1991*	*1981–1991*
Executive, Administrative, and Managerial Employees	29.0	38.7	44.5	4.3
Full-Time Faculty Members	1.0	2.3	2.8	10.3
Other Professionals	49.4	74.3	88.0	5.8
Clerical and Secretarial Employees	57.1	72.1	88.2	4.3
Technical, Paraprofessional Staff	6.1	9.2	14.0	8.3
Skilled Craft Workers	0.0	1.0	0.0	—
Service, Maintenance Personnel	0.0	0.0	0.0	—
Graduate Student Instructors	0.0	0.0	0.0	—
Other Students	12.1	19.7	18.5	4.2
Not Classified	0.0	1.0	0.0	—
Total	154.7	218.4	256.1	5.0

Source: Calculations using unpublished payroll data from Duke.
— No calculation could be made.

areas. The overall rate of growth in these areas, 5.0 percent per year, is more than that for the academic departments, but this comparison may mean very little because the number of units covered was small, and they probably are not representative of the entire administrative enterprise. In these units, the most rapid rate of growth (ignoring the faculty category, which has a very small base) was in the technical and paraprofessional group, followed by the "other professional" group. Secretarial, administrative/managerial, and student workers all increased at below-average rates. Among the two largest groups of workers in these administrative units, the "other professional" category appears to have grown relative to clerical and secretarial workers, a trend that seems consonant with the rising importance of computers.

CONCLUSION

In order to accomplish the mission that sets them apart from other firms and nonprofit organizations, colleges and universities perform certain service and administrative functions that are quite similar to what is done in the service sector of the corporate world. Three sets of factors affect how the scale, organization, and technological virtuosity with which these functions are performed in universities. The first factor is the demand from the customers of universities, most notably, students and government agencies. In their efforts to compete for students, institutions sought to provide new services; this attempt seems especially evident in the area of student services. Colleges and universities also are under pressure from regulatory agencies, which probably has led to some increases in staff size in such areas as cost accounting and sponsored programs.

A second set of influences, coming also from the outside, was the dramatic transformation in the technology of the workplace, epitomized by the gradual appearance over the period of study of a personal computer on a desk in almost every office. During the 15 years covered by this analysis, perhaps the most important effect of this technological transformation was to require a more highly trained workforce in university administrative positions—an effect that had a profound impact on the economy at large. Rather than reducing the workforce, computers appear to have forced it to become more professionalized. By the early 1990s, therefore, computers had not saved universities very much money. They may well have increased productivity, especially in research, but this improvement produced little in the way of cost savings.

The third set of forces affecting the size and operation of administrative staffs in universities are internal, comprising both the "administrative entrepreneurism" noted by observers Massy and Wilger (1992) and efforts intended to lean in the other direction, toward smaller staffs. Perhaps taking a cue from the corporate world, many universities undertook serious efforts in the 1990s to reduce non-faculty staff or to increase the quality of service provision, or both, as evidenced by prominent campaigns for "quality improvement" and "process re-engineering." If the experience of firms in service industries is any predictor, the failure of computers and other innovations to bring about reductions in staffing does not necessarily preclude the possibility that such reductions eventually will occur.

CHAPTER 7

The Allocation of Faculty Effort

> Writing is 'our work,' which we do alone.
> Teaching is our 'load,' which we also do alone,
> up there in front of the class. . . . And commit-
> tee work is the dues we grudgingly pay so that
> we can continue to read and write for a living.
> *Jane Tomkins, 1992*[1]

THE UNIVERSITY'S central and most distinctive activities—teaching, research, and public service—are carried out largely by its most distinctive set of employees: the faculty. As a consequence, the decisions about how to allocate faculty effort are basic to the functioning of colleges and universities, and to their cost. Although most day-to-day decisions concerning these activities are entirely in the hands of departments and faculty members themselves, the larger decisions of resource allocation related to these functions, such as who will teach undergraduates, what courses will be offered, and how large classes will be, are influenced strongly by deans and other officers in the central administration. As noted in chapter 2, the governance of private colleges and universities is neither hierarchical nor entirely decentralized. Whatever the precise locus of power, however, these institutions face alternatives about resource allocation, they make choices, and those choices have educational consequences. Perhaps the most striking fact about contemporary American colleges and universities—even among institutions that compete for the very same groups of applicants and face virtually identical input prices—is that they do not all make the same decisions about these basic resource allocation questions. Among the private institutions competing for the most sought-after high school seniors, for example, are marked differences in the use of graduate students in undergraduate course instruction and in the average size of undergraduate classes.

Given the importance of faculty compensation in arts and sciences budgets, the choice of approach has profound implications for the cost structure of these institutions. It is for this reason that an increase in emphasis on research, accompanied by a trend toward reduced teaching loads, pushes up total costs. Massy and Wilger (1992, p. 367) describe this trend impressionistically:

The American professorate has undergone an evolution since World War II. No longer do faculty members devote the majority of their time to teaching and related activities such as academic advising and mentoring. Rather, the primary focus of faculty effort increasingly is research, scholarship, and other professional activity.

They argue that this shift has been most pronounced in the "elite research institutions," where heavy demand by applicants has allowed institutions to determine the "output mix," and that other institutions have emulated the elite institutions in this regard. If these changes in faculty teaching loads have in fact occurred, they would imply changes in institutions' choices about the technique of undergraduate teaching, with implications not only for costs but also, possibly, for the quality of undergraduate education. It is therefore important to give explicit consideration to these allocation choices. However, as Massy and Wilger note, hard evidence documenting these changes is not plentiful.[2]

This chapter and the next focus on the central resource allocation choices open to universities—choices about how universities will employ the faculty in arts and sciences—and the consequences of those choices for students. The reader will observe quickly that most of the attention is directed toward the activity that can be measured most readily—classroom teaching. Research is given short shrift largely because we understand less about its "technology," and because it offers few measurable indicators, let alone a quantifiable output. To be sure, few adequate measures of the output of teaching exist, but the available measures at least are suggestive of process and quality. This chapter begins with an examination of the alternatives open to institutions for producing a service that is sold in a rather competitive market: undergraduate education. It notes the significant differences in the approaches that research universities and liberal arts colleges actually take and then proceeds to examine trends in faculty classroom teaching loads in the sample institutions. Following this discussion are two short sections presenting some evidence from one institution on trends in advising and committee work. The chapter ends with a brief concluding section.

ALTERNATIVE METHODS OF ORGANIZING UNDERGRADUATE INSTRUCTION

The university is a diversified enterprise in which several distinct but related activities are performed. Research occurs largely behind closed doors, in libraries, laboratories, and faculty offices, although field work is vital to the research in many disciplines as well. Public service, of course, assumes many forms. The primary focus of this and the next chapter is teaching. Professional schools aside, the teaching performed at research universities is carried out on two rather distinct levels. Undergraduates have most of their contact with faculty members in formal classes, although it is not uncommon for them to meet with faculty outside of class. Graduate students, most prominently those pursuing doctorate degrees, usually receive their classroom instruction in small classes early in their programs, moving to quite specialized work with individual faculty members— on faculty research projects and in their own dissertation research— toward the end of their graduate careers. A key element in the practices that research universities follow is the dual role played by many graduate students: not only are they students in their own right, but they also serve as instructors and teaching assistants for undergraduate classes, particularly in introductory courses.

In principle, like the generic firm studied in economics textbooks, a university can choose from a variety of techniques in deciding how to teach students. Although recent advances in computers and communications have the potential to bring about significant change in current practices, the typical "technology" employed in teaching remains on the primitive side. To teach undergraduate courses, for example, universities can make use of such time-honored techniques as lectures, discussion sections, and seminars. Historians of higher education tell us that the lecture replaced the individual recitation as the preferred teaching method in colleges during the 19th century.[3] Usually accompanied by visual aids transmitted by blackboard (first used at Bowdoin around 1823) and later often enhanced by microphones and overhead projectors, the lecture remains the mainstay of teaching at this level. The other principal organizational techniques used for classroom instruction are the seminar, which was first used in the form that we know it more than a century ago, and the discussion section, apparently first developed at Harvard at the turn of the century (Boyer 1987, p. 149). Colleges have options as to technique as well, albeit more limited ones, as they have no graduate students on whom they can call. Both colleges and universities also have options about how much faculty advising or undergraduate written work to expect. Given the considerable degree of discretion that institutions have along these dimensions (at least in the long run), and the implications of these decisions on their budgets, not to mention the potential effect on the quality of education, it is important that a study of expenditures look explicitly at how teaching is carried out.

In selecting how classes are staffed, an institution deals with several variables: the average size of classes, the number of courses, the classroom teaching load of faculty, the size of the student body, and the use of instructors who are not members of the regular faculty. Of these, perhaps the starkest trade-off is that between faculty classroom teaching load and average class size. This trade-off may be illustrated by considering a simple example of a college, in which the regular faculty does all the teaching and all classes are of the same size. For illustrative purposes, suppose the college has a faculty numbering 150, it enrolls 1,850 undergraduate students, and each student takes eight courses per year. If classes contain C students each, a total of $8(1,850)/C$ classes must be taught. This can be accomplished if the average faculty member teaches L courses per year, where C and L satisfy the equation:

$$150\ L\ =\ 8(1,850)/C. \tag{1}$$

Rewriting the equation yields

$$LC\ =\ 98.7, \tag{1'}$$

which makes it clear that the teaching load L and the class size C are inversely related, one falling only if the other increases. This inverse relationship is shown by the dark curve in Figure 7.1. Given the assumed student load of eight courses per year, the curve demonstrates, for example, that the college could achieve an average classroom teaching load of four courses per year if class size were about 25, but that if it wished to reduce class size to 15, the average load would have to be more than six courses per year. Illustrating another dimension of choice, if students were required to take nine courses per year rather than eight, then the options become more severe, requiring larger class sizes, heavier teaching loads, or both. Either line shows, for the given student course load, the feasible combinations available to the college (comparable to the "isocost" line for the firm, showing the combinations of inputs requiring a given amount of expenditure). Regardless of how it chooses its own preferred combination, the college must face the fact that it cannot have *both* smaller classes and a lower average classroom teaching load for its faculty.

When one adds the option of using other kinds of instructors, such as nonregular faculty and graduate students, the calculations become more complicated, but the essence of this trade-off remains the same. Figure 7.2 illustrates the feasible combinations of class-

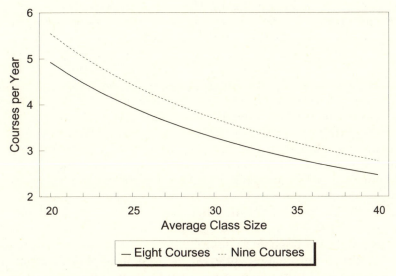

Figure 7.1 Combinations of Class Size and Teaching Load: Options for a College.

Source: Numerical example assuming 1,850 students and 150 faculty. See text.

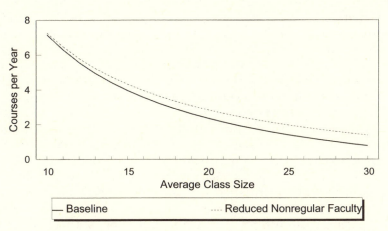

Figure 7.2 Combinations with Nonregular Faculty.

Source: Numerical example. See Appendix 7.1.

room teaching load and average class size for a hypothetical research university that uses both graduate students and nonregular faculty in addition to regular faculty in undergraduate courses.[4] Two alternative sets of choices are shown, differing only by the relative weight given to nonregular faculty in teaching undergraduate courses. The "reduced nonfaculty" scenario halves the number of courses taught by nonregular faculty in the baseline case and uses the budgetary savings to hire more regular-rank faculty, resulting in all points shown having the same cost. As is evident, this reallocation increases the average classroom teaching load of the regular faculty, because these faculty have a considerably higher average per-class cost than do nonregular faculty. Similar trade-offs exist and could be graphed involving other variables, including the number of graduate students, the amount of teaching that is expected of the graduate students, and the size of graduate classes.

Although it is possible to describe the options that are available to colleges and universities, little will be said here about factors that determine an institution's choice of technique. Questions of pedagogy are best left to experts, although some aspects of class size are noted in the next chapter. The essential points are simply that institutions do have choices about how teaching will be done, particularly at the undergraduate level, and that these choices have significant budgetary ramifications. For one of the institutions in the study, Carleton College, the published proceedings of its budget priorities committee reveal that the college remained constantly aware of its resource constraints and of the available trade-offs. In the face of the stagnation of real faculty salaries in the late 1970s and faculty pressure for improvements on that front, this committee debated the relative merits of increasing the enrollment of the college or reducing the size of the faculty. Although committee members expressed concerns about the effects of a larger student body on the "'intimate, personal freshman experience' that now characterizes Carleton," the committee more than once expressed reluctant support for the option of increasing enrollment. In fact, enrollment was allowed to increase over the period of study, from 1,700 to about 1,850. Increasingly, the committee also turned to tuition increases as a means of improving faculty salaries and maintaining the quality of its programs without increasing enrollment excessively. Concern also was expressed over what was perceived to be unduly burdensome teaching loads.[5] An institution may find that choices it has made in the past, manifested in the existence of programs, institutional traditions, and the architectural constraints of classroom buildings, greatly limit its latitude of choice at any given moment. Yet movement is possible at the margin, and it is the measurement of levels and trends in these variables—variables determined largely at the institutional level—to which we now turn.

WHAT DO FACULTY DO?

As noted in chapter 2, the culture of colleges and universities, particularly those in a position to be truly selective in their hiring of faculty and admission of students, allow faculty members considerable freedom, but this freedom is limited by institutionally determined constraints. These constraints include the prevailing classroom teaching load, a condition of work that is quantifiable, as well as the more amorphous but equally important set of expectations concerning research, student advising, administrative effort, service outside the institution, and the quality of teaching effort that usually are no more than an implicit part of the labor contract between faculty members and their employing institution. A major purpose of this chapter is to examine one of the measurable aspects of these conditions of employment that manifest themselves in the faculty's allocation of time: the classroom teaching load. For any one institution, trends in measured loads indicate changes in the institution's choice about how it will use faculty. The chapter also presents some information on advising at one institution.

Before turning to measures of classroom teaching loads at the sample institutions, it is important to emphasize that classroom teaching is only one of several important tasks that faculty perform. Research is, of course, another principal activity, and is an especially prominent one at research universities. To varying degrees, faculty also spend time participating in the administration and governance of their institutions, as well as in public service and consulting activities outside the institutions.

Often overlooked in enumerations such as this, however, are the unseen aspects of teaching and the set of faculty tasks that fall between the cracks of categorization. For every hour spent in classroom teaching, additional time is required to organize course materials, prepare for class, meet with students, read and grade student assignments, and write student recommendations. For faculty who advise graduate students, particularly those who advise doctoral students working on their dissertations, teaching takes the form of individualized mentoring—reading, reacting, questioning, and suggesting. In addition to these activities that relate directly to teaching are a host of functions that often pass without comment because they are so basic to what is assumed to go with the territory. Included in this group of activities are anonymous referee reports and reviews undertaken on behalf of academic journals, publishers, and university review committees. And, as Bowen and Schuster (1986, p. 69) emphasize, faculty are expected to "keep up" in their disciplines. About the whole set of duties undertaken by faculty, they state: "There is no end to the amount of time and effort that can usefully be devoted to them."

The time available is limited, however, and it is instructive to learn how faculty members actually allocate their time. As an aggregate, faculty report average work weeks exceeding 50 hours, with slightly longer work weeks at research universities than at other types of institutions. How they use that time differs markedly by type of institution. As shown in Table 7.1, research accounted for 30 percent of the average faculty member's time at private research institutions, compared with just 8 percent for faculty at liberal arts colleges. In addition, faculty at private research universities spent more time on consulting and other work outside the institution (11 percent) than did other faculty, particularly those at liberal arts colleges (4 percent). These differences reflect differences in teaching time between private research universities and liberal arts colleges (40 percent versus 65 percent). In most respects, the time allocation of faculty is similar in public and private research universities.

The differences in time allocation shown in the table are reflected in the incomes of faculty. In 1987, faculty at private research universities reported that the income they received from their institutions

TABLE 7.1
Percentage of Time Spent on Various Activities by Full-Time Faculty:
Selected Types of Institutions, Fall 1987

	All Institutions	Research Universities		Liberal Arts Colleges
		Public	Private	
Teaching	56	43	40	65
Research	16	29	30	8
Administration	13	14	14	14
Community Service	4	3	2	5
Other Work	7	7	11	4
Professional Development	5	4	4	4
Total	100	100	100	100

Source: Data are from U.S. Department of Education (1991), p. 55, Table 2.7.
Note: Components may not sum to total as a result of rounding.

over and above their base salaries, typically covering summer research, plus their consulting income equalled an average of 32 percent of their base salary. By comparison, these sources of income represented only a 9 percent enhancement of the base salaries of faculty in liberal arts colleges (U.S. Department of Education 1991, p. 95, Table 3.2).

One of the criticisms that has been leveled at higher education in recent years is that faculty increasingly have neglected undergraduate teaching. William Bennett's (1986) address at Harvard is one prominent example. There, he presented a tongue-in-cheek formulation of "Bennett's axiom," which held that the more money universities have, the fewer distinguished professors they have doing classroom teaching. Surveys appear to support the hypothesis that, to some extent, faculty, especially those at research universities, have turned their attention away from undergraduates. Table 7.2 reports on surveys conducted in 1975, 1984, and 1989, covering faculty in all institutions and in research institutions alone. The table shows both the median number of hours per week and the percentage of faculty who reported spending 10 or more hours per week in: (1) classroom instruction with undergraduates, (2) classroom instruction with graduate and professional students, and (3) office hours. The

TABLE 7.2

Faculty Time Typically Devoted to Classroom Teaching and Office Hours, 1975, 1984, and 1989

Activity and Type of Institution	Median Number of Hours per Week			Percentage Spending more than 10 Hours per Week		
	1975	1984	1989	1975	1984	1989
Undergraduate Classroom Instruction						
All institutions	8.2	7.8	8.9	41.0	38.9	43.8
Research universities	3.5	2.7	3.5	13.1	8.7	8.0
Graduate Classroom Instruction						
All institutions	0.3	0.0	0.7	4.8	2.7	2.9
Research universities	2.2	1.6	2.2	5.7	3.0	1.8
Scheduled Office Hours						
All institutions	5.4	4.8	3.5	22.3	15.1	7.0
Research universities	4.2	3.0	2.9	21.9	10.8	4.3

Source: Calculations by Ehrenberg (1991), pp. 202–4.

Note: Medians are calculated by interpolation from percentage distributions. For further explanation of methodology used, see footnote in Ehrenberg (1991).

only evident trend with respect to undergraduate instruction was the definite decrease in the percentage of faculty at research universities spending more than 10 hours per week in undergraduate classroom instruction. There was also an overall decline in the percentage spending as much as 10 hours per week in graduate instruction. The activity experiencing the most dramatic change was scheduled office hours. For all institutions and for research universities alike, both the median number of hours and the percentage scheduling more than 10 hours declined over this period. Whereas more than one-fifth of faculty in research institutions in 1975 scheduled more than 10 hours of office hours per week, the comparable fraction had dropped to less than 1 in 20 by 1989.

TRENDS IN FACULTY CLASSROOM TEACHING LOADS AT FOUR INSTITUTIONS

To assess trends in classroom teaching effort, administrative data from the four institutions in the sample were used to calculate average classroom teaching loads.[6] Calculations were made for regular-rank faculty in each of the three corresponding departments at each institution (one each in humanities, natural sciences, and social sciences and one engineering department at Duke) for each of the four years of study (1976/77, 1981/82, 1986/87, and 1991/92). The basic unit used to measure classroom teaching load is the course. In semester systems, a course consists of the equivalent of three 50-minute "hours" of meetings per week, which might, for example, be combined into two 75-minute meetings; in quarter systems, a course consists of the equivalent of five 50-minute sessions per week over a proportionately shorter term. Courses under the two systems generally are regarded as equivalent, and are treated as such here.

In the calculations presented in this chapter, a faculty member is credited only with time spent in the classroom conducting a regular class. Reductions are made for shared teaching, labs, or discussion sections conducted by teaching assistants, and for courses that normally consist of presentations by others. More important, the calculations omit time spent in course preparation, conferring with students after class or in office hours, grading examinations and other written work, and writing student recommendations. Classroom teaching was recorded for all regular (tenured or tenure-track) faculty in each department. In addition, the number of faculty not on leave (or the FTE effort, if available) was summed. Any administrative duties undertaken by faculty, from department chair to coordinator for a science course's labs, are ignored.

Although this approach may appear relatively straightforward, the customs and peculiarities of college and university teaching make it necessary to make use of several simplifying and, ultimately, arbitrary assumptions. As with the exclusion of all hours of teaching effort that do not occur in the classroom—an exclusion necessitated by the absence of data—these assumptions can be justified only by arguing that rough quantification of what can be observed will be a useful addition to our knowledge of resource allocation in these institutions. Several of the assumptions are noted briefly here. Appendix 7.2 provides a more detailed account of the calculations used.

Hours in all courses were given equal weight, and faculty who shared courses received the corresponding proportionate share of both the course hours and enrollment for those courses, with four major exceptions. The first exception was the exclusion from the calculation of hours of formally constituted credit courses for supervision of doctoral dissertations. The institutions differed in how they recorded this type of instruction. Moreover, this kind of instruction blends with the other personalized attention that is excluded from the calculations. The second exception was for graduate colloquium or workshop courses consisting mainly of presentations by faculty or graduate students, as this work normally does not require the level of preparation demanded by most courses. Where only one faculty member's name was listed for such courses, that person was credited with one-third of a course, to reflect this reduced responsibility. However, in the one university whose records contained all the participating faculty, the general rule of dividing the hours equally among faculty was applied. The third exception was for labs, which generally were supervised by regular faculty in only one of the institutions studied. Although these labs typically were scheduled for four hours, faculty were credited with only one hour of classroom teaching for each lab taught. The fourth exception deals with "independent study" courses, in which students typically work on reading or research projects and meet periodically with their sponsoring professors. Occasionally, these course designations are used when a professor teaches a new course to a small class. In order to reflect the more limited time commitment that is typical of these classes, a weight of one-sixth of a course (reflecting, for example, one hour of meeting every two weeks in the semester system) was given to each student enrolled in an independent course number per term, up to a maximum of six, after which the course was weighted as a regular course.

A second measure of classroom teaching used in this chapter replaces the number of contact hours with the number of students enrolled in a faculty member's classes. As with the measure based on hours, enrollments were divided in the case of team-taught courses, but no other distinction was made on the basis of the type of course taught.

Like most of the institution-specific data presented in this study, these measures of classroom teaching most appropriately are used to chart trends over time only within an institution (actually, only within an individual department). Although every attempt was made to ensure the comparability of the measure of classroom teaching load across institutions and among departments within each institution, differences in custom, teaching technique, and data make cross-section comparisons problematic. An average load of four courses in a department in which faculty are expected to undertake extensive individualized work with each student will mean something different from the same calculated load in a department in which this expectation does not exist. As long as customs and teaching techniques remain fairly stable over time, however, changes over time in these measures within a department can be assumed to signify a real shift in resource allocation.

Duke

Figure 7.3 shows the trends in classroom teaching loads in the four sample departments at Duke from 1976/77 to 1991/92. The bars in each graph represent the average amount of classroom teaching, measured in number of courses, for regular faculty, divided between undergraduate and graduate classes. It is quite evident that the general trend at Duke was downward: in every department, the level in the most recent year was lower than the level during the initial period. The largest absolute decline occurred in the humanities department, in which the average classroom teaching load fell from 5.6 to 4.2 courses per year, a decrease in classroom teaching of one-fourth. In the natural sciences department, the average load also fell by one-fourth, from 3.4 to 2.5 courses per year, which was the result of an increase in graduate teaching and a larger decrease in undergraduate teaching. Despite an overall decline in classroom teaching of 16 percent, the social sciences department likewise experienced an increase in graduate teaching. Graduate instruction did not play a large part in the engineering department, where average loads fell by more than 20 percent. Although they are based on only four departments, these figures strongly suggest that classroom teaching loads at Duke, measured in terms of classroom contact hours, declined markedly during this 15-year period.

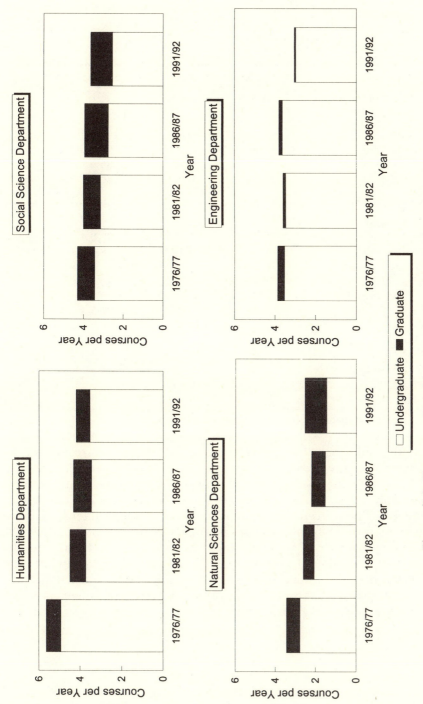

Figure 7.3 Classroom Teaching Loads, Four Departments: Duke.

Source: Calculations using unpublished data from Duke.

TABLE 7.3
Average Classroom Teaching Loads per FTE:
Duke, Four Representative Departments

Department and Year	Courses per Year		Enrollment	
	Total	Graduate	Total	Graduate
Humanities				
1976/77	5.63	0.70	111.7	3.6
1981/82	4.50	0.77	96.9	5.3
1986/87	4.33	0.87	86.0	6.6
1991/92	4.20	0.67	84.3	6.7
Social Sciences				
1976/77	4.30	0.87	145.6	7.4
1981/82	4.00	0.87	109.6	6.1
1986/87	3.93	1.20	137.0	18.3
1991/92	3.63	1.10	98.3	11.6
Natural Sciences				
1976/77	3.43	0.67	115.3	7.1
1981/82	2.60	0.53	109.1	5.8
1986/87	2.20	0.67	90.5	12.6
1991/92	2.53	1.07	86.2	10.2
Engineering				
1976/77	3.87	0.33	67.4	2.1
1981/82	3.60	0.13	82.1	0.8
1986/87	3.80	0.17	82.6	0.9
1991/92	3.03	0.07	61.3	0.3

Source: Calculations using unpublished data from Duke.

Teaching loads measured in terms of students enrolled also declined over the period, but the patterns are not as stark. As shown in
Table 7.3, the average enrollment per faculty member declined
steadily in two of the four departments (humanities and natural sciences). The percentage declines in these two departments matched
the declines in faculty contact hours, 25 percent. For example, the
average number of students taught by faculty in the humanities department declined from 112 to 84. Enrollments per faculty member
in the other two departments fell over the period, but not steadily.
The heaviest loads were in the social sciences department, in which
the average faculty's load fell from 146 to 98 students per year.

Harvard

The comparable calculations for Harvard are displayed in Figure 7.4
and Table 7.4. One striking difference between Duke and Harvard is

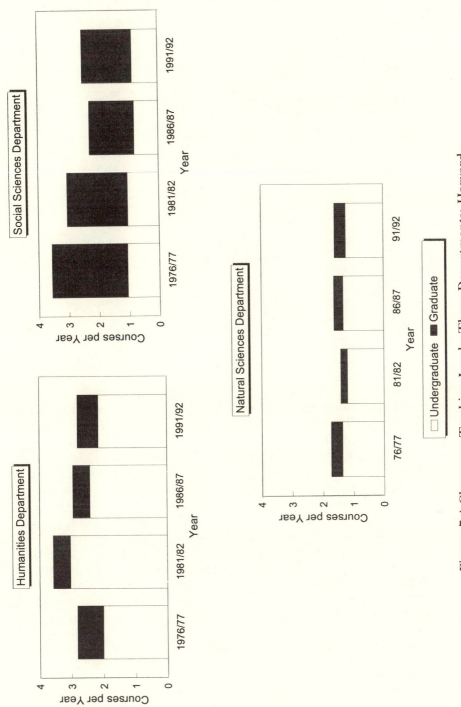

Figure 7.4 Classroom Teaching Loads, Three Departments: Harvard.
Source: Calculations using unpublished data from Harvard.

TABLE 7.4

Average Classroom Teaching Loads per FTE:
Harvard, Three Representative Departments

Department and Year	Courses per Year		Enrollment	
	Total	Graduate	Total	Graduate
Humanities				
1976/77	2.82	0.81	154.1	4.6
1981/82	3.57	0.54	145.6	4.3
1986/87	2.94	0.52	187.3	4.2
1991/92	2.80	0.66	152.2	5.6
Social Sciences				
1976/77	3.56	2.50	135.4	38.9
1981/82	3.04	2.00	143.5	18.0
1986/87	2.29	1.49	113.9	15.6
1991/92	2.52	1.66	129.5	24.5
Natural Sciences				
1976/77	1.74	0.36	133.0	2.9
1981/82	1.43	0.22	111.2	2.1
1986/87	1.63	0.30	105.0	4.0
1991/92	1.61	0.36	108.3	2.1

Source: Calculations using unpublished data from Harvard.

the overall lower teaching loads, measured in courses per faculty member, at Harvard. Even allowing for some differences between the universities that might lead to some lack of comparability, the calculated differences are simply too large to conclude anything other than that real differences in teaching loads did exist during this period. One other obvious difference is the larger share of total teaching accounted for by graduate courses in Harvard's social science department. As at Duke, the trend in average teaching load is downward, but the changes at Harvard generally were smaller than those at Duke. Measured by the percentage change in average classroom hours between the first and final years, teaching loads at Harvard decreased about 1 percent in the humanities department, 7 percent in the natural sciences department, and 29 percent in the social sciences department. In addition, overall classroom teaching loads as measured by enrollments in the departments declined somewhat. These enrollment average loads were larger than those for the corresponding departments at Duke, reflecting differences in the size of lecture courses.

Chicago

Figure 7.5 presents the corresponding data on average classroom teaching loads at Chicago for the sample years. These levels are expressed in numbers of courses, which at Chicago were quarter courses, representing only about three-fourths of the total number of hours of contact time as the semester courses at Duke and Harvard. The large relative size of the shaded portions of the bars reflects Chicago's strong emphasis on graduate instruction. As at Harvard, a majority of classroom teaching by faculty in social sciences was in graduate-level courses; in the other two departments, the graduate shares were roughly twice those at Harvard. The trends over time in the aggregate loads, as with Duke and Harvard, are downward, if only modestly so in two of the three departments. Calculated as a percentage change from the first to last years observed, the average loads for graduate and undergraduate courses declined about 6 percent in the humanities and social sciences departments and 29 percent in the natural sciences department. No consistent trend is observed in classroom teaching loads measured in terms of enrollments per FTE faculty, which is shown in Table 7.5.

TABLE 7.5
Average Classroom Teaching Loads per FTE:
Chicago, Three Representative Departments

Department and Year	Courses per Year		Enrollment	
	Total	Graduate	Total	Graduate
Humanities				
1976/77	4.58	1.99	78.1	12.2
1981/82	4.57	1.19	86.2	9.1
1986/87	4.36	1.42	82.0	12.0
1991/92	4.17	1.26	86.2	13.8
Social Sciences				
1976/77	3.32	2.71	90.3	70.4
1981/82	3.18	2.35	83.3	56.4
1986/87	3.24	2.52	79.7	58.0
1991/92	3.13	2.38	98.6	78.7
Natural Sciences				
1976/77	3.08	1.46	131.6	19.1
1981/82	2.67	1.78	73.7	17.6
1986/87	2.38	0.97	114.8	17.4
1991/92	2.20	1.01	100.0	17.0

Source: Calculations using unpublished data from Chicago.

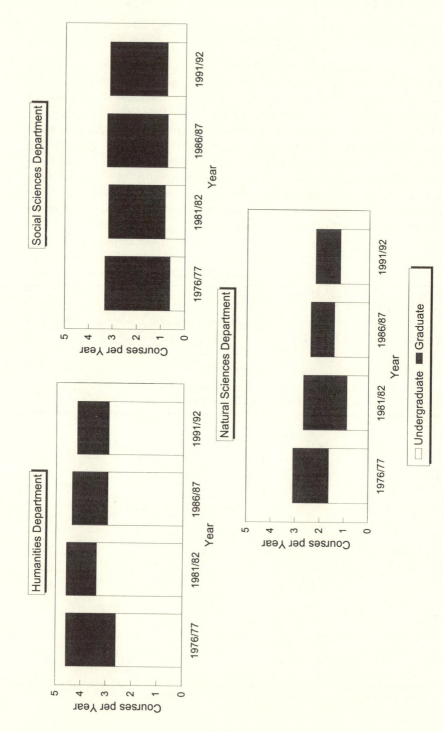

Figure 7.5 Classroom Teaching Loads, Three Departments: Chicago.
Source: Calculations using unpublished data from Chicago.

Carleton

The information on classroom teaching load at the one liberal arts college in the sample, shown in Figure 7.6, is striking evidence of one important difference in the nature of the faculty's work at colleges and at research universities. As in the previous figures, classroom teaching loads are measured in average number of courses taught per year. Although Carleton, like Chicago, was on a quarter system, its courses were roughly comparable to semester courses in total contact hours. Thus measured, the classroom teaching loads in the sample departments at Carleton were noticeably higher than their counterparts in any of the research universities studied. Even allowing for the unavoidable differences in measurement and culture among the institutions, these differences are too great to avoid concluding that faculty at Carleton spent considerably more time in classroom teaching than comparable faculty in any of these research institutions. Nevertheless, the measured loads at Carleton exhibit the same downward trend over this period that was evident in the universities. The average load in the humanities department dropped from 7.3 courses per year in 1976/77 to a low of 5.8 in 1986/87 and then rose to 6.8 in the last year, for a 7 percent overall decline over the 15-year period. In the other two departments, the declines in classroom teaching loads were both steady and steep. In the natural sciences department, the measured load fell from 6.8 to 4.8 courses per year, a decline of 29 percent. In the social sciences department, the drop was even larger, from 9.7 to 5.7 courses per year, or 41 percent.

Table 7.6 shows classroom teaching load as measured by enrollments per FTE. As with the universities, no consistent pattern is observed. These loads generally fell in the natural sciences department but rose in the humanities department. Taken together, loads in the three departments, as measured by enrollment, converged over the period.

ADVISING

In addition to classroom teaching, faculty at research universities typically perform several prominent functions, among which are research, professional activities (including peer reviews of scholarly work and participation in the activities of professional organizations), advising students, and service on departmental and univer-

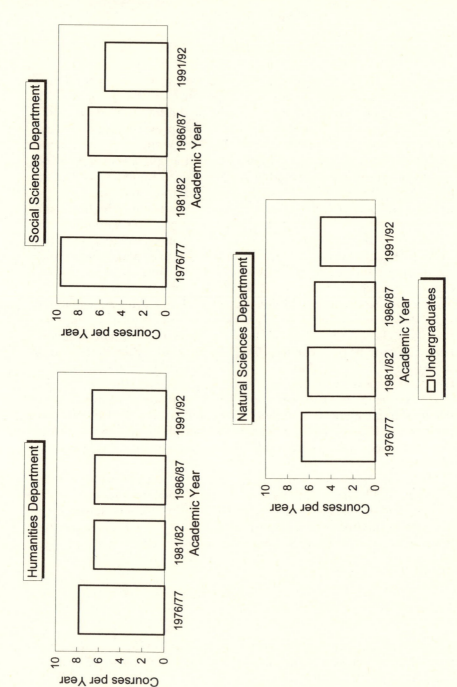

Figure 7.6 Classroom Teaching Loads, Three Departments: Carleton.
Source: Calculations using unpublished data from Carleton.

TABLE 7.6
Average Classroom Teaching Loads per FTE:
Carleton, Three Representative Departments

Department and Year	Courses	Enrollment
Humanities		
1976/77	7.3	130.5
1981/82	6.5	111.4
1986/87	5.8	136.2
1991/92	6.8	145.1
Social Sciences		
1976/77	9.7	179.2
1981/82	6.2	159.5
1986/87	7.2	153.8
1991/92	5.7	128.6
Natural Sciences		
1976/77	6.8	243.3
1981/82	6.2	253.5
1986/87	5.5	196.9
1991/92	4.8	163.3

Source: Calculations using unpublished data from Carleton.

sity-wide committees. In order to understand the changes in re-source allocation within research universities, it is helpful to know more about how faculty members spend their time. Surveys, such as those summarized above in Table 7.1, give a broad-brush impression of changes over time, but it is possible to do a better job of describing the work of faculty by using an unusual source of data—surveys that routinely were sent to Duke faculty requesting information on advising, independent study classes, and committee work. The next two sections use this information, as well as some administrative records from Carleton, to examine faculty advising and committee work. The tabulations use information from these data sources for the same representative departments previously referred to in this chapter.[7]

Formal student advising in research universities may take a number of different forms. At the level of the academic department, undergraduate majors, master's degree students, and doctoral students may have advisors to assist with course planning or for large research projects, ranging from undergraduate theses to doctoral dissertations. In addition, universities typically provide advising for first-year undergraduates who have not yet declared a major. Although the arrangements for advising of majors and graduate students often differ markedly from one department to another even in the same university, two forms of advising that tend to be measured consistently across departments are first-year (or pre-major) advising and the advising of doctoral dissertations. The former is obviously a university-wide service that goes beyond a department's narrow teaching requirements; more so even than with undergraduate classroom teaching, little in this activity can be seen as complementing research. Research is the ultimate manifestation of the personalized nature of doctoral training in a particular discipline and may be quite complementary with a faculty member's own research, even to the extent that dissertations may be based on aspects of a professor's research.

Using the Duke faculty surveys described in this section, information was collected on these two forms of advising. Pre-major advising at Duke was carried out at a central location on campus, and all advisors were required to see about the same number of students. At first, advisors were recruited on a volunteer basis. Later, beginning in the mid-1980s, they were compensated with small research grants. In contrast, the decision to chair a graduate student's dissertation review committee typically was made on a case-by-case basis, and departments sometimes rewarded this service. Table 7.7 presents data on advising for the four sample academic departments at Duke. The top section gives the percentage of faculty members, by rank, who

TABLE 7.7

Student Advising at Two Levels, by Faculty, by Rank:
Four Duke Departments, Selected Years

	Academic Year			
	1976/77	*1981/82*	*1986/87*	*1991/92*
Percentage of Faculty Who Were Freshman Advisors				
Professor	15.2	14.5	12.3	9.5
Associate professor	20.0	0.0	5.9	7.7
Assistant professor	7.7	7.7	6.3	5.0
All	15.2	11.0	10.0	8.3
Average Number of Dissertations Supervised				
Professor	1.9	1.8	2.2	2.0
Associate professor	2.6	0.6	2.4	1.9
Assistant professor	1.0	0.7	0.4	1.1
All	1.9	1.4	1.9	1.8
Concentration Index	0.55	0.65	0.62	0.61

Source: Calculations using unpublished faculty census data from Duke.

were pre-major advisors in each of the four sample years. Although this percentage fluctuated somewhat over time for associate and assistant professors, overall, a clear secular decline occurred: the proportion of regular faculty in the four sample departments serving as pre-major advisors declined from about 15 percent in 1976/77 to 8 percent in 1991/92 (emeritus and other nonregular faculty are excluded from all of these calculations). Unfortunately, this decline does not quite square with information in other administrative records. According to this information, the number of regular faculty who did pre-major advising increased in conjunction with a sizable increase in the program over this period. However, the administrative data also show that the share of pre-major advising by regular faculty fell by about one-half, the slack being taken up by administrators and nonregular faculty.[8]

Trends in the supervision of doctoral dissertations in the four departments are summarized in the remainder of Table 7.7. Not surprisingly, full professors tended to have the highest average number of dissertations to supervise, and assistant professors the least. Over the 15-year period covered by the table, there was no discernible trend in the amount of advising done at any level. The absence of an upward trend is somewhat puzzling, since the total graduate enrollment in these four departments grew by 87 percent over the period,[9] and it is rare for dissertations to be supervised by anyone other than a regular faculty member of a department.[10]

As in the case of pre-major advising and other voluntary activities, differences in the amount of advising can be large, even among faculty of the same rank. In order to measure the degree to which doctoral advising is spread out among the faculty, a gini coefficient was calculated for all faculty in each year. This coefficient is an index of concentration, with extreme values that range from 0, which would be the case if the distribution of advisees were perfectly even, to 1, which would signify the extreme case in which only one professor had every advisee. The calculated indices shown in the table indicate that little change in the distribution of advisees in these four departments occurred over this period.

COMMITTEE WORK BY FACULTY

An important component of a university's administration and governance is undertaken by faculty members in their roles as administrators and committee members. Little is known about trends in committee membership, and one reason for this ignorance may be the difficulty in measuring such membership consistently over time. The approach taken in this section is analogous to that used to track advising: consistent data on committee memberships for representative departments were collected for each of the sample academic years for two of the sample institutions. For Duke, the information on committee assignments was taken from the same faculty census forms discussed in the previous section. Each fall, faculty were asked to list the active university and departmental committees of which they were members. The faculty members' committee assignments usually were recorded as reported (the few exceptions are noted in the accompanying appendix). Carleton kept data on committee assignments as part of its administrative data.

Table 7.8 summarizes the committee memberships for the regular faculty members in the seven sample departments in each of the four sample years at Duke and Carleton. These departments had an average of about 25 faculty at Duke and about 7 at Carleton. For Duke, the assignments were divided into departmental committees, defined as those relating only to a faculty member's department, and university committees, which include college committees as well as university-wide committees. For Duke, the time trend in committee membership shows a peak in 1981/82 and a decline thereafter, whereas the average number of committee assignments at Carleton rose throughout the period.

Using data on individual committee assignments for Duke, it is possible to describe more fully the pattern of committee member-

TABLE 7.8
Faculty Membership in Committees, Four Departments:
Duke and Carleton, Selected Years

Average Number of Committees per Faculty Member	Academic Year			
	1976/77	*1981/82*	*1986/87*	*1991/92*
Duke				
University committees	1.7	1.9	1.5	1.3
Departmental committees	1.1	1.3	1.0	1.0
Total committees	2.7	3.2	2.5	2.3
Carleton				
Total committees	1.6	1.8	1.9	2.3
Concentration Index				
Duke	0.409	0.464	0.466	0.564
Carleton	0.394	0.466	0.428	0.417

Source: Calculations using unpublished faculty census data from Duke and unpublished administrative records from Carleton.

ships. Regressions were estimated explaining committee membership among the faculty for these four departments. The estimated coefficients, which indicate the differences from the omitted groups, reveal the existence of sizable departmental differences as well as a heavier commitment of full professors in university committees. Although there generally was no overall time trend, the decline in university committee representation of roughly one-half a committee assignment between 1981 and 1991 in the four departments is significant at the 95 percent level.[11]

One interesting aspect of these data on committee assignments is the degree to which responsibilities were distributed evenly across the faculty. In order to assess this distribution, concentration indices of the sort discussed above were calculated, where an index value of 0 would refer to a completely even distribution of assignments and 1 would indicate the polar opposite, the concentration of all assignments in one person. Indices were calculated for the sample departments at both institutions. Although virtually no trend is observed for Carleton, the figures for Duke suggest a steady increase in the inequality in number of committee assignments over time. Not only were salaries becoming more unequal at Duke, so, too, was the burden of university citizenship, as measured by committee memberships.

CONCLUSION

Like the theoretical firm featured in innumerable graphs in microeconomics textbooks, institutions of higher education have before them a menu of alternative techniques for the teaching of undergraduate students. They may offer large lectures or smaller classes, in which discussion is more feasible. They may enroll and compensate graduate students to perform some of the teaching, or they may employ as instructors individuals who are not members of the regular-rank faculty. The choice of techniques has implications for the cost of teaching undergraduates, the time available for faculty research, the number of courses that can be offered, and the kinds of classroom experiences that may be offered to undergraduate students. These choices are the result of a distinctive set of traditions and institutions for decision making. Moreover, the decisions are not always explicit. As Rosovsky (1992, pp. 186–7) notes:

> First, the dean has only a vaguest notion concerning what individual professors teach. Second, the changes that have occurred were never

authorized at the decanal level. . . . No chairman or group of science professors ever came to the dean to request a standard load of one half-course per year. No one ever requested a ruling concerning, for example, credit for shared courses. Change occurred through the use of *fait accompli.* . . .

Once made, however, these decisions are difficult to change dramatically in a short period, although incremental changes are possible at almost any time.

If the four institutions examined here are any indication, the period between 1977 and 1992 was one of gradual, but quite perceptible, change. Virtually without exception, average classroom teaching loads, measured in courses taught per year, decreased in the sample departments. Although these calculated loads by no means cover all aspects of teaching, they are suggestive of a significant movement away from teaching and toward research. It is noteworthy that this trend was observed in the one liberal arts college studied as well as in the three research universities, all of which started from different levels. At the same time, trends in another measure of teaching load, based on enrollments rather than on time, were less clear. Moreover, in one institution, the proportion of faculty who were advisors for first-year students declined, although there was no measurable trend in advising of doctoral students. Committee work became more common at one institution and became more concentrated among a minority of faculty at another.

What is the significance of the transformation in the use of faculty implied by these findings? If institutions did not increase the average size of classes to compensate for the reduced classroom teaching loads—and the next chapter supports that assumption—then the reduced loads must have increased total costs. In order to teach a given number of classes, institutions must either have increased the size of the regular faculty or hired additional graduate students or non-regular faculty to teach undergraduates. The evidence presented in chapters 4 and 5 suggests that they took both steps. Considering first the "output" of higher education, this shift surely meant more research, at the expense of teaching by regular faculty, and the net effect on total output may well have been positive. There is less ambiguity about its effect on costs, however: this shift pushed up the cost of operating the institutions. For a more complete assessment of the effects of these reallocations on undergraduate instruction, it is necessary to turn to evidence on the measurable characteristics of courses.

Appendix 7.1

Options for Providing Classroom Instruction

To SEE THE NATURE of the choices regarding teaching that are open to an institution, it is helpful to consider a simple model that links undergraduate teaching inputs and a budget constraint. Specifically, I consider a highly simplified model that assumes all undergraduate classes are of one equal size, C_u, and all graduate classes are of another size, C_g. The number of required undergraduate classes is equal to the number of undergraduates U multiplied by the number of courses each student takes per year R divided by average class size C_u; the number of required graduate classes is defined similarly. The supply of classes is given on the right-hand side of the equation and consists of the product of the faculty size F and faculty classroom teaching load L_f plus a similar term for graduate students plus the number of classes taught by nonregular faculty X.

$$U\, R/C_u + G\, R/C_g = F\, L_f + G\, L_g + X. \tag{7.1}$$

If income is derived from undergraduate tuitions of T per student and all graduate students are paid a stipend of S_g, then the institution's budget constraint is given by

$$T\, U = F\, S_f + G\, S_g + X\, P_n, \tag{7.2}$$

where S_f is the average salary for faculty and P_n is the average price per course for nonregular faculty.

For the purpose of calculating the possibility functions shown in Figure 7.2, this model was calibrated using a combination of estimates and actual figures for arts and sciences at Duke in 1991/92. The values for the baseline simulation were: $U = 6{,}055$, $G = 2{,}122$, $R = 8$, $C_g = 13$, $F = 506$, $L_g = .3$, $X = 742$, and $P_n = \$7{,}500$.

The alternative scenario assumed $S_f = \$62{,}818$; reducing X to 371 allowed \$2.28 million to be used to hire 44 (\$2.28 million/\$62,818) additional faculty.

Calculation of Classroom Teaching Loads
and Course Characteristics

THE MEASURES of classroom teaching load, average class size, and other classroom characteristics presented in the text use data sets for each of the institutions studied. Although there are minor differences among institutions in how various data components are defined, most variables used here are more or less standard and would be readily available to administrators who wished to calculate these measures for their own institutions.

DATA

For each of the four institutions, information was collected on every course offered by each of the three sample departments (one each in humanities, natural sciences, and social sciences, plus an engineering department at Duke), in each of the four sample academic years (1976/77, 1981/82, 1986/87, and 1991/92). The basic information required for these calculations generally is available from an institution's registrar. It includes the course number and name; the name of the instructor; the number of credits; whether the course included recitation sections or labs; and the enrollment, specified as undergraduates enrolled through that department, graduate students enrolled through the department, and other students enrolled in the course who were not arts and science students or who had enrolled in a cross-listed course.[12] Other data were collected to supplement this information for the purpose of determining the rank of instructors, clarifying the meeting schedule of classes, and obtaining information on sections. These supplementary data sources included course catalogs; lists of faculty, with ranks, provided by the institutions; faculty census forms at Duke, giving information on teaching, advising, and other professional activities; and information on the number of sections and meeting schedules provided by the institutions.

It is worth noting, as a word of both warning and encouragement to those unfamiliar with the kind of data that university registrars typically maintain, that information of this sort is seldom tidy or consolidated, and local knowledge is indispensable. For the present study, verification of information often took the form of specific questions that cannot be answered by examining official computer records of classes, such as: "How many sections did this course have in the fall of 1981?" and "Did this course normally meet for two or three lectures per week in addition to the section?" Although no two institutions follow the same record-keeping procedures or conventions, it is reasonable to expect that any comparable institution can construct a fairly similar data series, which is internally consistent over a period such as that employed in the present study.

In order to illustrate the kinds of data used and the calculations, Table 7A.1 presents information for a hypothetical music department. Each instructor for each course was listed as a separate observation. A team-taught course, such as Music Appreciation II, has more than one observation. If a class (or a part of class) met in a discussion section or lab, each section or lab was listed in addition to the lecture. The list of courses offered by a department includes those taught by faculty who are not in the department (for example, Music History is taught by a history professor). In addition, information was collected on courses outside the department that were conducted by faculty who were members of the sample department (for example, Economics of the Performing Arts is a course offered by the economics department, but taught by a music professor).

CLASSROOM TEACHING LOAD

The basic measure used in this study to measure classroom teaching load is based on the average weekly contact hours of courses taught by a full-time member of the regular faculty. A second, alternative measure is the total enrollment in courses taught by a faculty member over the course of a year. The discussion here refers to the basic measure, but most of the discussion applies to the alternative measure as well. The basic measure attempts to approximate the amount of time that faculty spend in formal classroom instruction. For example, if a faculty member meets with a class for two 50-minute "hours" per week, with the class meeting in sections led by graduate student teaching assistants a third time, this counts as two hours. Subject to several modifications noted below, this measure of teaching load therefore counts only teaching time spent in the classroom. As such, it fails to account for several important activities that are central to teaching, among them, preparing for classes, meeting with

TABLE 7A.1

Hypothetical Data for Calculating Teaching Loads and Classroom Characteristics

Course #	Course Name	Instructor	DEPTINS	Rank	DEPTOFF	TEAM	PERHRS	SHRS
MU 101	Music Appreciation I	Nelson	MUS	Assistant Professor	MUS	1	1	3
MU 102	Music Appreciation II	Nelson	MUS	Assistant Professor	MUS	0.5	0.5	3
MU 102	Music Appreciation II	Reynolds	MUS	Professor	MUS	0.5	0.5	3
MU 121	Music Theory I	Stevens	MUS	Visiting Professor	MUS	1	1	3
MU 122	Music Theory II	Summers	MUS	Lecturer	MUS	1	1	3
MU 129	Ear Training	Nelson	MUS	Assistant Professor	MUS	1	1	1
MU 141.01	Independent Study: Cello	Reynolds	MUS	Professor	MUS	1	0.167	3
MU 141.02	Independent Study: Violin	Davis	MUS	Associate Professor	MUS	1	0.333	3
MU 146	Music History	Miller	HST	Professor	MUS	1	1	3
MU 155	Great Russian Composers	Reyonds	MUS	Professor	MUS	0.5	0.5	3
MU 155	Great Russian Composers	Miller	HST	Professor	MUS	0.5	0.5	3
MU 161	Conducting	Kane	MUS	Professor	MUS	1	0.75	4
MU 161.01	Conducting Laboratory	Lewis	MUS	Graduate Student	MUS	1	0.25	4
MU 169	Advanced Music Theory	Smith	MUS	Associate Professor	MUS	1	0.667	3
MU 169.01	Advanced Music Theory Discussion	Lewis	MUS	Graduate Student	MUS	1	0.333	3
MU 169.02	Advanced Music Theory Discussion	Lewis	MUS	Graduate Student	MUS	1	0.333	3
MU 181	Advanced Composition	Smith	MUS	Associate Professor	MUS	1	1	3
MU 202	Workshop: Conducting	Nelson	MUS	Assistant Professor	MUS	1	0.333	3
MU 205	Workshop: The String Quartet	Davis	MUS	Associate Professor	MUS	1	0.333	3
MU 299.07	Dissertation Research	Reynolds	MUS	Professor	MUS	1	1	3
MU 299.21	Dissertation Research	Kane	MUS	Professor	MUS	1	1	3
EC 149	Economics of Performing Arts	Marshall	MUS	Professor	ECO	0.5	1	3

Note: Course #: Course number.
DEPTINS: Department of the instructor.
DEPTOFF: Department sponsoring a course.
TEAM: Instructor's share of the teaching of a course.
PERHRS: Percentage of the hours per week of a course attributable to the instructor.

SHRS: Hours a course meets per week.
PHRS: Number of hours alllocated to an instructor for a class (SHARE × SHRS × (1-RDUM)).
PENR: Number of students allocated to an instructor for a class (TEAM × TOTAL ×(1-RDUM)).
GHRS: Number of hours allocated to an instructor for a graduate class.

PHRS	PENR	GHRS	GENR	CRED	TOTAL	UNDER	GRAD	OTHER	GDUM	RDUM	SHARE
3	21	0	0	3	21	21	0	0	0	0	1
1.5	7.5	0	0	3	15	15	0	0	0	0	0.5
1.5	7.5	0	0	3	15	15	0	0	0	0	0.5
3	33	0	0	3	33	33	0	0	0	0	1
3	25	0	0	3	25	24	0	1	0	0	1
1	7	0	0	1	7	7	0	0	0	0	1
0.5	1	0	0	3	1	1	0	0	0	0	1
1	2	0	0	3	2	2	0	0	0	0	1
3	13	0	0	3	13	12	0	1	0	0	1
1.5	6	0	0	3	12	10	0	2	0	0	0.5
1.5	6	0	0	3	12	10	0	2	0	0	0.5
3	3	0	0	3	3	0	3	0	0	0	0.75
1	3	0	0	0	3	0	3	0	0	0	0.25
2	18	0	0	3	18	15	3	0	0	0	0.667
1	10	0	0	0	10	8	2	0	0	0	0.333
1	8	0	0	0	8	7	1	0	0	0	0.333
3	2	3	2	3	2	0	2	0	1	0	1
1	9	1	9	3	9	0	9	0	1	0	1
1	6	1	6	3	6	0	6	0	1	0	1
0	0	0	0	3	3	0	3	0	1	1	0
0	0	0	0	3	2	0	2	0	1	1	0
3	7.5	0	0	3	15	13	1	1	0	0	0.5

GENR: Number of graduate students allocated to an instructor for a class.

CRED: Number of credit hours assigned to a course.

TOTAL: Total enrollment in a course.

UNDER: Number of undergraduates enrolled in a course.

GRAD: Number of graduate students enrolled in a course.

OTHER: Number of other students enrolled in a course.

GDUM: Equal to one if a graduate course; zero otherwise.

RDUM: Equal to one if course was dissertation research; zero otherwise.

SHARE: Share of a student's time spent in each section of a course.

students outside of class, working alongside graduate students in labs, reading student drafts, and grading assignments. Therefore, this measure is by no means a complete measure of "teaching load."

In calculating the basic measure, several modifications and assumptions, some of them rather arbitrary, were used.

1. In accordance with the usual convention used in describing teaching loads, the total number of hours for all courses taught over the course of the year are added together. In addition, courses taught in institutions using the quarter system are taken to be equivalent to courses taught in semester systems. Thus, a professor teaching two courses per quarter, each carrying three contact hours per week, would have a classroom teaching load of 18 hours; this load would be comparable to three similar courses per term in a semester system.

2. In cases in which actual hours per week and credit hours differ, measured hours are based on actual number of hours in class per week, or contact hours, rather than on credit hours.[13]

3. Team teaching is reflected by dividing hours (and enrollment) evenly among all listed instructors for the purpose of measuring classroom teaching loads. In most cases, this assumption seems to be a fair reflection of the actual teaching load per instructor. Occasionally, single instructors were listed for colloquia courses, which consist largely of invited presentations by invited speakers or graduate students enrolled in the course. Because these courses typically require significantly less time than do conventional lecture courses or seminars, the listed faculty leader of a workshop or colloquium received credit for one-third of the class time.[14]

4. One set of courses that required special attention were those designed to give credit to a student who is under the direction of a faculty member and who is engaged in a largely independent project; these courses may be called "advanced topics in . . ." or independent study. In some instances, some of these courses may be used to "try out" a new course that might later receive a more permanent course number and title. Although not normally conducted in classrooms, these courses require meeting time similar to that required by conventional courses, and so it is important to reflect their contribution to faculty teaching loads. Data on the number of contact hours between the professor and student simply are not available for independent study-type courses. Furthermore, data on the number of hours per week that a listed faculty member spent teaching students in a workshop or a dissertation research section are not available. Because of the difficulty in distinguishing the various possibilities, the calculations of course load in this study use the following arbitrary weighting system. Courses that were formally designated as independent study or had the characteristics of a flexible course that might be used in the same way (courses of this type often had low enrollments) were designated "independent study-type" courses. Using a benchmark that an independent study course might require a professor to meet with a student for at least one hour every two weeks, a course was assumed to take up one-sixth of a three-hour commitment for each student enrolled, up to six students, beyond which the course was assigned a full three-hour credit. Thus, an independent study-type course in which three students were enrolled would be assigned a weight of 1.5 hours.[15]

The number of hours per week that a student spends in a class, designated *SHRS* in the table, and the number of hours that a particular instructor spends conducting the class are not necessarily the same. To accommodate this fact, variables were created describing whether the lecture, discussion, or laboratory portion of the class was team taught (*TEAM*, a variable showing an instructor's share of a team-taught course) and the percentage of the hours per week attributable to a particular instructor for an entire course, *PERHRS*. If a class is team taught, the percentage of the hours per week had to be allocated to the various instructors. For the present study, the hours per week were divided evenly among instructors in team-taught classes. For example, in the hypothetical team-taught Music Appreciation II class, each professor is allocated 50 percent of the class's hours per week.

5. Professors listed as leading dissertation research sections were given no credit for classroom teaching for such advising. For ease of calculation, a dummy variable was created, equal to one if the course is for dissertation research and equal to zero otherwise, as illustrated by *RDUM* in the example.

6. One other arbitrary rule used in the present study to calculate classroom teaching loads was to credit instructors and students with only one hour of class time for laboratory sections, in keeping with the practice of giving only one hour of credit for lab sections even though an instructor or student may spend as much or more time in lab than in lectures for a course.

Average classroom teaching loads were calculated for each department by dividing the total number of hours (or enrollments) by the number of faculty available for teaching each term or, where available, by the FTE number of faculty available. In cases in which FTE were not available, faculty were considered available for teaching in any semester during which they were not on sabbatical or other leave of absence. The data were not always sufficient to identify official leaves of absence, so, for institutions that did not have FTE information, faculty doing no teaching during a term were assumed to be on leave. However, no correction was made for reductions in teaching loads given for administrative duties; these reductions serve to reduce the total classroom teaching load without reducing the number of faculty FTEs available for teaching.

These assumptions are applied to the example in Table 7A.2. The product of *SHARE* (the share of a student's time spent in each section of a course), *SHRS*, and (1-*RDUM*) is an estimate of the number of hours per class attributable to each instructor, *PHRS*. The number of students per class allocated to each instructor, *PENR*, is equal to the product of *TEAM*, *TOTAL*, and (1-*RDUM*).[16]

As noted, the calculation of classroom teaching loads per class does not reflect time spent reading, preparing syllabi, preparing lecture notes, or meeting outside class with students. Because of the nature of graduate training, preparation for graduate classes often is more demanding on professors than is preparation for undergraduate classes. Thus, it is useful to distinguish between graduate classes

TABLE 7A.2

Average Classroom Teaching Loads per FTE and Course Characteristics: Hypothetical Example

Description	Calculated Value
Classroom Teaching Load	
Courses per week	
Total	7.67
Graduate	1.67
Enrollment	
Total	97.5
Graduate	17.0
Average Class Size	
Undergraduates	21.3
Graduate students	7.4
Percentage of Undergraduates Taught by	
Graduate students	3.7
Nonregular faculty	47.7
Subtotal	51.4
Percentage of Undergraduates enrolled, by Size of Class	
18 or less	42.4
19–35	57.6
36–75	0.0
More than 75	0.0
Total	100.0

Source: Calculations based on hypothetical figures in Table 7A.1.

and undergraduate classes when calculating classroom teaching loads. One mechanism for making this is to use a dummy variable to designate graduate courses. For instance, in the example, *GDUM* equals one for graduate-level courses and zero otherwise. The hours per instructor for graduate classes, *GHRS*, equals *PHRS* multiplied by *GDUM*, and enrollment per professor in the graduate classes is the product of *PENR* and *GDUM*.

After these variables were constructed, observations were summed, by professor. The sums of *PHRS*, *PENR*, *GHRS*, and *GENR*, by professor, show individual teaching loads. In this study, to calculate average classroom teaching loads by department, total classroom hours are divided by the sum of the department's faculty FTE. Average teaching loads for this case are translated from hours to courses, where three hours per week for a 14-week semester is one course.[17]

CLASS CHARACTERISTICS

Several measures are used to describe the courses taught in the sample departments in each institution. In contrast to the measures of teaching load, which are calculated from the perspective of regular faculty members, the class characteristics attempt to describe salient aspects of the course from the perspective of the enrolled student. As illustrated in Table 7A.2, four measures are calculated: (1) average class size for undergraduates; (2) average class size for graduate students; (3) the size distribution for undergraduate classes; and (4) the distribution of undergraduate enrollments, by type of instructor (regular faculty, nonregular faculty, and graduate students). Regular faculty are tenured or tenure-track faculty, usually having the rank of professor, associate professor, or assistant professor. Nonregular faculty include visiting instructors and instructors with such ranks as professor of the practice, lecturer, research professor, and artist-in-residence. Several aspects of the calculations are worth mentioning.

1. Average class size is weighted, as appropriate, by the number of undergraduates or graduate students enrolled in the course through the sample department. In calculating average class size for undergraduates in the philosophy department, for example, a course with 30 undergraduates who enrolled through the philosophy department, 3 graduate students, and 2 undergraduates who enrolled in the cross-listed course from another department would have a total class size of 35 and would receive a weight of 30. In calculating the average class size for graduate students in the department, the class would still be entered as 35 with a weight of 3.

2. Courses that meet in sections or labs in addition to lectures imply different class sizes and different instructors for different portions of the course, and these different meeting arrangements are weighted roughly according to the time spent. For example, a student in an introductory natural sciences course might spend two hours per week in a lecture with 235 students, one hour in a section of 28 students, and one hour (the official weight for what usually is more than one hour) in a lab with 22 students. If the section and lab are run by graduate students and the lecture is given by a professor in the department, this student sees a regular faculty member half the time and, on average, is in a class of 130 (.5 × 235 + .25 × 28 + .25 × 22). Lecture classes with sections and no labs typically imply a weight of three-fourths for the lecture and one-fourth for the section, although most core courses at Harvard met only twice per week in lecture, implying a two-thirds/one-third split.

In illustrating the calculation of these measures, it is useful to begin with a variable that defines the share of the student's time spent in each section of a course, as illustrated by the variable *SHARE* in Table 7A.1. If a course does not meet outside of the lecture and has only one instructor, *SHARE* equals one. If a course has two hours of lecture as well as a one-hour discussion section each week, then the share of a student's time for the course spent in lecture is two-thirds and the share for the discussion section is one-third.

The average class size for undergraduates enrolling in the courses of a given department, *UAVESIZE*, is obtained by calculating a weighted average of the class sizes for all the components of all the courses offered by that department, the weight being undergraduates who enrolled in that department's courses. This is formulated as the sum of the product of *SHRS* (credit hours), *UNDER* (the number of undergraduates in the course), *SHARE*, and *TOTAL* (the total enrollment, including graduate students and those enrolled in the course via another department or program), divided by the sum of the product of *SHRS*, *UNDER*, and *SHARE*, or

$$UAVESIZE = \frac{\sum_i SHRS_i * SHARE_i * UNDER_i * TOTAL_i}{\sum_i SHRS_i * SHARE_i * UNDER_i}, \quad (7.3)$$

where i represents all of the *n* meetings of each undergraduate class. The denominator is the sum of undergraduate credit hours for all the department's courses, and this constitutes the weight for the average. The average graduate class size is calculated by using the students' total enrollment hours of each graduate course weighted by graduate enrollment.[18] In chapter 7, the average class sizes are calculated by the department offering the course (*DEPTOFF* in Table 7A.1). However, the identities of the departments used in the calculations are not revealed.

Another description of class size presented in chapter 8 is the distribution of undergraduate enrollment, by class size. This calculation is accomplished by sorting the total enrollment of undergraduates into four categories based on the total enrollment in each course or part of a course: (1) 18 or less, (2) 19 to 35, (3) 36 to 75, and (4) 75 or more. For each category, the sum of the product of *SHRS*, *SHARE*, and *UNDER* (in other words, undergraduate enrollment hours) is calculated and, in turn, the sum of undergraduate enrollment hours for each of the categories. The percentage distribution is equal to the product of *SHRS*, *SHARE*, and *UNDER* for each category divided by the sum of all undergraduate enrollment hours across all categories such that

$$\frac{\sum_j \sum_i SHRS_{ij} * SHARE_{ij} * UNDER_{ij}}{\sum_i SHRS_i * SHARE_i * UNDER_i} = 1, \qquad (7.4)$$

where j represents each category, one through four. This distribution approximates the proportion of a students' time spent in sections of different sizes.

Undergraduates' exposure to regular rank (tenure or tenure-track) faculty, to nonregular faculty, and to graduate students in the classroom was calculated by, first, summing the undergraduate enrollment in undergraduate classes by these three categories, and then, dividing the undergraduate enrollment hours for each category by the sum of all undergraduate enrollment hours. This reveals the portion of students' time spent in sections led by regular-rank faculty as distinguished from nonregular rank faculty and graduate students (if any).

Appendix 7.3

Data on Committee Membership

DATA ON FACULTY committee membership at Duke were obtained from the annual faculty census surveys described in chapter 7. These forms were circulated each term over the entire period covered by the sample years of the study. In each term, they asked faculty to list the active university committees and departmental committees on which they served. The responses of all regular tenured and tenure-track faculty in the four sample departments were recorded and tabulated. The data are imperfect, in that they rely on professors' own evaluations of which committees are sufficiently significant to merit listing or which may be otherwise incorrect. With a few exceptions, however, the responses of faculty are recorded as reported. Committees related to departments were classified as departmental, and those related to schools or colleges were classified as university-wide. In general, subcommittees were not counted, the exception being the executive committee of the faculty senate. Administrative positions, such as departmental chair, director of graduate and undergraduate studies, liaison with some outside group not involving a committee, advisor to an academic honorary society, or coordinator of some function, were excluded from consideration. However, all departmental chairs were credited with serving on their dean's council of chairs even if this committee had not been listed. Committee memberships that were not counted on the grounds that they were indistinguishable from other scholarly duties of professors included editorial boards, doctoral examination committees, committees to evaluate candidates for appointment or promotion, and administrative duties connected with professional associations. On the other hand, formally constituted search committees were counted because they normally involve at least some months of continuing administrative work.

TABLE 7A.3
Regressions Explaining Committee Membership at Duke

	Dependent Variable			
	Departmental Committees		University Committees	
Department				
A	2.35	(12.4)	−0.52	(1.7)
B	0.63	(3.3)	−0.91	(3.0)
C	0.57	(3.1)	0.34	(1.2)
(Omitted: D)				
Rank				
Full professor	0.08	(0.5)	0.92	(3.8)
Associate professor	−0.08	(0.4)	−0.24	(0.8)
(Omitted: Assistant professor)				
Year				
1981	0.31	(1.8)	0.14	(0.5)
1986	0.07	(0.4)	−0.23	(0.9)
1991	0.10	(0.6)	−0.43	(1.7)
(Omitted: 1976)				
Intercept	−0.01	(0.1)	1.45	(4.2)
R^2	.40		.14	

Source: Estimated regressions using unpublished data on committee membership in four sample departments at Duke.

CHAPTER 8

Classes and Course Offerings

> We concluded that one important way to mea-
> sure a college's commitment to undergraduate
> education is to look at class size in general ed-
> ucation. Do these courses enroll hundreds of
> students? Are they taught by senior pro-
> fessors? Do students have an opportunity to
> meet with their teachers?
>
> *Ernest Boyer, 1987*[1]

UNDERLYING an institution's measured expenditures are choices that it makes about how to allocate its teaching resources, notably, its faculty and graduate students. The previous chapter presents data showing that one evident trend in the sample institutions during the period of study was a decline in the average amount of classroom teaching by regular faculty members, at least in the departments examined. This trend is certainly consistent with the notion that an increasing emphasis on research had affected the entire labor market for academic labor, by way of changing the expected conditions of work for faculty. Whatever its genesis, it would be surprising if a change such as this one had no impact on the production processes of colleges and universities, and, in turn, on the outputs. Owing to the primitive nature of our understanding of these processes and the difficulty in measuring the outputs, however, it is impossible to say exactly what the effects might be. The best that can be done is to observe some of the corollary effects of these changes. In particular, it is possible to measure the size of classes and the share of teaching by regular-rank faculty. If characteristics such as these affect the quality of educational experience for students—and there is evidence that they do—useful, if not ideal, information can be obtained. The aim of this chapter, then, is to examine several measurable indices that help to assess the real, as opposed to the purely financial, changes that occurred during the sample period at the four institutions.

The first section of the chapter presents measures describing two major characteristics of courses offered by each institution: the size of classes and whether the instructors are regular faculty, graduate students or other, nonregular faculty. The second section examines the number of courses offered in several departments. It also touches on several related aspects of the courses offered.

CHARACTERISTICS OF COURSES: HOW LARGE AND WHO TEACHES

The conventional wisdom among practitioners of college and university teaching is that class size matters, but that its effect is not necessarily proportional. Smaller classes give instructors the option of using teaching techniques, principally those that require give-and-take between student and teacher, that are infeasible in larger classes. Beyond the size at which these techniques become impossible, however, it is often claimed that increasing a class's size has little further deleterious effect. Some scientific evidence appears to support the notion that class size matters. In his surveys of Harvard undergraduates, Light (1992, pp. 50–1) finds that students who take at least one small course report higher levels of satisfaction and are "noticeably more engaged, by their own rating, than students who take only larger classes."

The other measurable characteristic of classes is the type of instructor. The general presumption is that, other things equal, a member of the regular faculty usually will do a better job of teaching than will a graduate student. The student lacks not only the training signified by the degree but also lacks experience in the job at hand. A similar presumption can be defended with respect to the comparison between regular (tenured and tenure-track) faculty and non-regular faculty. One would be hard put to argue that either class size or the category of the instructor functionally determines teaching quality (assuming the latter could be measured), but it seems reasonable to pay attention to both indices.

Given the presumption that class size is important, at least within limits, it seems best to measure it directly, by the number of students who share a given classroom or laboratory experience. Interestingly, this measure is completely different from the statistic that is most commonly reported and compared for the same purpose—the student-faculty ratio. Lower ratios are considered preferable to higher ratios, and indeed, private, selective, and expensive institutions do tend to have the lowest ones. For example, the 1994 *Peterson's Guide* reported the following ratios for the sample institutions: Duke, 12:1; Carleton, 11:1; Harvard, 8:1; and Chicago, 3:1. Assuming that total faculty was used to calculate these ratios, the ratios would be heavily influenced by the presence and size of graduate and professional schools. Moreover, as chapter 7 shows, even between two institutions with undergraduate, graduate, and professional schools of equal size, there is no necessary correspondence between this ratio and average class size. In the simple model presented in chapter 7, average class size depends not only on enrollments and faculty size—the raw material for the student-faculty ratio—but also on the normal course load taken by students, the classroom teaching load of faculty, the use of graduate students as instructors, and the use of other nonfaculty instructors.

Although average class size seems to be a more useful descriptive statistic than the gross student-faculty ratio, it is not without its own shortcomings. For one, average class size suffers from the drawback of all averages; a more complete description of the size of classes would account for the variation across classes by size as well as the overall average. Another shortcoming of average class size is its dependence on patterns of student enrollment: the inevitable ebb and flow of student enrollments by department stands against the relative fixity in the number of faculty in each department, creating strong forces for larger classes in popular departments and making small classes easier to achieve in less popular fields.

As described in chapter 7 and appendix 7.2, data were collected for three corresponding departments in each institution, one each in humanities, natural sciences, and social sciences, plus an engineering department at Duke. For every course in each department in each sample academic year, information was obtained on the number of undergraduates registered through the department, the number of graduate students so registered, and the number of students who had registered for the same courses through some other department's designation (for cross-listed courses only). For courses that met in discussion sections or labs in addition to lectures, information on the size of each meeting group was collected or estimated. Using a variety of data sources, it also was possible to determine whether the instructor of any class or component section was a regular tenure-track faculty member, a graduate student, or other instructor. The latter group includes visitors, adjunct faculty, and those with a nonregular rank, such as lecturer.[2] Calculations were then made, taking the perspective of students rather than of faculty members, and asking how the changes in the scheduling and staffing of courses, combined with enrollment shifts, affected the sort of learning environments that students experienced. Despite the common presumptions alluded to here, the calculations incorporate no judgment about the relative quality of teaching provided by instructors in each of these categories. The objective simply is to examine the composition and determine whether it changed over time. Much the same can be said about class size.

In keeping with the approach of taking a student's perspective, the calculation of average class size weights the various courses by the number of students rather than equally. Consider, for example, the calculation of average class size when 300 students are spread among 10 classes. Regardless of their distribution, the size of the average class (unweighted) will be 30. However, the class size for the average student will depend on the distribution of students among courses. If the 300 students are enrolled equally in 10 classes, then all students and, therefore, the average student, would be in a class of 30. If there were 9 classes with 10 students each and 1 class with the remaining 210, then the average student's class size would rise dramatically, to 150, reflecting the experience of the large number of students enrolled in the 1 large class.[3] This example also serves to illustrate the importance of measuring the size distribution as well as the average size of courses. In cases in which courses met in more than one venue, such as in discussion sections and lectures, the class size of each gathering was calculated and was weighted according to the amount of class time (with the exception of science labs, which were assigned one hour's weight). Special assumptions were made to account for some types of courses, such as independent study and colloquia. Appendix 7.2 provides more detail on the calculations.

Class Size

Duke

Graphs showing average class size for Duke's four departments are presented in Figure 8.1. The bars show the averages corresponding to undergraduate and graduate classes, respectively. (Table 8A.1 in the appendix gives values corresponding to these figures, along with summaries of enrollment trends.) Corresponding to the overall growth in arts and sciences graduate programs at Duke over this period, the graduate enrollments in all four sample departments increased as well. Enrollment patterns of undergraduates differed from those of graduate students, showing steady growth in the engineering department, a dip and then sharp growth in the humanities department, and general declines in the social science and natural sciences departments.

One feature that is immediately evident from the graphs is the

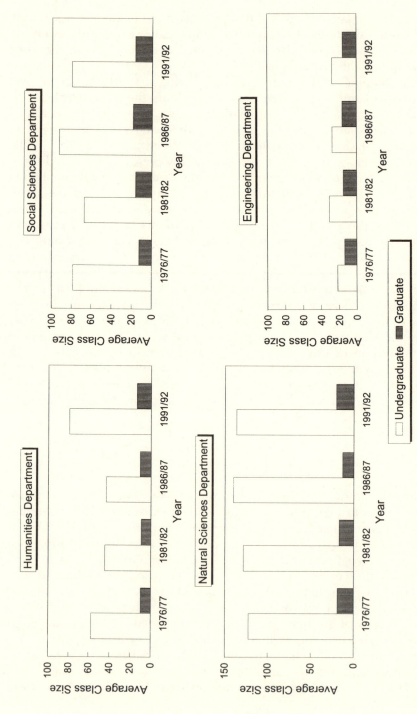

Figure 8.1 Average Class Size, Four Departments: Duke.

Source: Calculations using unpublished data from Duke.

much higher average class sizes in undergraduate courses, which is not surprising in light of the large effect that large classes have on the average. For 1991/92, the average graduate class size ranged from a low of 14 to a high of 20, whereas the average undergraduate class ranged from 28, in the engineering department, to 136, in the natural sciences department. Although they are averages that hide considerable variation among individual classes, these calculations of average class size are sufficient to suggest how little can be learned from a single, university-wide student-faculty ratio. Looking at the changes in these averages, there appears to be little trend in either the natural sciences department or the engineering department. The decline in undergraduate enrollments appeared to be matched by a similar decline in faculty size over the period. In the remaining two departments, average class size for undergraduates varied somewhat. In the case of the humanities department, the average followed the trend for total enrollments, dipping in 1986/87 and rising sharply in 1991/92; the average in the last year reflects enrollments in two survey courses that the department offered as large lectures.

Figure 8.2 shows the distribution of undergraduate classes by size. The most interesting trend, evident in the humanities and the social science departments, was an increase in the percentage of students taking both the smallest classes and the largest classes. Although the percentage of students in classes with more than 75 students increased from 1981/82 to 1991/92, the percentage taking seminars and other classes with enrollments of 18 or less did not fall.

Harvard

Regardless of whether the discussion section as a teaching format actually was developed at Harvard,[4] undergraduate education at Harvard College is widely associated with a style of teaching that features large lectures and sections run by graduate students. Thus, Harvard presents an interesting case study for applying the measures developed in this study. Unfortunately, data limitations significantly restricted what could be learned about trends in course characteristics in the sample departments at Harvard. Although official enrollment data were available for the sample departments for all years, with the exception of the social science department, it was not possible to obtain complete information on either the size or number of sections. It was possible to obtain two years of data on the humanities department, but no data on the years before 1991/92 could be located for the natural sciences department. Because of the em-

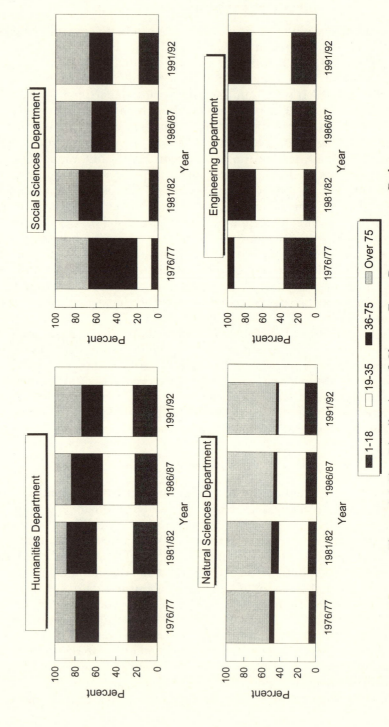

Figure 8.2 Size Distribution of Classes, Four Departments: Duke.

Source: Calculations using unpublished data from Duke.

phasis in this study on time-series comparisons, the natural sciences department was dropped in these calculations.

More recently, Harvard has become known for its "core," a collection of courses that are listed separately from the traditional departments, but some of which were in fact plucked out of those departments and are taught by many of the same professors. For the calculations, performed for the current analysis, the core courses that would in other colleges be part of one of the sample departments were included in the calculation for that department. Because many of these courses featured the lecture-and-section format, their inclusion tends to raise the calculated averages from what they otherwise would have been.

Figure 8.3 shows average size of classes in the two departments. Although the general admonition against comparisons among institutions applies here, as it does in other cases, it seems safe to conclude that the average class sizes for undergraduates and graduate students at Harvard are markedly larger than for the corresponding departments at Duke. In the social science department in 1991/92, for example, the average size for undergraduate courses was 242, compared with 80 at Duke. For graduate classes, the numbers were much closer, 24 versus 17. No trend in the average size of classes in the social science department is evident. Instead, this average appears to track the department's total enrollment, with both figures hitting their highest levels in 1981/82 and their second highest levels in 1991/92.[5] With respect to the size distribution, shown in Figure 8.4, the percentage of students in the smallest classes appears to have grown; this increase is evident in the two-year comparison for the humanities department as well as over the entire period for the social science department.

Chicago

Unlike Harvard, Chicago did not make extensive use of the large lecture as a teaching format, and this fact becomes evident in the summary measures shown in Figure 8.5. Using 1991/92 as a reference point, the average undergraduate class sizes in Chicago's sample departments were smaller than those of the corresponding departments at Duke and Harvard—strikingly so in the humanities and social science departments, the two departments where these averages also fell over the period. Graduate class sizes were somewhat smaller in these two departments and quite a bit smaller in the natural sciences department.

Data on the distribution by class size, shown in Figure 8.6, also

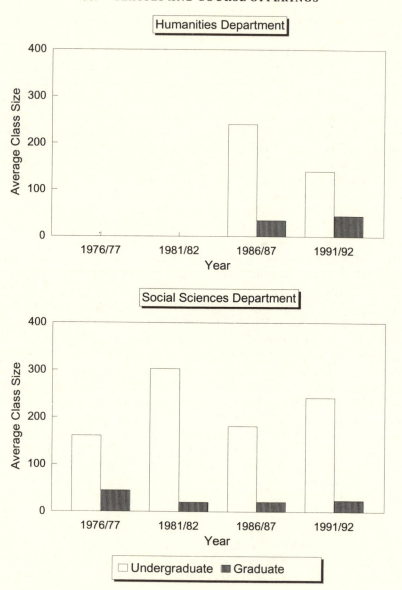

Figure 8.3 Average Class Size, Two Departments: Harvard.

Source: Calculations using unpublished data from Harvard.

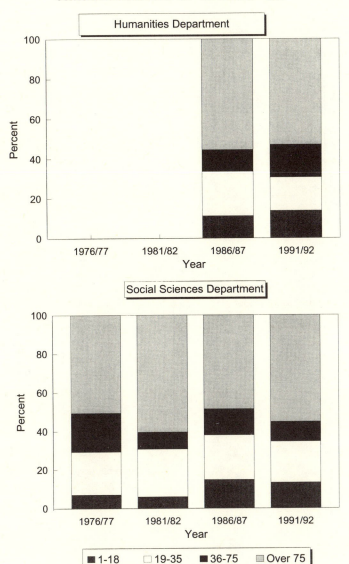

Figure 8.4 Size Distribution of Undergraduate
Classes, Two Departments: Harvard.
Source: Calculations using unpublished data from Harvard.

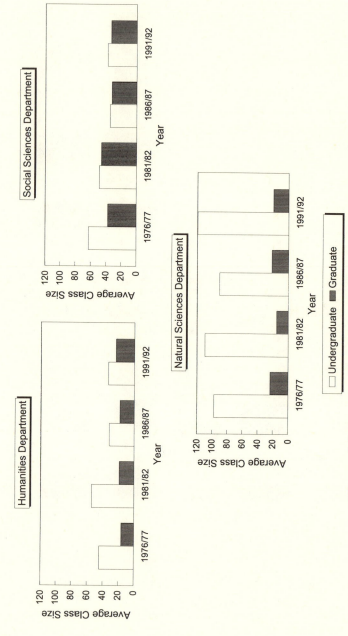

Figure 8.5 Average Class Size, Three Departments: Chicago.
Source: Calculations using unpublished data from Chicago.

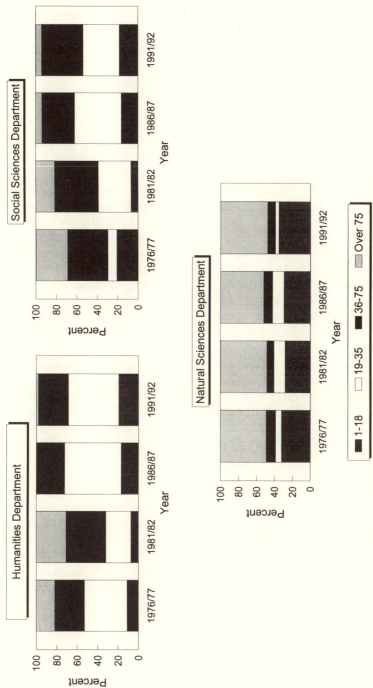

Figure 8.6 Size Distribution of Classes, Three Departments: Chicago.
Source: Calculations using unpublished data from Chicago.

reflects the relative scarcity of large lectures other than in the natural sciences department. The humanities department significantly changed the size distribution of its classes, doubling the percentage of undergraduates in the smallest courses and practically eliminating classes of 75 students or more.

Carleton

In stark contrast to the mode of course organization at Harvard and in the natural sciences department at Duke and Chicago, Carleton made little use of large lectures in the departments examined. Taking advantage of its relatively heavy classroom teaching loads, Carleton was able to offer its students small classes almost across the board, as the graphs in Figure 8.7 reveal. Using the social science department as a point of comparison, the average class size at Carleton in 1991/92 was 24, compared with 80 at Duke, 242 at Harvard, and 38 at Chicago. Over the period, the class size in Carleton's humanities and social science departments averaged about 30 students; its natural sciences department averaged almost 40 students per class. Average enrollment declined between 1981/82 and 1991/92 in both the social science and natural sciences department, paralleling the decline in enrollments in both. Examining the size distribution of classes, summarized in Figure 8.8, indicates how the humanities and social science departments were able to arrive at the same approximate size by quite different routes, the former enrolling higher portions of students in both the largest and smallest classes. It is striking that in 1991/92, no class in the social science department had more than 35 students.

Summary

Data on class characteristics for the four institutions are presented in Table 8.1. Unlike most of the measures used in this study, these calculations are comparable across institutions, as well as over time. Because of data limitations, no information is given for Harvard's natural sciences department or for some years in other departments at Harvard and Duke. The top part of the table, showing average class size, illustrates three points. First, owing to different modes of instruction and to the prevalence of large introductory courses in some departments, average class size differs among departments in the same institution. For each of the three institutions with complete data in 1991/92, the natural sciences department had the highest average class size. Second, differences in class size also exist between

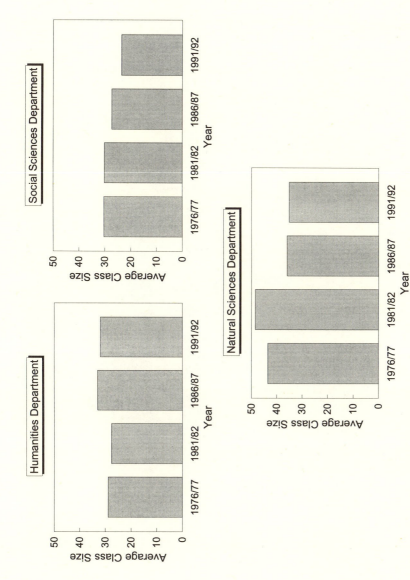

Figure 8.7 Average Class Size, Three Departments: Carleton.
Source: Calculations using unpublished data from Carleton.

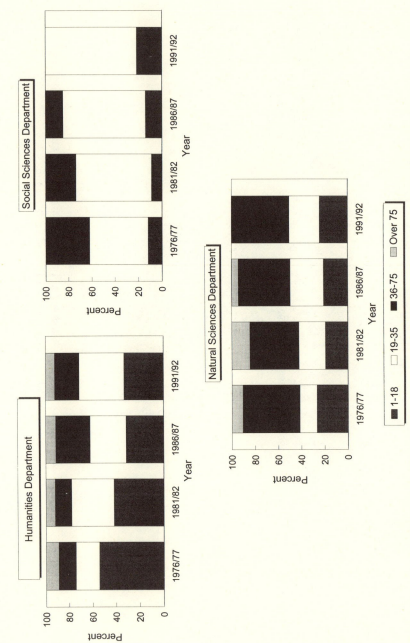

Figure 8.8 Size Distribution of Classes, Three Departments: Carleton.

Source: Calculations using unpublished data from Carleton.

TABLE 8.1
Undergraduate Classes in Three Departments at Four Institutions:
Average Size and Percentage Taught by Regular Faculty, Selected Years

Average Class Size	1976/77	1981/82	1986/87	1991/92
Humanities Department				
Duke	57	42	42	76
Harvard	NA	NA	241	139
Chicago	45	54	32	33
Carleton	29	28	33	32
Natural Sciences Department				
Duke	122	128	140	136
Harvard	NA	NA	NA	NA
Chicago	97	109	90	119
Carleton	44	49	36	35
Social Sciences Department				
Duke	79	67	91	80
Harvard	162	303	181	242
Chicago	63	49	35	38
Carleton	30	30	27	24

Percentage of Teaching Conducted by Regular Faculty				
Humanities Department				
Duke	NA	82	87	61
Harvard	NA	NA	55	54
Chicago	74	78	79	69
Carleton	91	91	91	99
Natural Sciences Department				
Duke	NA	61	57	61
Harvard	NA	NA	NA	NA
Chicago	66	37	67	68
Carleton	100	100	100	82
Social Sciences Department				
Duke	94	66	69	72
Harvard	56	50	46	48
Chicago	78	47	38	42
Carleton	88	91	77	85

Source: Calculations using unpublished data from the four sample institutions.
NA: not available.

institutions. Especially striking are the low average class sizes at
Carleton. Third, there is no discernible trend in these departments
over time. Whatever was happening to average faculty teaching load
did not translate into larger classes.

Instructors

The bottom part of Table 8.1 summarizes findings on the share of enrollments in the sample departments taught by members of the regular faculty. (Separate shares for graduate students and other instructors are given in the detailed tables in the appendix.) Significant differences among the institutions are evident. In the social science department, the shares of teaching by regular faculty at Chicago and Harvard in 1991/92 were the lowest, being under one half in the latest year; these compared to 72 percent at Duke and 85 percent at Carleton. In the humanities department, the share of classroom teaching by regular faculty in the latest year ranged from 54 percent at Harvard to 99 percent at Carleton. In the natural sciences departments, the differences among Duke, Chicago, and Carleton are much smaller. What is more interesting, however, is the trend shown in these graphs. In six of the eight departments for which complete data were available for the entire period, the share of undergraduate teaching by the regular faculty declined over the period of study. At Carleton, no trend was evident: these proportions remained high throughout the period.

COURSE OFFERINGS

One of the most prominent descriptions of the educational program of any college or university is its published description of course offerings. Determined largely by individual academic departments, these course listings give substance and a degree of order to that portion of the body of knowledge for which each department takes responsibility for teaching. In a rough way, they can be thought of as a description of one set of the institution's outputs. Together with the requirements set down for obtaining degrees, course offerings define the curriculum—an area that has become the focal point of vigorous debate in American higher education for the last decade. Although much of this debate has little direct bearing on university expenditures, the charge that universities have allowed undergraduate courses to proliferate while emphasizing research at the expense of teaching is relevant. According to this argument, courses are offered not because they are part of a carefully constructed introduction to existing knowledge on a subject but rather because they cover topics of special interest to individual faculty members. The result, according to critics, is that curricula have become little more than agglomerations of uncoordinated courses, the operative metaphor being a smorgasbord, as opposed to a planned meal.[6] If a proliferation of courses has occurred, even holding teaching loads constant, at least one of the following would be required: more faculty, an increase in class sizes in introductory courses, or the use of more nonfaculty instructors in the teaching of undergraduates.

It is therefore pertinent to seek evidence of increases in course offerings. To be sure, the growth of knowledge alone would constitute one reason to expect some change in the curriculum over time, and evidence suggests that academic disciplines have undergone increased specialization[7]; an increased number of courses may reflect these developments. Although it is beyond the scope of this study to examine in detail issues of curriculum structure, as Massy and Zemsky (1994) have, it is possible to make several straightforward measurements that are relevant to these concerns. One measure is simply the number of courses, which is applied to several departments in the sample institutions. A proliferation of courses should show up in such a count. In addition, it is useful to investigate the charge that the curriculum is determined by research interests of faculty, rather than by a set of abiding educational principles. One implication of this view is that courses would tend to change when faculty arrive or depart. Conversely, if courses were set as a matter of educational policy, they generally would be taught regardless of who is a member of the faculty. Therefore, the association between faculty turnover and course continuity is examined for a few departments.

Course offerings in several selected departments were compared for the beginning and ending years of the 15-year period of analysis. The departments chosen for these comparisons are not necessarily the same as those in the calculations of classroom teaching loads and course characteristics. Course lists were compared, and courses with similar titles and descriptions were considered to be the same course. For the purpose of these comparisons, generic courses (such as independent study, general senior seminars, courses of reading and research, or the direction of doctoral dissertations) were not included. In general, each of the components of a related series of courses was counted as a separate course if it had a different number, but the precise number of courses, and course changes, ultimately is a judgment call. Any concerted departmental effort to rationalize or rearrange its offerings may result in a large number of changes in its course listing, which may overstate the actual change in course material. For these reasons, the calculations presented here should be considered illustrative only.

Summary measures for 13 departments in the four institutions are

TABLE 8.2
Number of Courses Offered in Selected Departments,
1976/77 and 1991/92

	Number of Courses					
	Total		*Courses Offered in*			*Turnover*
Institution and Department	*1976/77*	*1991/92*	*Both Years*	*1976/77 Only*	*1991/92 Only*	*Rate[a] (%)*
Duke						
Chemistry	29	34	26	3	8	17
English	127	138	68	59	70	49
Political science	136	144	65	71	79	54
Electrical engineering	53	68	18	35	50	70
Harvard						
Chemistry	36	34	19	17	15	46
Government	111	86	24	87	62	76
Romance languages and literatures	64	123	27	37	96	71
Chicago						
Chemistry	46	44	34	12	10	24
English	195	260	46	149	214	80
Political science	184	173	5	179	168	97
Carleton						
Chemistry	14	17	10	4	7	35
English	53	79	23	30	56	65
Political science	34	52	15	19	37	65

Source: Calculations using unpublished data from the four sample institutions.

Note: Courses listed but not scheduled in the sample year are considered as having been offered in that year.

[a]Average number of courses offered in only one year as percentage of average number of courses.

presented in Table 8.2. The total number of courses for the beginning and ending years, the number of courses that appeared in both years, and the number of courses that appeared in only one of the two years are shown. The number of courses increased in nine of the departments, and in five the number increased by more than 25 percent. Although the growth in a few of the departments was impressive, "proliferation" seems too strong a term to apply to the changes in most of the departments. Generally, the dominant characteristic was the substitution of new courses for old ones, rather than growth in the total number of courses. The last column in the table shows the rate of turnover in courses, defined as the average number of courses offered in one year as a percentage of the average total number of courses. This rate exceeded 50 percent in more than one-half the cases. It seems likely that both differences in turnover rates and growth in numbers largely are discipline-specific, with some disciplines experiencing greater change than others in how topics of inquiry are organized. Among the sample departments in each institution, chemistry exhibited the highest degree of stability in course offerings.

In addition to changes in a discipline's organization of inquiry, another possible reason for course turnover is faculty turnover. If a department offers a course primarily because one of its faculty specializes in the topic, the course is likely to be dropped if that faculty member departs. In order to suggest the importance of this effect in explaining course turnover, data were gathered for a few departments on the faculty members listed in course catalogs in the course descriptions. Accompanying the description of most courses in the course catalogs is a list of faculty who might teach it. For each course offered in 1976/77, the listed faculty were compared with the department's complete faculty roster in 1991/92 in order to determine whether any faculty were available to teach at the end of the period. If no overlap in faculty was observed, the course was deemed to have complete faculty turnover for the period. Similarly, the listed faculty for courses in the 1991/92 catalog were checked against the roster of faculty in the department at the beginning of the period, with faculty turnover for each course defined analogously.[8] As is clearly evident in Table 8.3, courses offered in only one of the two years were much more likely to have had complete turnover than those offered in both years. This result suggests that changes in courses offered tended to be associated with faculty turnover. As indicated by the chi-square values in the last column, these differences are significant at the 1 percent level in four of the departments and at the 5 percent level in the other.

CONCLUSION

The findings presented in this chapter are intended to be read along with other evidence on expenditure trends and classroom teaching loads. Although these changes are far from definitive, even for the

TABLE 8.3

Course Continuity and Faculty Turnover, Five Departments

| | Percentage of Courses with Complete Faculty Turnover from 1976/77 to 1991/92 | | |
Department	Courses Offered in Both Years	Courses Offered in Only One Year	Chi-Squared Value
Duke			
Chemistry	0	18	5.00[b]
English	7	35	17.82[a]
Electrical engineering	0	31	6.98[a]
Political science	6	33	17.36[a]
Harvard			
Romance languages and literatures	70	92	10.99[a]

Source: Calculations using unpublished data from Duke and Harvard.
[a]Significant at 1% level (critical value, 6.64).
[b]Significant at 5% level (critical value, 3.84).

four sample institutions, they are suggestive of changes that could well have an impact on the nature of undergraduate education. With respect to the measures of classroom size, marked differences among departments were observed. One clear implication is that an institution's student-faculty ratio provides little useful information about the likely classroom environment for undergraduate students. There were changes over the period of study in some of the sample departments. In particular, in Chicago's social science and humanities departments, the use of nonregular faculty increased as a means of reducing the average size of undergraduate classes. At Duke, the use of graduate students in undergraduate instruction in the social science department and of nonregular faculty in the humanities department increased, with a concomitant increase in the reliance on larger lecture courses. Nonregular faculty were increasingly used in some but not all, departments. One very rough interpretation of the developments in the sample departments at Duke was that they implied an increase in the emphasis on graduate education and, probably, on research, at the expense of undergraduate teaching. It is worth noting that an issue of debate at Duke over this period, as in the wider higher education community, was the quality of undergraduate education.[9] More than one person has suggested that the increasing emphasis on research in universities sets the stage for what Keohane (1993) referred to as a "tacit unholy alliance" between students and faculty: "'You leave me alone, and I'll leave you alone.'"[10]

One feature of undergraduate teaching that appears to be complementary with specialization and research emphasis is the seminar. Data on both Duke and Harvard indicate an increase in the use of small classes, defined as those with enrollments of 18 or less. Still, the differences in the measurable aspects of courses between Duke and Harvard that remained by 1991/92 were substantial. Just as striking were the differences between Carleton and the universities in average class size and the reliance on regular-rank faculty. The absence of graduate students appears to be only one of the factors differentiating the structure of undergraduate classes; Carleton's heavy classroom teaching load and its modest reliance on nonregular faculty appear to be important as well, at least in the sample departments.

Appendix 8.1

Supplementary Tables for Chapter 8

TABLE 8A.1
Trends in Faculty, Enrollment, and Class Size: Duke

Humanities Department	1976/77	1981/82	1986/87	1991/92
As Percentage of 1976/77 Levels				
Undergraduate enrollment	100	100	85	131
Graduate enrollment	100	90	128	157
Regular faculty	100	85	100	106
Average Class Size				
Undergraduates	57.6	44.4	43.2	79.4
Graduate students	9.7	9.3	10.4	13.7
Percentage of Undergraduates Taught by				
Graduate students	NA	5.9	0.7	5.0
Nonregular faculty	NA	11.5	10.0	33.3
Subtotal	NA	17.4	10.7	38.3
Percentage of Undergraduates Enrolled, by Class Size				
18 or less	28.5	23.3	21.7	23.5
19–35	28.4	35.9	31.5	29.4
36–75	22.4	28.9	30.3	20.5
More than 75	20.7	12.0	16.5	26.5
Total	100.0	100.0	100.0	100.0
Natural Sciences Department				
As Percentage of 1976/77 Levels				
Undergraduate enrollment	100	101	78	88
Graduate enrollment	100	149	114	167
Regular faculty	100	92	88	88
Average Class Size				
Undergraduates	122.3	128.3	140.0	136.4
Graduate students	18.8	17.0	13.2	20.3
Percentage of Undergraduates Taught by				
Graduate students	NA	33.9	34.9	38.0
Nonregular faculty	NA	4.9	8.2	0.6
Subtotal	NA	38.8	43.1	38.6
Percentage of Undergraduates Enrolled, by Class Size				
18 or less	7.7	9.1	12.1	13.7
19–35	38.6	32.9	32.5	29.5
36–75	5.5	8.1	3.5	2.6
More than 75	48.2	50.0	51.9	54.2
Total	100.0	100.0	100.0	100.0

TABLE 8A.1 (*cont.*)

Engineering Department	1976/77	1981/82	1986/87	1991/92
As Percentage of 1976/77 Levels				
Undergraduate enrollment	100	168	234	219
Graduate enrollment	100	185	222	241
Regular faculty	100	109	118	155
Average Class Size				
Undergraduates	21.7	30.6	27.4	27.6
Graduate students	13.8	15.1	16.2	15.8
Percentage of Undergraduates Taught by				
Graduate students	0.0	0.0	0.0	0.0
Nonregular faculty	5.0	3.7	29.3	24.6
Subtotal	5.0	3.7	29.3	24.6
Percentage of Undergraduates Enrolled, by Class Size				
18 or less	36.2	13.4	26.9	28.1
19–35	56.4	54.8	43.4	45.9
36–75	7.4	31.8	29.7	26.0
More than 75	0.0	0.0	0.0	0.0
Total	100.0	100.0	100.0	100.0
Social Sciences Department				
As Percentage of 1976/77 Levels				
Undergraduate enrollment	100	111	95	68
Graduate enrollment	100	149	199	229
Regular faculty	100	108	104	108
Average Class Size				
Undergraduates	78.6	66.9	92.7	80.1
Graduate students	12.5	16.1	18.9	16.8
Percentage of Undergraduates Taught by				
Graduate students	3.8	26.4	29.7	22.5
Nonregular faculty	1.8	7.9	1.3	5.9
Subtotal	5.6	34.3	31.0	28.4
Percentage of Undergraduates Enrolled, by Class Size				
18 or less	6.3	8.6	8.6	18.9
19–35	13.8	45.3	32.6	25.3
36–75	47.4	23.0	23.4	22.7
More than 75	32.5	23.2	35.4	33.1
Total	100.0	100.0	100.0	100.0

Source: Calculations using unpublished data from Duke.
NA: not available.

TABLE 8A.2
Trends in Faculty, Enrollment, and Class Size: Harvard

Humanities Department	1976/77	1981/82	1986/87	1991/92
As Percentage of 1986/87 Levels				
Undergraduate enrollment	a	a	100	61
Graduate enrollment			100	118
Regular faculty			100	103
Average Class Size				
Undergraduates			240.3	139.6
Graduate students			34.4	44.6
Percentage of Undergraduates Taught by				
Graduate students			23.1	20.0
Nonregular faculty			4.8	8.8
Subtotal			27.9	28.8
Percentage of Undergraduates Enrolled, by Class Size				
18 or less			11.2	13.8
19–35			22.4	16.7
36–75			10.9	16.5
More than 75			55.6	53.1
Total			100.0	100.0
Social Sciences Department				
As Percentage of 1986/87 Levels				
Undergraduate enrollment	104	141	100	122
Graduate enrollment	112	62	100	113
Regular faculty	83	88	100	98
Average Class Size				
Undergraduates	161.2	303.2	181.1	241.7
Graduate students	45.0	20.4	20.8	24.2
Percentage of Undergraduates Taught by				
Graduate students	25.8	25.3	28.8	26.2
Nonregular faculty	14.0	3.9	13.2	12.4
Subtotal	39.8	29.2	42.0	38.6
Percentage of Undergraduates Enrolled, by Class Size				
18 or less	7.1	6.0	14.8	13.3
19–35	22.2	24.8	23.2	21.4
36–75	20.1	8.8	13.5	10.2
More than 75	50.7	60.4	48.4	55.2
Total	100.0	100.0	100.0	100.0

Source: Calculations using unpublished data from Harvard.

[a]Complete data necessary for calculations not available for the Harvard humanities department for 1976/77 and 1981/82.

TABLE 8A.3

Trends in Faculty, Enrollment, and Class Size: Chicago

Humanities Department	1976/77	1981/82	1986/87	1991/92
As Percentage of 1976/77 Levels				
Undergraduate enrollment	100	108	83	101
Graduate enrollment	100	77	73	80
Regular faculty	100	85	100	106
Average Class Size				
Undergraduates	44.7	54.3	31.8	33.1
Graduate students	16.3	18.8	18.2	23.5
Percentage of Undergraduates Taught by				
Graduate students	0.0	0.0	0.0	3.9
Nonregular faculty	25.6	21.7	21.4	27.0
Subtotal	25.6	21.7	21.4	30.9
Percentage of Undergraduates Enrolled, by Class Size				
18 or less	11.0	7.3	16.9	19.3
19–35	41.6	24.7	55.6	49.5
36–75	29.2	38.9	27.6	29.0
More than 75	18.2	29.1	0.0	2.1
Total	100.0	100.0	100.0	100.0
Natural Sciences Department				
As Percentage of 1976/77 Levels				
Undergraduate enrollment	100	118	118	112
Graduate enrollment	100	63	95	77
Regular faculty	100	108	96	92
Average Class Size				
Undergraduates	97.3	109.3	90.1	119.4
Graduate students	23.6	15.0	21.4	19.7
Percentage of Undergraduates Taught by				
Graduate students	33.5	33.4	31.3	31.4
Nonregular faculty	0.9	29.5	2.0	1.1
Subtotal	34.4	62.9	33.3	32.5
Percentage of Undergraduates Enrolled, by Class Size				
18 or less	32.3	28.4	29.6	35.4
19–35	6.4	12.2	12.6	3.8
36–75	10.6	7.8	10.0	8.5
More than 75	50.7	51.5	48.8	52.3
Total	100.0	100.0	100.0	100.0

TABLE 8A.3 (*cont.*)

Social Sciences Department	1976/77	1981/82	1986/87	1991/92
Social Sciences Department				
As Percentage of 1976/77 Levels				
Undergraduate enrollment	100	203	202	201
Graduate enrollment	100	103	94	105
Regular faculty	100	105	105	110
Average Class Size				
Undergraduates	62.7	48.9	34.9	38.0
Graduate students	37.6	46.2	32.6	33.5
Percentage of Undergraduates Taught by				
Graduate students	0.0	5.0	41.8	25.5
Nonregular faculty	21.8	48.0	20.7	32.9
Subtotal	21.8	53.0	62.5	58.4
Percentage of Undergraduates Enrolled, by Class Size				
18 or less	20.8	6.7	16.2	18.1
19–35	8.8	32.3	45.7	35.3
36–75	39.4	42.7	32.0	40.7
More than 75	30.9	18.4	6.2	5.8
Total	100.0	100.0	100.0	100.0

Source: Calculations using unpublished data from Chicago.

TABLE 8A.4
Trends in Faculty, Enrollment, and Class Size: Carleton

Humanities Department	1976/77	1981/82	1986/87	1991/92
As Percentage of 1976/77 Levels				
Enrollment	100	116	139	146
Faculty	100	100	110	130
Average Class Size				
Undergraduates	28.9	27.6	33.1	32.0
Percentage of Undergraduates Taught by				
Nonregular faculty	8.8	9.3	9.0	0.6
Percentage of Undergraduates Enrolled, by Class Size				
18 or less	54.4	41.8	31.2	32.8
19–35	19.9	36.0	30.8	38.5
36–75	15.0	14.4	29.5	21.0
More than 75	10.8	7.8	8.5	7.7
Total	100.0	100.0	100.0	100.0
Natural Sciences Department				
As Percentage of 1976/77 Levels				
Enrollment	100	102	84	81
Faculty	100	100	117	133
Average Class Size				
Undergraduates	43.5	48.5	35.9	35.1
Percentage of Undergraduates Taught by				
Nonregular faculty	0.0	0.0	0.0	18.3
Percentage of Undergraduates Enrolled, by Class Size				
18 or less	26.7	19.2	20.8	24.1
19–35	14.7	23.0	28.8	26.2
36–75	49.3	42.3	44.7	49.8
More than 75	9.3	15.5	5.6	0.0
Total	100.0	100.0	100.0	100.0

TABLE 8A.4 (*cont.*)

Social Sciences Department	1976/77	1981/82	1986/87	1991/92
As Percentage of 1976/77 Levels				
Enrollment	100	125	114	102
Faculty	100	140	140	160
Average Class Size				
Undergraduates	30.3	30.1	27.2	23.5
Percentage of Undergraduates Taught by				
Nonregular faculty	12.0	8.7	23.3	15.4
Percentage of Undergraduates Enrolled, by Class Size				
18 or less	11.8	8.9	13.9	21.2
19–35	50.2	64.8	70.9	78.8
36–75	38.0	26.3	15.2	0.0
More than 75	0.0	0.0	0.0	0.0
Total	100.0	100.0	100.0	100.0

Source: Calculations using unpublished data from Carleton.

CHAPTER 9

Ambition Meets Opportunity

Can I really afford to raise tuition above inflation? If so, I can afford this program. You
quickly persuade yourself you ought to have
the program. We prospered as an institution
by following that strategy, but the world has
changed and we can't do that any more.

James N. Rosse, 1990[1]

In his 1978 report, *Planning for the Eighties*, Duke Chancellor Kenneth Pye spoke for many in higher education when he wrote that the
coming decade would require stringency and selective retrenchment.
Chancellor Pye called for a 15 percent reduction in the size of the
faculty through selective elimination of programs. Although he did
in fact bring about a few cutbacks, the decade of the 1980s, both at
Duke and at other private research universities, was anything but
austere. Buoyed by tuition increases that outpaced inflation by an
average of four percentage points per year, the country's top private
universities experienced a decade of steadily increasing expenditures. The example of Duke is especially striking: rather than
shrinking, its arts and sciences faculty grew by 14 percent in the
decade beginning with the 1981/82 academic year.[2] The preceding
chapters have examined this period of rising outlays by focusing on
four institutions. In this final chapter, the study's approach and
principal findings are reviewed, and the causes of these increases are
suggested. The chapter's last section discusses three issues arising
from the study that have implications for future directions in higher
education.

THE STUDY AND ITS LIMITATIONS

For its empirical findings, the present study relies principally on information covering the period beginning with the 1976/77 academic
year and ending with the 1991/92 year for three private research
universities—the University of Chicago, Duke University, and Har-

vard University—and one private liberal arts college—Carleton College. Owing to the small size of this sample, it is obviously impossible to make any claims of statistical representativeness. Nor can it be said that the group of institutions to which these four belong is representative of American higher education in general. One reason for eschewing the advantages of a large and representative sample is the prospect of learning new things from the deeper level of detail made possible by restricting the number of institutions. Moreover, although the findings are not necessarily applicable to the rest of American higher education, these institutions do stand as nonstatistical representatives of a subset of institutions of higher education whose small share of total enrollments belies their national significance. The three universities are among a relatively few private research universities that produce a disproportionate share of the country's scholarly research and train a disproportionate share of the world's scholars. Adding to these universities the equally small number of elite private liberal arts colleges, of which Carleton is one, these institutions also provide undergraduate education to a strikingly large share of the nation's leaders of all fields. Without minimizing the accomplishments of other private institutions or the giant public sector in higher education, one must conclude that the social and economic impact that these elite private institutions exert makes them well worth studying.

In some respects, these institutions are decidedly unrepresentative of American higher education. They enroll only a small fraction of the nation's undergraduates.[3] Their tuitions are far above the average. In 1991/92, the median amount that the 32 COFHE colleges and universities charged for tuition, fees, room, and board was $21,876, more than half again higher than the average for all private institutions in that year ($13,983) (U.S. Department of Education 1992, p. 308). Their students, both undergraduate and graduate, were among the best in the country. The faculty of the universities in this group evince loyalty to their disciplines, as well as to their institutions, attending more national and international meetings and publishing far more than the average faculty member. One visible corollary of the research orientation of the universities in the sample is the high ratio of arts and sciences graduate students to undergraduates, suggesting the great degree of complementarity of research and graduate training. In their internal governance, these institutions tend to give a more substantial role to their faculty, and sometimes to their students, than is the case in less prestigious colleges and universities.

But, as is so often the case when one looks closely at real examples within any category, the four institutions exhibited remarkable variety, with observable differences in the way that activities were organized and carried out. Perhaps the most striking contrast in the present sample is in the methods used in undergraduate classroom instruction. The same introductory course that is taught by a professor to a class of 30 at one institution might be taught in a large lecture, with smaller sections led by graduate students meeting once a week, at another. At a third institution, the same course might be taught by a graduate student in its entirety. The best single predictor of the format used in undergraduate instruction appears to be the ratio of doctoral students to undergraduates; the greater the number of graduate students, the smaller the share of the faculty's attention that the undergraduate students will receive. Yet despite the substantial differences in format and in the amount of faculty attention given to undergraduates, remarkably, all the institutions vied for virtually the same students, and the bachelor's degrees offered by all of them generally were treated as close substitutes by employers and graduate schools alike.

A second difference that is evident (largely between the liberal arts college and the research universities) is the sharp contrast in the duties of faculty. Even accounting for some degree of noncomparability across institutions, the number of hours that faculty devoted to classroom teaching differed sharply, with loads being the smallest at institutions at which faculty and graduate programs were rated the highest. Left unmeasured in this study are two activities that undoubtedly occupy a significant share of the time of faculty at research universities: research, and the one-on-one teaching that is an integral part of doctoral training.

The four institutions studied differed in numerous other ways, although many of the differences amounted to no more than accounting details. A particular function that resided in one department at one institution might have been placed elsewhere at another. One institution might have accounted for a given category of expenditure separately, whereas a second might have lumped it with other similar items. Missions differ as well, even within a reasonably consistent definition of arts and sciences; the presence or absence of museums, university presses, and major intercollegiate athletics programs illustrates this diversity. Indeed, differences such as these, and the problems they pose for making comparisons among institutions, are one of the major justifications for using case studies rather than cross-section financial data.

As a means of overcoming these differences among institutions in function, quality, and structure, the present study focuses primarily on *changes* over time in quantities for given institutions. When expenditures are analyzed, primary attention is paid to internally financed expenditures, those funded from unrestricted revenues and endowment income. When they use internally financed funds—the most fungible of funds—institutions show their highest level of commitment to the activities so funded. Increases in spending on these activities have important implications for the continued well-being of the institutions. But they are not the whole story, of course. Externally funded spending, even though it does carry earmarked revenues to cover it, may have very real impacts on internally financed spending—for example, when universities take over funding for activities previously supported by outside grants.

PRINCIPAL FINDINGS

Because this study examines the experiences of only four institutions, strictly speaking, the results are applicable only to those four. However, it is useful to summarize the patterns that emerge when viewing all the findings together, for there is good reason to believe that general trends in this small group will have wider applicability. Most prominent among the findings—and one that does apply to other private institutions—is the overall increase in tuition levels and expenditures. For the entire 15-year period, the mean tuition and fees at the four institutions increased at a real annual rate of 4.6 percent; for the decade 1981/82 to 1991/92, for which most of the expenditure data apply, the rate was even higher, 5.3 percent. These increases apply to the advertised tuition, or sticker price; they overstate the increase in cost to the average student because financial aid to students has grown faster still.[4] A notable aspect of the increases in private tuitions is the breadth with which they covered private colleges and universities, extending far beyond the relatively small group of elite institutions. Although tuition and fees increased at an annual rate of 5.7 percent in the 32 COFHE institutions between 1981/82 and 1991/92, the 4.8 percent average for all private universities was only one percentage point slower. For all private institutions, the rate was 4.5 percent. The similarity of these rates suggests that other private institutions were willing and able to follow the price leadership of the elite ones.[5]

Total expenditures for arts and sciences components of the sample institutions likewise grew rapidly. For the period from the early 1980s to the early 1990s, internally funded expenditures grew at real annual rates of 5.3 percent at Harvard, 5.7 percent at Carleton,

6.0 percent at Chicago, and 6.8 percent at Duke. Faculty salaries, which accounted for a large portion of arts and sciences spending, grew in real terms, although less rapidly than total spending. Owing in part to the surprisingly low inflation in the early 1980s, by 1992, faculty salaries had regained, in real terms, levels that had not been achieved for two decades. Average faculty salaries rose most rapidly at Duke, which followed a policy during this period that emphasized the recruitment of senior scholars from outside the university. In part, expenditures on faculty also rose because the numbers of faculty increased at these institutions. The categories of compensation showing the highest growth rates, however, were nonregular faculty and professional staff.

Other than compensation, the types of expenditures experiencing the most rapid growth were financial aid—a big gainer at all four institutions—and, at more than one institution, computers and other capital expenditures. Although not one of the largest items, expenditures for computers grew rapidly in importance, as mainframe machines waned in significance and personal and minicomputers gained. These and other capital expenditures, including new construction, building renovations, and large equipment, were an important item of increase at Harvard. All the research universities expressed heightened concern over start-up costs, the up-front commitments that became a necessary part of the offers made to scientists and other scholars. Most of this increase in spending can be attributed to the growth in existing programs, as opposed to the creation of new programs. Perhaps the most important conclusion that arises from the scrutiny of spending increases, however, is that a large portion of increases simply cannot be attributed easily to any identifiable cause. Such widespread expenditure growth is consistent with across-the-board commitments to quality improvement and service enhancements. New services were offered to students, interdisciplinary seminars were launched, computer service staffs were upgraded, and research support to faculty was increased.

Using data for selected departments in the sample institutions, the study also examines measures of faculty teaching and characteristics of classes taught. One general trend over the period of study was a decrease in measured classroom teaching loads. On the basis of data for three departments in each of the four institutions over the period 1976/77 to 1991/92, the unweighted average classroom teaching load fell by 12 percent in the representative humanities department, 26 percent in the natural science department, and 28 percent in the social science department.[6] The decreases occurred principally in undergraduate teaching, with some departments showing increases in graduate teaching. These declines in classroom teaching loads go hand in hand with the increases observed in the size of the arts and sciences faculty at the institutions. Moreover, this growth definitely contributed to higher spending, although, as the calculations in chapter 5 show, it explains only a small part of the overall increase. No consistent trend was observed in the average size of classes in the sample departments, at either the undergraduate or graduate level. At the undergraduate level, the average size tended to increase in years of high enrollments. At the same time, in more than half the sample departments, the percentage of undergraduates enrolled in seminar-size classes increased through the period. Finally, in apparent reflection of the decline in faculty classroom teaching loads, the percentage of undergraduates who were taught in class by regular-rank faculty tended to fall.

WHY DID EXPENDITURES RISE?

Certainly the motivating fact of the present study is the impressive increase in spending by the nation's leading private research universities, an increase that was mirrored in tuition rates and matched in percentage terms by spending increases among other private institutions. At the outset of the study, the possible explanations for any increase in spending were divided into three generic reasons: (1) an increase in the cost of purchased inputs, (2) an expansion in the level or quality of activities being performed, and (3) an increase in inefficiency. On the basis of the evidence presented here, it is safe to ascribe spending increases in the four sample institutions to the first two explanations. Prices of inputs, most importantly labor inputs, increased in real terms over the period of study, although this increase may well be seen largely as making up for real declines occurring during the 1970s. The cost of providing other services, such as campus security and compliance with regulations, also appeared to rise. Based on the decomposition presented in chapter 5, one-fifth or less of the increase can be ascribed to increases in the market price of faculty and other purchased inputs. Spending also increased because institutions did more things, or attempted to do them better. Although new activities rarely showed up as new departments, existing entities took on new activities and expanded old ones. As for the third explanation, the study found little evidence that increasing inefficiency played an important role in the growth in spending, unless the drop in classroom teaching is prima facie evidence for such inefficiency. This view seems unreasonable, however, because it would imply that research has little or no value. This is not to say that inefficiency was absent, but only that it did not grow so as to contribute importantly to the overall increase in expenditures.

In summarizing the sources of higher spending, it is useful to look beyond these broad categories of explanation to name in particular the major influences motivating the growth in spending. I believe four major causes deserve attention. The first two are more or less inherent characteristics of the institutions and cannot by themselves explain why spending would have increased during one period but not during any other. In contrast, the remaining causes are rather specific as to time, perhaps representing the spark that ignited a combustible collection of ready conditions.

Unbounded Aspirations

The first basic cause, or precondition, is the nature of the university as an organization. Featuring weak central control, a remarkable degree of freedom accorded to its faculty, and traditions of collegiality in governance, the university lacks any corporate goal other than the pursuit of excellence. When it comes to the research that it undertakes, the university has little to guide it other than an uncompromising devotion to the highest standards of inquiry. Limits do exist and compromises must be made, of course, but the official policies of any university provide few guideposts for making these compromises. Furthermore, administrators face a decidedly uneven set of incentives when considering the possibility of eliminating or downsizing any program that they oversee. In the same way it has been observed that, once established, government programs are difficult to eliminate, owing to the intense interest among the beneficiaries (and providers) in their continuation, so it appears to be for programs within universities. Moreover, the university's aim of excellence contains little that can be used to justify cuts in the same way a profit objective can be used to guide such decisions in corporations. This is not to say that universities never eliminate programs, of course, but only that the forces militating against cuts are powerful.[7]

This institutional imperative for excellence might also apply to activities other than research, but if so, certainly to a lesser extent. During the period of study, the universities appeared to have increasingly emphasized research at the expense of teaching. One piece of supporting evidence is the decline in average classroom teaching loads observed in the sample departments. Rosovsky's plaintive observation in 1992 about Harvard was that these shifts simply occurred, with no official sanction. By all appearances, the reduction in classroom teaching loads was a widespread phenomenon. These reduced loads became part of the expectations of faculty in the same way that salary rates for scholars by field and reputation became established, through the national labor market for faculty. The reasons for the increased emphasis on research and for the accompanying changes in the expectations of faculty are not obvious, but the mechanism by which their effects were distributed to campuses across the country was the national market for faculty, which is one of the important dimensions of competition among institutions.

The Nature of Competition

A second precondition necessary for understanding the increase in spending is the nature of the competition that exists among institutions. For the private institutions that are the subject of this study, competition exists at two levels among two overlapping sets of institutions. First is the competition for students, which takes place largely among a group of prestigious public and private colleges and universities. The second arena of competition, and here it is confined largely to research universities and other research organizations, is for faculty. In both of these dimensions there exists active and continuous competition among institutions. Some information in the relevant markets, on such characteristics as tuitions, admissions success, and faculty salaries, was readily available, if not perfectly known. Institutions were both aware of what their competitors were doing and willing to adjust their behavior accordingly. At the same time, other information, especially indications of quality that would be helpful to consumers, was virtually nonexistent.

In the market for students, especially that for undergraduates, two features seem especially noteworthy. The first relates to the nature of the commodity, this amorphous thing called a college education. Because it is little understood and even less perfectly measured, suppliers have abundant opportunities to provide signals to potential consumers about the quality of their services. In addition to tangible indicators, such as buildings, prominent alumni, and published professors, one possible indicator is price itself. Indeed, evidence indicates that institutions did not necessarily view tuition increases as harmful to their attractiveness, so long as their tuition did not depart from those of the pack of competing colleges. The other, complementary aspect of competition in the market for students was an effective compact on financial aid to which all suppliers subscribed. Virtually all the colleges and universities that competed with the sample institutions for the nation's top high school graduates had pledged to provide need-based financial assistance according to a fairly uniform formula. Each would offer applicants a package of loans, employment, and grants equal to the difference between the student's theoretical ability to pay and the total cost of attendance.[8] Consequently, tuition increases largely would be cushioned,[9] easing concerns that rising tuition would close the college's doors to low-income applicants. Together, these two features of the competitive environment made it feasible for institutions to finance their ambitious goals by increasing tuition, subject only to the strength of the market's demand and the behavior of their competitors.

The second major dimension of competition among these colleges and universities covers the several arenas related to faculty and research, the most important of which is the market for faculty. Owing to their strong disciplinary orientation and a degree of specialization that limits the number of professors in a subfield who can find work in any given local labor market, the market for research faculty is decidedly national in scope, if not international. Most of the professional expertise that a scholar builds up over the course of a career is easily portable from one institution to another. Accordingly, institutions that aspire to excellence in research must, within limits, meet the prevailing standards for salary and conditions of work to hire and retain faculty.[10] The significance of this aspect of competition is in the interpretation of rising faculty salaries as a factor contributing to rising costs: because the market is competitive in the sense described, individual institutions had little choice but to meet the going price and conditions of work. Only when an institution chose to upgrade the quality of its faculty, as Duke did during the study period, can a portion of the increasing cost of faculty be laid to a deliberate policy to modify the quality of its purchased inputs. In contrast, increased spending to finance lower classroom teaching loads or higher start-up costs that merely meet the market might be viewed more appropriately as increases in the cost of inputs.

A Surge in Demand

The conditions described under the first two headings might never have been given the chance to contribute to a rise in spending were it not for a push from a force outside higher education. That push came principally from a surge in the demand for the kind of high-quality undergraduate training that the most selective colleges and universities offered. Whether caused by the dramatic increase in the economic payoff to college, the rapidly advancing affluence of the affluent, or merely the snob appeal of purchasing a conspicuously expensive service, the premium on acceptance at one of the nation's most selective colleges appeared to grow during the 1980s. Applications to Ivy League and other selective institutions rose steadily at the same time that their enrollments remained virtually constant.

In almost any other unregulated market, an increase in demand against a fixed supply is sure to push up the equilibrium price. It is a distinctive feature of the market for higher education, however, that the supplying firms made it a practice *not* to charge what the market might bear, choosing instead to ration demand by electing talented and diverse student bodies who would best fit their institutional objectives.[11] At the same time, however, the trustees and administrators of these favored institutions could not fail to observe that their admissions offices were being besieged by eager applicants, and that an unusually large tuition increase would not cool the ardor of prospective students. And, tuition increases would be safer still if competing institutions were to increase their tuitions by comparable amounts. Indeed, to be left behind when all of one's competitors were announcing healthy increases in tuition might invite the suspicion among imperfectly informed consumers that the quality of one's product lagged behind those of its rivals. Thus, the strong demand from consumers enabled the selective institutions—as a group—to increase tuitions faster than the rate of inflation. Individual colleges and universities, for which such actions would be suicide if pursued alone, were protected from adverse consequences in their admissions by staying safely within the pack.

From their perspective, colleges and universities were not hiking tuition as a simple reaction to the strong demand. Rather, these extraordinary increases meant extra revenue to finance priority items, items that stood at the top of long lists on the desk of every provost and president, items that would serve their institutions' lofty aims for excellence. The opportunity for extra revenue was a rare chance to enhance the quality of a few departments by hiring a handful of nationally known scholars, or to compete more successfully for the best graduate students by increasing stipends, or to upgrade the quality of services provided to undergraduate students. One specific area of opportunity lay in attracting renowned faculty from the public research universities, the financial stringencies of which limited their ability to match the high salaries that some top scholars were being offered. During the 15-year period covered by this study, the average earnings advantage of faculty in private universities over those in public universities more than doubled.[12] During the 1980s, then, the ever-present urge for improvement met an opportunity to make some of that possible. In short, the surge in demand served as a catalyst, activating the pent-up institutional imperative for excellence.

Uncontrollables

The fourth cause for the rise in spending is a grab bag of contributing factors over which colleges and universities, even when taken together, could exert little control. Perhaps the most important of these was the worldwide increase in the earnings of highly educated professionals, of which university faculty are a part. The real earnings of doctors, lawyers, and business executives rose significantly during the 1980s. Those of university faculty rose as well, although at a somewhat slower rate. Although the job offers made by colleges and universities, taken together, had some effect on the rate of increase in faculty salaries—spurred in part by the demand for college training discussed above—these rising salary levels were largely exogenous, reflecting economy-wide shifts in the value of technical and professional training.[13] As purchasers of labor services in a competitive labor market, then, colleges and universities had little choice but to pay the market price.

A different type of uncontrollable influence was the technological revolution that manifested itself in the thousands of personal computers that seemed to materialize overnight throughout universities. As in virtually every industry in the economy, administrators in higher education found that computers appeared on purchase orders and desks in every department. These new machines enabled some economies to be realized, but their initial impact simply was to increase costs and improve productivity. Not only were the machines themselves expensive, the dizzying rate at which improved models were produced made it necessary to replace machines at a rapid rate. Most important, the introduction of this technology made it imperative to hire or train a new cadre of professionals to ensure that ordinary employees could make use of the machines on their desks. The net effect on costs of this technological onslaught is exceedingly difficult to distill, combined as it was with undeniable advances in productivity and improvements in service quality. Furthermore, it appears likely that the full impact of computers on university costs—like that on costs in other industries—cannot yet be fully assessed. It is possible that larger cost savings may be realized from the reconfiguration and reduction in administrative staffs.

A third uncontrollable element, largely unique to higher education, arose from the changing role of the federal government in its support of higher education. Although the aggregate dollars of federal expenditures for research, student financial aid, and other programs involving payments to institutions kept pace with inflation, some aspects of that support necessitated increased spending by colleges and universities. In the area of student financial aid, limitations in programs offering grants and the substitution of increasing amounts of loan moneys left the expensive private institutions with the responsibility of paying, out of their own internal funds, for virtually all the incremental costs in the need-based financial aid system. In the area of sponsored research, federal funding agencies increasingly tended to require institutions to share the cost of equipment and other direct costs of research. On top of these trends were layered real increases in the compliance cost of federal regulations, from the accounting requirements concerning indirect costs embodied in the continuously evolving rules for the calculation of indirect costs to regulations on handicap-access and drug-free workplaces. Some of these costs were evident in the growth in offices of sponsored programs at the sample institutions. Others no doubt were buried in numerous administrative budgets. The overall magnitude of these practices and regulations is difficult to assess.

ISSUES FOR THE NEXT 15 YEARS

The 15-year period between 1976/77 and 1991/92 was one of rapid growth in spending in the nation's leading private research universities. As Shapiro (1993, p. 15) wryly noted, there has to be some limit to the portion of national income taken up by the amount spent on higher education. Assuming this to be the case, that a continuation of past rates of real expenditure increases will not be sustainable, how will colleges and universities slow the growth in spending? The last section of this chapter examines three issues that seem likely to be central in determining how a new stringency will affect the operation of colleges and universities, with particular attention given to the private research universities.

The Arrangements for Work

Central to the cost structure of research universities are the everyday modes of getting work done, the methods of accomplishing ordinary tasks, the traditions of assigning work, and the customs followed in distributing responsibilities. The visible manifestations include such mundane matters as who types manuscripts, how telephones are answered, how classroom teaching assignments are made, who advises undergraduates about academic matters, and how administrative offices are organized. Arrangements concerning the amount and nature of teaching also are relevant. The substantial freedom traditionally enjoyed by faculty—over topics for study, methods of teaching, hours of work, and outside activities—is believed to be vital to effective production of the creative work demanded of them, and with justification. This freedom is especially valued at the research universities, such as those examined in the present study. As Rosovsky and Bok have pointed out with eloquence,[14] however, it is possible for the social contract under which faculty operate to be stretched too far. These observers have cited as areas of concern unsanctioned declines in teaching loads and excessive consulting. Because of tenure, it is impossible to consider the mechanisms conventionally employed in the corporate world for enforcing compliance with specific organizational guidelines. And, now that mandatory retirement is a thing of the past, the issue of faculty productivity will become all the more important.

How universities deal with these challenges largely will determine their success in reducing costs. Partly out of a reluctance to tread on the traditional prerogatives of faculty and partly from a belief that such methods as total quality management and process re-engineering simply do not transfer easily to teaching and research, management remedies now in vogue have been applied in universities almost exclusively in administrative units.[15] In those administrative areas, it seems reasonable to expect that work processes will be transformed gradually so as to adapt to the capacities of computers and other equipment. But there is no reason to believe that productivity increases cannot also be achieved in the traditional domain of faculty work processes. Nor does it seem obvious that such improvements must necessarily do violence to the freedom that has been a characteristic of faculty work, or of the institution of tenure. Whatever else happens, the change in retirement rules may well necessitate regular evaluations of tenured faculty less perfunctory than has been the norm. In the end, the traditions of independence and collegiality, which often seem to be quaint anachronisms, may turn out to offer exactly the kind of environment most amenable to the redesign of work processes.

The 15 years covered by this study already witnessed changes in the ordinary work arrangements for faculty. Although faculty have been relieved of a part of their traditional tasks, including a portion of academic advising and some administrative tasks, it is the ironic fact that they have assumed some of the clerical duties previously performed by secretaries, such as answering their telephones and doing more of their own typing, simply because the new technology increases the efficiency of this arrangement. Techniques of classroom teaching appear to be the most resistant to the incorporation of new technology, but evidence of change is here, too. Taken as a whole, electronic innovations probably will serve to exacerbate the outward-looking nature of university faculty. It is hard to anticipate any other result when a professor finds it easier to send a message to a colleague a continent away via electronic mail than to go downstairs to chat with a fellow department member. An increase in national and international exchange of ideas seems a likely result of these advances. More uncertain is whether "distance learning" through electronic communication will become a standard technique of education at universities.

The Teaching-Research Trade-off

The second issue that inevitably will persist as universities cope with cost pressures in the next decade and a half is the tension between research and undergraduate teaching. Unlike the issue of productivity, which is essentially independent of an institution's purposes, the teaching-research trade-off involves both matters of efficiency and matters of mission. Because both research and teaching are basic activities for which universities are known, their relevance to mission is obvious. In considering this trade-off, it is useful to consider these two aspects separately.

From the standpoint of efficiency, the question is whether there really *is* a trade-off at all. It is the oft-repeated mantra of deans and provosts in research universities that good research makes for good teaching, or, in the words of economics, that the two activities are complementary. The professor who has an active research program, it is argued, can offer students fresh insights and the sense of active inquiry. Granting that there is truth to this argument, and leaving open the possibility of future improvements in efficiency that may make it possible to improve teaching and research at the same time, it seems self-evident that the complementarities between under-graduate teaching and research can only go so far. Once they are exhausted, a trade-off between these two activities must be made: at some point, it becomes possible to increase one only at the expense of the other. In contrast to graduate instruction, which often is car-ried out in conjunction with research, undergraduate teaching nec-essarily takes up time that cannot be used for research, and vice-versa. It seems safe to assume that, to the extent that their faculty is being engaged efficiently, research universities now operate in that range in which the two activities are in fact rivals. The trade-off is real.

A choice remains, of course, and this is the aspect of the trade-off that is relevant to institutional mission. During the past 15 years, a period of increasing emphasis on research, it has been observed that undergraduates and faculty were content with a "tacit bargain" by which both sides agreed to limit their demands on the other.[16] The descriptive measures of undergraduate course characteristics pre-sented in chapter 8 also provide scattered evidence consistent with a view that undergraduate education may have suffered. The question for the research universities is whether they will maintain the cur-rent relative emphasis between research and undergraduate teach-ing. Judging from the interest that prospective students have shown in attending, there seems little reason to think that the private re-search universities will come under much market pressure to give more attention to undergraduate teaching. But, should demand slacken, the teaching-research trade-off may well be an issue that commands the increasing attention of administrators.

Comprehensiveness

The third issue likely to arise as universities consider ways to cope with rising costs is whether they can afford to continue to be "full-service" institutions, offering degrees, conducting research in all or virtually all of the recognized academic fields, and performing many other services as well. To use one of the sample institutions as an illustration of the panoply of a university's functions, in 1992, the University of Chicago offered graduate degrees in 74 fields and un-dergraduate majors in 51; it operated a massive medical center, four world-famous science research facilities, an observatory, the editorial offices of numerous scholarly journals, a university press, four mu-seums, a library with more than 6 million volumes spread over numerous buildings, a laboratory school for elementary and secondary students, an intercollegiate athletics program fielding varsity teams in 20 sports, a bus service, a travel agency, a news agency, a printing department, numerous dormitories and dining halls, and the largest private police force in Illinois.[17] In addition to offering degree programs to graduate, professional, and undergraduate students, research universities routinely undertake research supported by government agencies, corporations, and foundations; offer executive training to business professionals, government officials, and foundation executives; and provide continuing education classes to adults.

More than one observer of research universities has suggested that a range of activities this broad is problematic. Gray (1992, p. 236), who presided over the activities enumerated in the preceding paragraph, has argued that this comprehensiveness represents the most serious problem of research universities, that they are "burdened by too many tasks, too many demands, and too great a confusion of expectations." In her opinion, a major cause is the competition among institutions that, as we have seen, involves matching quality for quality. In his essay two decades before, Coleman (1973) advanced a similar theme, suggesting that some of the functions carried out by universities must be partitioned or jettisoned. In particular, Coleman argues that undergraduate education is ultimately incompatible with the research and graduate training functions and ought to be separated, which responds of course to the tension between research and teaching discussed above and is in effect accomplished in liberal arts colleges.[18] Regardless of whether these functions are compatible, the broad scope of the enterprise as a whole certainly has cost implications, as Gray and others have stressed. In his plan for reducing expenditures at Duke, for example, Kenneth Pye argued forcefully for selective retrenchment rather than across-the-board cuts. One approach is simply to learn to "do without." Where resources can be shared among institutions, however, this degree of stringency may not be entirely necessary. One can find numerous examples of neighboring institutions that share computing facilities, coordinate library acquisitions, and even allow cross-registration for courses. Such sharing has long been institutionalized in interlibrary loan. With the advent of widespread access to electronic communication, this kind of cooperation should become significantly easier to accomplish.

Ultimately, the degree to which comprehensiveness will be restricted largely will be like the extent to which expenditure growth will be restrained, a function of the growth in revenues. As has been the case in the past, revenues will largely determine the growth in spending. As long as universities hold the high aspirations that have characterized them in the past, the imperative for excellence will place pressure on spending. Only when revenue growth slows will spending growth slow. As to that possibility, it does indeed seem likely that the major sources of university funding will grow more slowly during the next 15 years. Although periods of scarcity have been forecast before but have not materialized, all indications now seem to point to a tightening of constraints. If every challenge presents an opportunity, then these institutions have an opportunity to employ new technologies and techniques to improve the manner in which they accomplish the traditional aims of the research university.

Notes to the Chapters

Preface

1. Derek Bok, "Reclaiming the Public Trust," *Change*, July/August 1992, pp. 13–9.

Chapter 1

1. President of Princeton University; Shapiro (1993, p. 12).

2. U.S. Department of Education (1992, Table 31, p. 34). These costs refer to the explicit, out-of-pocket expenditures for higher education. They do not measure the significant implicit component of costs in the form of forgone earnings by students.

3. The educational and general category excludes expenditures on construction, auxiliaries, and sponsored research. Inflation is measured by increases in the GDP price deflator.

4. Between 1978/79 and 1987/88, Getz and Siegfried found that educational and general spending per FTE student in all institutions of higher education rose 2.7 percent per year faster than the overall rate of inflation. The comparable rate for all private institutions was 4.0 percent; for private research universities without medical schools, 4.1 percent; for private research universities with medical schools, 3.9 percent; for private liberal arts colleges with enrollments of less than 1,000 students, 4.3 percent; and for private liberal arts colleges with enrollments of more than 1,000 students, 4.8 percent (Getz and Siegfried 1991, pp. 380, 382).

5. The discount, calculated here as the ratio of scholarships and fellowships financed out of unrestricted funds to all tuition and fee revenues, increased for all private institutions from 8.7 percent in 1975/76 to 15.3 percent in 1991/92, and from 7.9 to 8.7 percent over the same period for public institutions (Clotfelter 1991, p. 71; and U.S. Office of Education 1994, Tables 317-8 and 327-8). Because the net cost is the product of stated tuition and the net price (one minus the discount percentage), the growth of net tuition is the difference between the growth rates of stated tuition and the net price. For example, the net price of private college fell from 0.913 to 0.847 between 1975/76 and 1991/92, for a growth rate of -0.0047, or -0.5 percent.

6. From 1975 to 1992, the annual rate of increase in all prices (Consumer Price Index) was 5.6 percent; for medical costs, it was 7.6 percent (U.S. Council of Economic Advisers 1994, p. 335). At private universities, the rate of increase for the period 1975/76 to 1991/92 for tuition, room, and board at private universities was 8.6 percent (U.S. Department of Education 1992, p. 308). The financial aid discount for private institutions rose from 8.7

percent in 1975/76 to 15.3 percent in 1991/92, for an annual growth rate of −0.5 percent over this 16-year period (U.S. Department of Education 1989, Tables 270 and 280). Applying this rate to the 8.6 percent rate in stated tuition rates yields a growth in net tuition of 8.1 percent.

7. See Cook and Frank (1993) for an analysis of the concentration of top students in these institutions. To indicate their relative size, the authors note that the 33 colleges and universities designated by the *Barron's* guide as "most competitive" enrolled just 2.4 percent of the seniors who took the Scholastic Aptitude Test in 1980 (p. 127).

8. Edward R. Fiske, *New York Times*, May 12, 1987.

9. "Colleges: A Machine with No Brakes," *Washington Post Weekly*, August 21–27, 1989; *Washington Post*, January 28, 1993.

10. "Time to Prune the Ivy," *Business Week*, May 24, 1993, pp. 112–8. For similar attacks on the growth of administration in universities, see Bergmann (1991) or Wagner and Bowermaster (1992).

11. Gene I. Maeroff, "College Teachers, the New Leisure Class," *Wall Street Journal*, September 13, 1993, sec. A; and Sykes (1988, p. 5).

12. Sowell (1993, p. 13).

13. See, for example, Gary Putka, "Tracking Tuition: Why College Fees Are Rising so Sharply," *Wall Street Journal*, December 11, 1987, or *Business Week*, May 24, 1993.

14. William Bennett, "Our Greedy Colleges," *New York Times*, February 18, 1987, sec. A. Similar themes are raised by another member of the Reagan administration, Chester Finn. See Finn (1984).

15. Representative Wyden's comment expressed the indignation with which the committee greeted these revelations and Kennedy's apparently unrepentant attitude: "I think that this is a very sad day for one of the world's great universities. Speaking both as a Stanford graduate, as a taxpayer, I never thought that one would see this day where the president of Stanford University was going to be sitting where you are and asked to explain why antique fruitwood commodes were billed to the taxpayer. . . ." U.S. House of Representatives (1991, p. 193).

16. Among the initial stories on the investigation was Barbara Vobejda's, "Antitrust Probe Targets College Tuition Aid," *Washington Post*, August 9, 1989, sec. A.

17. See, for example, Davidson Goldin, "Full-Tuition Students Increasingly Pay for Others," *New York Times*, March 22, 1995, sec. A, or Fred M. Hechinger, "About Education," *New York Times*, April 25, 1990, sec. B.

18. See, for example, Kennedy (1985) or Joseph Berger, "College Officials Defend Sharply Rising Tuition," *New York Times*, March 23, 1988, sec. B.

19. For a bibliography relevant to the economic impact of both university and corporate research, see Trajtenberg, Henderson, and Jaffe (1992).

20. For a comparison to Japan, see Clotfelter et al. (1991, p. 12).

21. See, for example, Clotfelter (1991, p. 89).

22. For a discussion of explanations for increasing costs in higher education, see chapter 2.

23. To be sure, some variation exists even among the most selective insti-

tutions in the application of this dual commitment, with some institutions offering "merit" scholarships or athletic scholarships in addition to need-based aid. For the purposes at hand, it seems most useful to group together those institutions that make this commitment, regardless of whether they also offer other forms of aid.

24. Sowell (1992, p. 26) states, "colleges and universities use the same methods as business cartels or monopolies. Like monopolistic price discriminators in the commercial world, private colleges and universities set an unrealistically high list price and then offer varying discounts. In academia, this list price is called tuition and the discount is called 'financial aid.'" For a contrary view, however, see Bowen and Breneman (1993).

25. The Higher Education General Information Survey and its successor, the Integrated Postsecondary Education Data System, both undertaken and maintained by the U.S. Department of Education, have been the standard data sets for empirical analysis of higher education. See Getz and Siegfried (1991, ch. 11) for a description of these surveys.

26. The Carnegie scheme of classification divides colleges and universities into six major types: (1) research universities, (2) doctoral-granting universities, (3) comprehensive universities, (4) liberal arts colleges, (5) two-year institutions, and (6) specialized institutions. For a short description of this classification scheme, see Clotfelter et al. 1991, Table 2.

27. Getz and Siegfried (1991), for example, divide research universities in this way in their analysis.

28. See Getz and Siegfried (1991, pp. 271–85) and Halstead (n.d.).

29. The growth rates calculated in the present study are exponential growth rates, corresponding to instantaneous compounding. Where X_0 is a beginning quantity and X_1 is a comparable quantity after t years, the average annual growth rate is g in the equation:

$$X_1 = X_0\, e^{gt}.$$

Chapter 2

1. Clark (1987, p. 264).

2. In the parlance currently in use in the theory and application of business "reengineering," activities such as those described here often are characterized as business "processes," which refer to functions of a business that may or may not correspond to existing organizational divisions within the business. See, for example, Davenport (1993).

3. See, for example, Keohane (1993, p. 114) or Stigler (1993, p. 175).

4. Carleton College, *Academic Catalog 1993–94*, p. 3.

5. Surveys of faculty indicate a marked increase in the perceived importance of research in obtaining tenure. The percentage of all faculty who strongly agreed with the statement, "In my department it is difficult for a person to achieve tenure if he or she does not publish," increased from 21 to 42 percent between 1969 and 1989. Among faculty in research universities, the percentage strongly agreeing rose from 44 to 83 percent (Boyer 1990, p. 12).

6. Caplow and McGee (1958, p. 221) note the irony of the situation: "It is only a slight exaggeration to say that academic success is likely to come to the man who has learned to neglect his assigned duties in order to have more time and energy to pursue his private professional interests."

7. Cole (1993 p. 6).

8. The view of Sykes (1988, p. 7) is at one extreme: "Professors, after all, control everything that matters in the universities."

9. Quoted in Clark (1987, p. 156). In assessing their role in governance, Clark (p. 264) states that faculty in the research university:

> [D]evelop a strong sense of nationhood in their own department, ruling it by collective decision making and holding administrators at arm's length from the core tasks. Since trustees have ultimate authority and make occasional large decisions, and since the administrative staff steadily elaborates bureaucratic controls, the setting is far from innocent of contrary forces. But the greater power lies in subjects, the stuff of academic work itself.

10. Arnold R. Weber (1989), then president of Northwestern University, remarked, "A few imaginative college administrators have raised prices above competitive levels to try to persuade consumers that a higher price indicates a higher-quality product." For another expression of this idea, see Noah (1983, p. 18).

11. See McPherson and Winston (1993b). The study by Spies (1978) of admissions trends at selective colleges and universities provides empirical support for this argument. He observes, "[A]n institution faced with the choices of increasing tuition or damaging its academic reputation by cutting back programs might do more to discourage applications if it followed the latter course" (p. 17). As noted in chapter 3 of this book, at least some institutions appeared to believe that raising tuition would not necessarily hurt their admissions outcomes.

12. See McPherson and Winston (1993b, pp. 69–105) for a discussion of this issue.

13. See, for example, Massy and Wilger (1992, p. 370).

14. I believe this wish to make a difference is one of the central reasons for the existence of endowments, an issue that has been discussed at length by Hansmann (1990). Endowments are stocks of financial assets generating spendable revenue, most of which are designated for named funds that are restricted to specified uses. To me, the wishes of the donor to have recognition, to make a difference—and to do both in perpetuity—and the amenability of the tax law in making virtually all such gifts, in life or after death, fully deductible, explain the prevalence of this form of giving.

15. For a discussion of their calculations, see the appendix to this chapter.

16. In the view of some observers, studies examining per-student costs are inherently flawed, in that they may be interpreted as taking constant returns to scale (that is, constant per-student costs) to be the norm. Moreover, if enrollments were to fall very rapidly, these costs almost certainly would increase, owing to the stickiness of many expenditures. To interpret such increases as increases in cost would be misleading, according to this view.

17. The Higher Education Price Index (HEPI) gives more than one-half of its weight to professional salaries and more than four-fifths to compensation of all kinds (Halstead 1983, p. 52). Between 1976/77 and 1989/90, the HEPI increased by 128 percent, whereas the Consumer Price Index rose by 116 percent (U.S. Department of Education 1992, p. 41, Table 38).

18. Massy and Wilger (1992, p. 366) cite this effect.

19. See also Shapiro (1993, p. 13) or Bowen (1992, p. 175).

20. See, for example, Meisinger and Dubeck (1984, pp. 16–9), Getz and Siegfried (1991, p. 266), or Massy and Wilger (1992, p. 365).

21. Massy (1990, p. 3) defines growth force as the "constant pressure to layer new courses, programs, and disciplines on old ones, to increase the specialization and hence the size of the faculty. . . ." Bergmann (1991), in contrast, focuses on growth in administrative areas, ascribing it to "the desire of each administrator for more underlings" and the absence of effective curbs on administrative growth. See also Getz and Siegfried (1991, p. 266).

22. Bowen (1968) discusses the importance of revenues in a slightly different way in his analysis of rising expenditures by private universities: "[T]he level of expenditures depends to a considerable extent on the amount of income available—just as the amount of income available depends to a considerable extent on the strength of the pressures for increased expenditures. The interdependence of the expenditure and income sides of the budget is a basic characteristic of all non-profit organizations. . . ."

23. For general statements of this widely cited hypothesis, see, for example, Baumol and Bowen (1966) or Baumol (1967). Bowen (1968, pp. 12–6) applies the thesis directly to private universities and to the increase in their expenditures during the 1950s and 1960s.

24. See also Cole (1993), who argues that administrators embraced and pushed the emphasis on research during the 1980s, and Massy and Wilger (1992, pp. 367–8), who refer to the increased emphasis on research as "output creep."

25. See, for example, Niskanen (1971).

26. See also Breneman (1994, p. 106) for a reference to logrolling in determining college budgets.

27. He states (p. 39): "Lacking the power to make changes without painful confrontation and lacking the personal incentive to overcome that obstacle, administrators are likely to prefer the status quo and to avoid initiatives that would make their institution different from others."

28. See, for example, Kennedy (1993, p. 139).

29. For a summary of these admissions indicators for 1991/92, see Table 3.2.

30. *Peterson's Guide to Four-Year Colleges 1994* (Princeton, NJ: Peterson's Guides, 1994).

31. Address to the Board of Trustees, September 28, 1984.

32. Graduate students in education were counted with professional students, although Duke had no separate school of education. The number of education graduate students was large, constituting about one-fifth of the graduate school's enrollment in 1976.

33. This committee, the Administrative Planning Committee, was composed of four faculty members, three administrators, and three students.

34. Minutes of the Administrative Policy Committee, January 25, 1984.

35. This relationship is discussed at greater length in the remainder of this appendix.

36. The assumption in the model that direct costs are fully covered may not be correct. One practice that apparently became more common during the 1980s was for granting agencies to insist that institutions contribute matching funds for certain research-related expenditures. Furthermore, direct costs might not be covered fully if the depreciation schedules used for scientific machinery tend to overstate useful lives or if grants end before the useful lives of this equipment have ended.

37. Although Figure 2.1 may be viewed as a picture of cross-subsidy, it remains impossible to pick any point of demarcation showing whether research subsidizes instruction or vice-versa. To say, for example, that at levels below D^* instruction is subsidizing research implicitly would assume that donors and students have no interest in research; to the extent that they do, one would expect the net costs of research to be positive. This may be what Kennedy (1993, p. 148) has in mind when he refers to the growth in restricted expenditures as taxing the general fund.

38. Two empirical studies of institutional response are those by McPherson and Schapiro (1991) and by Ehrenberg, Rees, and Brewer (1993).

39. Where the growth in X over t years can be described by the exponential function $X_1 = X_0 \, e^{rt}$, then the growth rate of any product is $r(bc) = r(b) + r(c)$, and the growth rate of any quotient is $r(b/c) = r(b) - r(c)$.

Chapter 3

1. Farewell Address to the Nation, January 11, 1989 (Reagan 1989, pp. 412–3).

2. For a discussion of the components of this increase, see Clotfelter et al. (1991, chap. 1).

3. The rise in applications is reflected in an annual survey of freshmen. Among those attending private universities, the percentage who applied to as many as seven institutions increased from 12.1 percent in 1979 to 22.5 percent in 1992 (Astin, 1979, 1992), tables entitled, "Weighted National Norms for All Freshmen." For a description of the increase in applications to the most selective institutions, see Deirdre Carmondy, "Better Students Finding Colleges Reject Them," *New York Times*, April 20, 1988, sec. B.

4. Calculations are based on data from U.S. Bureau of the Census, *Current Population Reports*, Series P-60, No. 184, *Money Income of Households, Families, and Persons in the United States: 1992* (Washington, DC: Government Printing Office, 1993), Table B-7. See Table 3A.1 in the appendix to this chapter.

5. These rates applied to ordinary, as opposed to capital gains, income and do not reflect the 33 percent marginal tax rate "bubble" applying to one band of income classes.

6. According to one set of tabulations, the effective tax rate for the top 20 percent of households fell from 27.2 percent in 1977 to 26.4 percent in 1989 (U.S. House of Representatives, Committee on Ways and Means, *1992 Green Book*, p. 1510, Table 14). Similarly, Kasten, Sammartino, and Toder (1992, Table 12) estimate that the average federal tax rate on the top one-fifth of households declined over the period 1980 to 1989.

7. Between 1981 and 1988, median sales prices increased by 50 percent in Washington, DC, 73 percent in San Francisco, 126 percent in Boston, and 150 percent in the New York metropolitan area (Phillips 1990, Appendix I-2). See also Richard W. Stevenson, "Housing Prices Expected To Be Sluggish in the 90's," *New York Times*, April 6, 1990, sec. A.

8. U.S Bureau of the Census, *Current Population Reports*, Series P-60, No. 118, *Money Income in 1977 of Families and Persons in the United States* (Washington, DC: Government Printing Office, 1979), Table 22; and *Money Income of Households, Families, and Persons in the United States: 1992* (Washington, DC: Government Printing Office, 1993), Table 9. Using the Gross Domestic Product price deflator, the dollar value in 1977 corresponding to $65,000 in 1992 was $30,004. The estimate of average family size for families with incomes of $30,004 or more in 1977 was computed using interpolation. Cook and Frank (1993, p. 133) also make this point.

9. For evidence, see, for example, Clotfelter (1991, p. 46, Table 2.13) or Hearn (1990).

10. See Freeman (1976). For further discussion of the return to college education, see Clotfelter (1991, pp. 64–9).

11. The exact timing of the trough in the earnings advantage depends on the measure used. One time series presented in Clotfelter et al. (1991, p. 66, Figure 3.1) suggests 1980 for men. For further discussion of the economic returns from college, see also Murphy and Welch (1989).

12. Minutes of the Administrative Policy Committee, Carleton College, May 8, 1986.

13. For analyses of the academic labor market and salaries, see Hansen (1986) or Ehrenberg (1991).

14. Calculations are based on data in *The Lawyer's Almanac*, various years (Englewood Cliffs, NJ: Prentice Hall Law and Business), and American Medical Association, *Socioeconomic Characteristics of Medical Practice*, 1987 through 1994 editions. Data on starting salaries, comparing three doctoral fields with MBAs and lawyers, similarly show that increases in academic salaries were well within the range of those in other professions (Ehrenberg 1991, p. 182, Table 8.3).

15. For a description of the methodology for computing the Higher Education Price Index, see Halstead (1983).

16. A monopsonist is a firm that is the only buyer in a factor market. See Ransom (1993) for an application of the monopsony model to the market for faculty.

17. Conversation with Irwin Feller, November 17, 1994. Similarly, Kennedy (1985) argues that there has been a general decline in the federal gov-

ernment's commitment to pay for scientific equipment and cites attempts by the National Institutes of Health to reduce research support by withholding a portion of indirect costs.

18. That reimbursements systematically fail to cover costs is suggested, for example, by Richardson (1992, p. 182) and Rosovsky (1992, p. 184).

19. Institutions themselves made up for some of the declines in federal student aid grants. See, for example, Clotfelter et al. (1991, p. 105).

20. For a discussion of this econometric work, see Clotfelter et al. (1991, pp. 107–13).

21. A listing for 1987/88, for example, showed 9 national universities, including such universities as Harvard and Chicago, with an average tuition and fees of $16,767; 9 national colleges other than Carleton, including such colleges as Wellesley and Oberlin, with an average of $15,658; and 10 Midwestern colleges other than Carleton, including such colleges as Grinnell and St. Olaf, with an average of $12,192. Carleton's figure for that year was $13,640, the highest of the its group, $3,100 below the average for the national universities, and $2,000 below that of the national colleges.

22 The minutes of the Administrative Policy Committee, February 28, 1978, made specific reference to the empirical study by Spies (1978): "Citing passages from a COFHE report entitled 'The Effect of Rising Costs on College Choice' to support his point, Mr. Sullivan urged that since it has been demonstrated that students in the market for a school like Carleton are less influenced in their choice by the cost than by the academic quality of the institution, we should not hold down Carleton's comprehensive fee at the risk of lowering its quality." At a meeting a decade later, committee members heard a report on research indicating that some students, particularly those from the East, were likely to equate price with quality (Minutes, April 3, 1989).

23. Minutes of the Administrative Policy Committee, Carleton College, May 13, 1980.

24. He also noted that this would be a good time for an increase because of favorable press that Carleton had received in an article in *U.S. News and World Report* (Minutes of the Administrative Policy Committee, Carleton College, February 1, 1988).

25. Minutes of the Administrative Policy Committee, Carleton College, April 3, 1989.

26. For evidence that selective colleges and universities enroll a disproportionate share of students from affluent families, see McPherson and Winston (1993a, chap. 5).

27. Hauptman (1990, pp. 80, 82) makes a similar argument, emphasizing the ability of institutions to raise tuitions and their wish to enhance their academic and student service offerings.

Chapter 4

1. Bowen (1980, p. 15).

2. Defining a cost function is more difficult even than assigning costs,

because it requires a measure of the firm's output. In the case of higher education, it is the unfortunate fact that we cannot adequately describe, let alone measure, the output. Higher education produces many different outputs, and we have only a vague idea of the "technology" involved. (Although it is generally believed, for example, that teaching a seminar is different from teaching a lecture, and that student time and effort are vital inputs in the process, our understanding of these differences is rudimentary.)

3. It is worth noting one inherent difficulty in the omission of medical schools and centers. To varying degrees, most major university medical centers contain faculty whose work would be judged as "basic," as opposed to applied research, in such fields as genetics and microbiology. Although such fields could be classified in arts and sciences, the approach taken here is to omit such departments when they are part of the university's medical center.

4. University accounting systems typically place all fringe benefits in the same account. In order to estimate the fringe benefits applying to each category of employee, the appropriate fringe benefit rate for the year and class of worker was added to salaries and deducted from total fringe benefits. To the extent that this method did not exhaust the fringe benefit totals precisely, the difference was reflected in the residual category.

5. For example, annual capital outlays for the University of Chicago were available for the years 1983/84 to 1992/93. These expenditures were divided by departmental group and converted into constant 1991/92 dollars. Averages then were formed: for 1983/84, the average of capital spending in 1983/84 and 1984/85; for 1986/87, the average of 1985/86, 1986/87, and 1987/88; and for 1991/92, the average of 1990/91, 1991/92, and 1992/93.

6. The departmental groups include four sets of academic departments (humanities, social sciences, natural sciences, and engineering), library, student services, plant, admissions and financial aid, arts and sciences administration, provost, alumni affairs and development, and other general administration. A 13th department, athletics, is shown separately. The expenditure types are as follows: compensation for regular faculty, other faculty, administrative staff, nonexempt workers, and students; professional services; contract work; computers; financial aid (including stipends for graduate students); supplies; general operating expenses; capital expenditures; maintenance; and a residual, which includes excess or insufficient fringe benefits. For a detailed listing of departmental components and spending categories used to create the table, see appendix Table 4A.2.

7. The specific proportions used for Duke were: 90 percent of the library, 95 percent of student services and alumni affairs and development, 75 percent of the provost's office, and 20 percent of plant and general administration. All other categories were assigned exclusively to arts and sciences and engineering. These percentages reflect administrators' estimates. The 20 percent figure for general administration reflects the large number of buildings, employees, and financial transactions in the university's medical center. By comparison, the percentages of departmental groups assigned to arts and sciences at the University of Chicago were: 60 percent of the library, 53 percent of the provost, and 80 percent each of student services, plant, and

general administration. All other categories were assigned to arts and sciences entirely. The first of the above estimates for Chicago was based on the proportion of students in arts and sciences and the second on the proportion of faculty. The 80 percent figure was an estimate made by administrators in the budget office.

8. The interested reader can verify this assertion by applying alternative allocation percentages to the tabular data given in this chapter.

9. As noted in the appendix, however, the inclusion of transfers combined with the apportioning of nonallocatable general expenditures means that internal transfers do not necessarily cancel out completely.

10. During this period, the way in which payments to graduate students were allocated between fellowships and salaries for teaching changed significantly. For this reason, most categories covering salaries to graduate students are included in the category of fellowship spending.

11. For the purpose of computing full compensation, wages and salaries in each category were multiplied by the applicable fringe benefit rate, and the resulting amount was transferred from the separate fringe benefit account to the appropriate compensation category. These calculated fringe benefits did not equal exactly the totals in the university's fringe benefit accounts; the residual category shown in the table consists almost entirely of the difference.

12. As noted in the text, the use of the eight-year period 1983/84 through 1991/92 was necessitated by the lack of computer-readable accounting data before 1983/84. As a check on the validity of relying on this shortened period in the analysis of expenditure trends, a comparison using data for Duke was made, using other data between the period 1976/77 to 1983/84 and the more recent period covered in the tables. This comparison is presented in appendix 4.3.

13. Where X_1 and X_2 are expenditures for one category in years 1 and 2, respectively, and T_2 is total expenditure in year 2, the percentage increase in total spending attributable to increased expenditures for category X is $(X_2 - X_1)/T_2 = (X_2/T_2)((X_2 - X_1)/X_2)$, or the product of the category's share of the total and the percentage growth in that category.

14. The large change in the federal share for admissions/financial aid and arts and sciences administration is due apparently to a change in the unit to which ROTC scholarships were assigned.

15. For the Harvard tables, the General Academic group includes the Core Curriculum, Freshman and House Seminars, and General Education; Natural Sciences includes departments 44, 49, 52, and 66; and Plant includes Physical Resources and Grounds and Buildings.

16. As noted in Table 4A.3, faculty compensation refers to Harvard's classes 01 (tenured professors) and 02 (faculty on term appointments longer than one year, mostly associate and assistant professors). Class 01 also includes some administrators who were grandfathered into that classification by virtue of being in their jobs in 1976, when administrators first were included in class 03.

17. See the appendix for a brief discussion of internal transfers and recharges.

18. Where to classify history has been a subject of debate for some time. See, for example, Sills (1968, p. xxi).

19. Further use is made of fund codes in the next chapter.

20. The departmental group into which any expenditure item was classified in the detailed analysis of financial data was determined by the "primary component," usually the unit responsible for the expenditure.

21. These amounts may differ for several reasons. First, the "unrestricted" expenditures taken from the detailed financial data include "allocated" expenditures, which were spent out of special fund codes, using money that might have been taken out of previous years' unrestricted budgets. The payments into these allocated fund codes were not counted in the detailed analysis; only the expenditures out of them were counted. However, the fund codes examined included no accounts for such allocated expenditures.

22. As is shown in chapter 6, because the staff size of the counsel's office grew modestly over the period, this increase in spending by the university counsel appears to be the result of hiring of outside counsel.

Chapter 5

1. President, University of Chicago. Gray (1992, p. 235).

2. For data on broader averages of faculty salaries, see Table 5A.1 in the appendix to this chapter.

3. In a steady state, in which the number of professors retiring and being replaced is constant, the difference would depend on the average growth in real salaries for continuing faculty and the average length of service from promotion to full professor to retirement. In actual institutions, the difference also would depend on the age distribution of the faculty.

4. Report of the Faculty Compensation Committee to the Executive Committee of the Academic Council, "Additional Information on Faculty Salaries," March 8, 1993.

5. It seems likely that some portion of the increase in the calculated fringe benefit rate for Duke overstates the actual increase. At least one category, benefits administration, reflects costs that were incurred in previous years but that, apparently, were noted only in the most recent years for the purpose of indirect cost recovery.

6. Exponential growth rate for 15 years of 1.1528 to 1.2269.

7. For a discussion of journal price inflation, see Noll and Steinmueller (1992).

8. Between 1981/82 and 1991/92, a period in which prices overall increased by 47 percent, the increases in the following components of the Higher Education Price Index were: professional salaries, 72 percent; nonprofessional salaries, 49 percent; library acquisitions, 99 percent; supplies and materials, 18 percent; services, 53 percent; construction, 39 percent; and capital equipment, 36 percent.

9. See, for example, Bowen and Rudenstine (1992, chap. 10).

10. As explained in chapter 4, each of the lines of the expenditure tables for Duke and Chicago has been multiplied by a constant that approximates the arts and sciences share of each departmental group. In the case of arts

and sciences academic departments and arts and sciences administration, in addition to all the lines at Harvard and Carleton, this constant is 100 percent, since these units were by definition wholly in arts and sciences.

11. For each of 10 expenditure categories, price indices P_i from Research Associates of Washington (1994) were used to calculate changes in factor market prices. The increased spending in any category attributable to the increase in prices of that category is $E_{1i}I_1(P_{2i}/P_{1i}) - E_{1i}$, where I_1 is the general price level in period 1 relative to 1991/92 and E_{1i} is expenditures for that category in the base year, in 1991/92 dollars. The categories are: professional salaries, nonprofessional salaries, library acquisitions, supplies and materials, services, capital (the average of the construction and capital equipment indices), and faculty salaries. The index of faculty compensation at the universities was based on a weighted average of full, associate, and assistant professor salaries plus fringe benefits for private independent doctoral institutions (category I) from the American Association of University Professors (AAUP) annual survey (Academe 1982, p. 18; 1984, p. 9; and 1992, pp. 19, 28). Data on private, independent, baccalaureate colleges (category IIB) were used to make the comparable calculation for Carleton.

12. Averages in Tables 5A.1 and 5A.2 reflect changes in the distribution of faculty by rank, whereas the index used in the current chapter uses weights of three ranks based on the relative number of faculty in those institutions in 1991/92.

13. Where C_1 is first-period compensation for regular faculty, the portion deemed attributable to growth in the size of the faculty is $C_1(N_2/N_1) - C_1$, where N refers to the faculty size in years 1 and 2, respectively.

14. Harvard figures are full-time-equivalents; figures for other institutions are numbers of regular faculty.

15. Where S is average salary for the institution and S^* is average salary for the market, the over-market increase in salaries is given by $(S_2/S_1 - S^*_2/S^*_1) C_1$. Where f is the institution's fringe benefit rate and f^* is the average for all institutions, the increase attributable to an extraordinary increase in the fringe benefit rate is $[(1+f_2)/(1+f_1) - (1+f_2^*)/(1+f_1^*)] C_1$.

16. Where N is the number of graduate or undergraduate students, as applicable, and A_1 is the amount of aid awarded in period 1, the portion of increased financial aid expenditure is $A_1 (N_2/N_1) - A_1$. The portion attributable to aid per student is the residual increase in financial aid, or $A_2 - A_1 (N_2/N_1)$.

17. For a description of the formula used in calculating need-based aid, see Clotfelter (1991, pp. 95–8).

18. At Duke, the percentage of total arts and sciences spending devoted to administration rose from about 38 to 41 percent; at Harvard, the increase was from 30 to 34 percent.

19. Negative values in expenditure accounts ordinarily signify repayments for services rendered. Thus, significant negative amounts as well as positive amounts would indicate existence.

20. Calculation by Office of Dean of Arts and Sciences.

21. The four primary entities here are: (1) the Division of Applied Sciences, (2) Organismal and Evolutionary Biology, (3) the Museum of Comparative Zoology, and (4) the Harvard Observatory.

22. The federal government's share of academic research and development expenditures declined from 67 to 59 percent from 1980/81 to 1991/92 (Feller 1995, p. 7). Blasdell, McPherson, and Schapiro (1993, p. 29) show that private universities experienced the same trend for the period 1979 to 1989.

23. For a discussion of the manifestations and effects of such cost-shifting, see Feller (1995, pp. 16–20).

Chapter 6

1. Comment on Shapiro in *Minerva* 30 (summer 1992): 185.

2. "Here is a partial list of new undergraduate services provided at Harvard during the past decade: special advice and counselling for minority students and personnel to work on race relations issues; special resources for disabled students; additional public service programs; programs pertaining to sexual harassment; expansion of office of career services; increased security costs, i.e., shuttle buses, police, guards, escort services, improvement in lighting; major increases in women's athletics and recreational sports; increased staff for financial aid services; greater supervision of extracurricular activities. There have also been major increases in services to graduate students" (Rosovsky 1992, p. 185).

3. See, for example, Getz and Siegfried (1991, p. 263).

4. One of the most well-known pieces of federal regulation is Circular A–21, which establishes the rules for determining reimbursement to universities for the indirect costs of research. One paragraph chosen at random, C5 (b), suggests the degree of complexity that may be involved in compliance with regulations: "In some instances, the amounts received from the federal government to finance institutional activities or service operation should be treated as applicable credits. Specifically, the concept of netting such credit items against related expenditures should be applied by the institution in determining the rates or amounts to be charged to sponsored agreements for services rendered whenever the facilities or other resources used in providing such services have been financed directly, in whole or in part, by federal funds. (See Sections F8 and J44 for areas of potential application in the matter of direct federal financing.)" (U.S. Office of Management and Budget, *Office of Management and Budget Circular A–21—Cost Principles for Educational Institutions*, Washington, DC: Government Printing Office, November 1991, p. 3.)

5. They state (1992, p. 367): "Consensus management . . . has become the norm for conducting business throughout higher education. Administrative and academic support staff personnel are widely consulted on a variety of issues. Agreements are hammered out before decisions are made. Although this process has the merit of being broadly participatory, it has many drawbacks." Among the drawbacks mentioned are the time required to reach

decisions and the lack of accountability. For a complementary interpretation of the role of university administrators, see Feldstein (1993).

6. For inefficiency, or any cause, to cause costs to increase, it also must increase; to raise the rate of cost increase, it must rise at a more rapid rate than other components of the total. In the present discussion, in consideration of the abstractness of the causes themselves, these distinctions are taken for granted.

7. Economists distinguish two kinds of inefficiency. *Allocative inefficiency* is the uneconomic use of resources. Allocative inefficiency may manifest itself, for example, in a capital-labor ratio that makes it more expensive to produce a given unit of output, or in an excessive amount of an output, which might be higher education itself. A second kind, which probably corresponds more closely to the common interpretation of the term, is what Leibenstein (1966) termed *x-inefficiency*, the failure to employ whatever resources are used in their best way. This type of inefficiency may show up as disorganization, old-fashioned routines, or long coffee breaks.

8. For a study of innovation in higher education, including some of the computing and communications equipment mentioned here, see Getz, Siegfried, and Anderson (1994).

9. For ease of data collection, I chose a set of seven administrative component codes rather than try to follow the changing set of codes corresponding to the four administrative areas discussed here.

10. One estimate made around 1980 was that 40 percent of commercial applications of computers had proven uneconomic, in the sense that the cost to perform the same job had increased as a result of computerization (Kidder 1981, p. 244).

11. Committee to Study the Impact of Information Technology on the Performance of Service Activities (1994, pp. 156–70). In explaining the lag in the impact of new technology, this report states: "In many cases, knowledge workers have used IT [information technology] to do more busy work without necessarily enhancing output—spreadsheets can be recalculated, presentations fine-tuned, or manuscripts revised more frequently with little noticeable benefit" (p. 170). See also Sylvia Nasar, "90's May Be the Growth Decade," *New York Times*, February 17, 1992, sec. C.

12. Shapiro (1992) suggests the proposition that productivity is directly related to the speed with which information can be gathered and processed. Of the innovations in higher education noted by Getz, Siegfried, and Anderson (1994), several have had dramatic effects on this speed, including on-line databases, automated circulation and public catalogs in libraries, and interbuilding data networks, not to mention personal computers.

13. At various times, other functions have been housed in the counsel's office at Duke, including public affairs and patents. The first of these functions was excluded from the present tabulations, and the second was included in the area of sponsored research.

14. At Duke, the administrative units that existed during the period of study in this area include the Office of Research Support, the Office of Research and Development, the Office of Research Administration and Pol-

icy, the Patent Office, the Office of Technology Transfer, the Office of Sponsored Programs, and the Office of Cost Accounting. At Harvard, they include the Office for Sponsored Research and the Office for Technology and Trademark Licensing.

15. The entities covered at Duke were counseling and psychological services, plus all offices under student affairs with the exception of cultural affairs, religious activities, university union, and the Mary Lou Williams Center for Black Culture. Several parts of student affairs at the University of Chicago were omitted from the tabulations in Table 6.6: registrar, graduate admissions and financial aid, resident halls, and physical education.

16. Also included at Duke were employee health fitness programs and employee discrimination, the latter being covered by a special assistant to the president for equal opportunity and the university ombudsman.

17. See note 2 above.

18. Data from Harvard were provided on a full-time-equivalent (FTE) basis. In the case of Duke, the FTE basis was calculated by multiplying the percentage of weeks of the year worked by the percentage of hours out of 40 typically worked.

19. See Table 4A.6 in chapter 4, appendix 4.3.

20. See Table 5.4 in chapter 5.

21. It is worth noting that information on nonregular faculty at universities tends to be of poor quality. One reason may be the highly individualized arrangements that often accompany this kind of employment, ranging from a lump payment for teaching one course to no payment whatever for university administrators who teach occasional courses.

Chapter 7

1. "The Way We Live Now," *Faculty Newsletter*, Duke University 4 (October 1992).

2. Massy and Wilger (1992, p. 367) state: "While quantitative data to demonstrate the ratchet are sparse, the discretionary time model developed by Massy and Zemsky . . . shows that faculty do behave in ways that are consistent with the concept."

3. By the 1903/04 academic year, Harvard's introductory lecture courses had enrollments in the hundreds. Economics 1 had an enrollment of 529; Geology 4, an enrollment of 489; and History 1, an enrollment of 408 (Veysey 1965, p. 339a).

4. This simulation is described in more detail in appendix 7.1.

5. Minutes of the Administrative Policy Committee, Carleton College. See, for example, minutes from meetings on January 31, 1978; April 25, 1978; and October 31, 1985.

6. The basic data for each institution were registrar lists of courses taught, with accompanying information on instructors and enrollments. These lists were complemented by faculty lists with ranks. For two institutions, information on full-time-equivalent status also was used; for another, "census forms" also were used. These forms were distributed to faculty each semester and

asked for verification of data on teaching assignments compiled by the registrar. They were a means of obtaining additional information on shared teaching, advising, and other duties.

7. In 1991/92, these four departments had an average of 25 regular faculty and slightly more than 100 graduate students.

8. According to administrative records, 41 of the 48 pre-major advisors in 1976/77 were regular-rank faculty, compared with 51 of the 122 in 1991/92—a decline from 85 to 42 percent.

9. The growth in graduate enrollment counts both master's and doctoral students. The inclusion of master's students, plus the lag between matriculation and dissertation writing would explain why the number of supervisions would not necessarily have grown by 87 percent.

10. Two trends in graduate education, noted by Bowen and Rudenstine (1992), namely increased time-to-degree and higher attrition rates, could explain the relative constancy in dissertation advising in the face of growth in total graduate enrollments.

11. The regressions are given in appendix Table 7A.3 of this chapter.

12. For example, Public Policy Studies 114, The Politics of the Policy Process, also might be listed separately as Political Science 114, but with the same title. Thirty-five undergraduates might be enrolled in the course under the Public Policy number, and another 10 might be enrolled in it as a Political Science course. The total class size would, of course, be 45.

13. In several cases at Harvard, data from course catalogs and discussions with administrators revealed that actual contact hours occasionally differed from the number of contact hours recorded in official records. In such cases actual hours were used.

14. Harvard's course catalog provides the names of all of the professors participating in workshops. These workshops were treated as team-taught classes, following the methodology noted in Appendix 7.2.

15. At Duke, all the courses described as independent study-type were three hours. At Carleton, students can sign up for one to six credit hours of independent study-type courses, with six considered a full course; therefore, a faculty member's load of such courses for a term was calculated as the total number of credits for independent study-type divided by six.

16. *TOTAL* is the total enrollment in the class. It is the sum of undergraduate enrollment (*UNDER*), graduate enrollment (*GRAD*) and other students (*OTHER*).

17. For the present study, these were calculated for regular (tenured and tenure-track) faculty only.

18. In equation (1), substitute $GRAD_i$ for $UNDER_i$ and sum over all m meetings of the graduate courses to perform this calculation.

Chapter 8

1. Boyer (1987, p. 145).

2. For the purpose of these calculations related to the size and instructors of classes, both instructors who would become assistant professors

after they had earned their doctoral degree and emeritus faculty who had been tenured professors were counted as regular tenure-track faculty. By contrast, emeritus faculty were not included in the calculations of teaching loads.

3. The weighted averages are (300 × 30)/300 in the first case and (90 × 10 + 210 × 210)/300 in the second. In practice, the weights are not necessarily the same as class size (as they are in this example). The calculations presented in the chapter were made separately for graduate and undergraduate students in the universities. In the calculation for undergraduates, for example, the number of undergraduates enrolled in each course of a department is the weight, whereas the total class size includes undergraduates as well as graduate students and other students enrolled in the course through some other department (for cross-listed courses).

4. Noted in chapter 2. See Boyer (1987, p. 149).

5. In the same way that average class size is sensitive to the distribution of classes by size, it also can be affected by a single large course. This effect can be seen by comparing the two years' of data for the humanities department. A large lecture class that was offered in 1986/87 was not offered in 1991/92; this class accounts for most of the very significant difference in the department's enrollments between the two years.

6. For statements to this effect, see, for example, Bennett (1986) or Massy (1990).

7. Bowen and Rudenstine (1992, pp. 234–47), citing English, history, and political science as illustrations, argue that the number of subfields in various disciplines has increased. They note the growing importance of interdisciplinary work, non-Western and other international perspectives, and the application of approaches from one discipline to other disciplines as factors in the growth of subfields. They note this effect on overall curricular structure: "[T]here has obviously been some loss of articulated coherence in the formal curriculum, some measurable loss of structure and control in program definition and management, and an increased sense of uncertainty about where to draw sensible boundary lines . . ." (p. 235).

8. If the catalog listed staff or gave no list of faculty, the assumption was made that complete turnover of available faculty had not occurred.

9. One public critique that gained attention was an address by Price (1993).

10. Clearly, a full investigation of this issue would require a careful analysis that is well beyond the scope of this study. One suggestive piece of information that may be relevant is the trend at Duke in the use of final examinations in courses. Any instructor who does not plan to give a final examination is asked to submit a form to the registrar listing any such courses. The ratio of forms to the total number of courses, an imperfect measure of the proportion of courses in which no examinations were given, increased from 0.121 in 1978/79 to 0.155 in 1991/92. Although this trend obviously is open to more than one interpretation, it is one concrete measure of a teaching technique for which comparable data over time exist.

Chapter 9

1. Provost, Stanford University, quoted in Susan Chira, "How Stanford, Wealthy and Wise, Is Cutting Costs to Stay that Way," *New York Times*, July 8, 1990, p. 1.

2. Duke Provost's Office. Part of this growth was offset by a decline in nursing faculty.

3. The 32 colleges and universities belonging to the Consortium on Financing Higher Education (COFHE) enrolled 122,000 undergraduates in 1993/94, which was 1.4 percent of the approximately 8.6 million full-time-equivalent undergraduates reported for the 1990/91 year nationwide (U.S. Department of Education 1992, p. 177, Table 165).

4. As noted in chapter 1, the growth of financial aid in private institutions had the effect of moderating the growth of net tuition by about 0.6 percent per year.

5. COFHE (1991, appendix A) and U.S. Department of Education (1994, p. 312, Table 304). In a similar vein, Rothschild and White (1993) remark on the similarity of tuition levels among private institutions of quite different quality.

6. The changes in the unweighted average classroom teaching loads from 1976/77 to 1991/92, respectively, were: 3.74 to 3.79 in the departments corresponding to the natural science discipline, 5.22 to 3.74 in social science, and 5.08 to 4.49 in the humanities. See chapter 7 for further discussion of these measures.

7. The example of Kenneth Pye's retrenchment efforts at Duke could serve as the exception that proves the rule. With much fanfare, university committees deliberated over the possible elimination of five academic units. In the end only two of the five were dropped—the nursing school and the education department. These changes were significant, allowing a large increase in arts and sciences undergraduate enrollments to take the place of nursing students and the elimination of the university's largest PhD program, that in education. Nevertheless, no tenured faculty member had to be let go as a result of these changes, and, within a decade, the university was offering graduate degrees in both nursing and education.

8. Some of these institutions offered, in addition to need-based aid, scholarships awarded strictly on the basis of merit. For a description of the uniform methodology that served as the basis for the financial aid awards made by these institutions, see Clotfelter (1991).

9. Such cushioning is rarely complete, however, as self-help amounts typically are increased when tuition and fees are increased.

10. As noted in chapter 5, universities may exploit an employee's ties to a locality to a certain extent, by offering less to continuing faculty than it would to attract new hires.

11. See, for example, Rosovsky (1990, p. 71) and Rothschild and White (1993) for discussions of the unwillingness of colleges and universities to charge the theoretical equilibrium price.

12. The gap, based on the average salaries of all faculty in public and

private independent category I universities, was 10.0 percent in 1976/77 and 23.2 percent in 1991/92 (*Academe*, 1977 and 1992).

13. For a discussion of the role of education in the shifts in relative earnings during the 1980s, see, for example, Murphy and Welch (1989).

14. See Rosovsky (1991) and "Bok's Outline of Right Role for Academy," *New York Times*, September 7, 1984.

15. An apparent exception is Antioch's reengineering effort, which combines a rearrangement of administrative functions and the introduction of new teaching techniques. See Guskin (1995) for a description of this effort.

16. In using this phrase, Riesman (1980, p. 5) excluded the most selective private research universities; similar ideas have been applied to those universities as well.

17. University of Chicago *Directory*, 1991/92; *Peterson's Guide to Four-Year Colleges 1993*; and unpublished data from the University of Chicago.

18. Comparing research and undergraduate teaching to the lions and zebras on the Serengeti Plain, Coleman summarized his argument for separation: "[L]ions eat the zebras, and the research or consulting time eats the teaching time" (1973, p. 381). Recently, Shapiro (1992) has questioned whether such a separation ought not be instituted.

Bibliography

Astin, Alexander W., et al. 1979, 1992. *The American Freshmen: National Norms*. Los Angeles: Cooperative Institutional Research Program.

Baumol, William J. 1967. "Macroeconomics of Unbalanced Growth: The Anatomy of Urban Crisis." *American Economic Review* 57 (June): 415–26.

Baumol, William J., and William G. Bowen. 1966. *Performing Arts—The Economic Dilemma*. Cambridge, MA: Twentieth Century Fund.

Bennett, William J. 1986. Address at Harvard University. *Chronicle of Higher Education* (15 October).

———. 1987. "Our Greedy Colleges." *New York Times*, 18 February, p. A31.

Bergmann, Barbara R. 1991. "Bloated Administration, Blighted Campuses." *Academe* (November/December): 12–16.

Blasdell, Scott W., Michael S. McPherson, and Morton Owen Schapiro. 1993. "Trends in Revenues and Expenditures in U.S. Higher Education: Where Does the Money Come From? Where Does it Go?" In *Paying the Piper: Productivity, Incentives, and Financing in U.S. Higher Education*, edited by Michael S. McPherson, Morton Owen Schapiro, and Gordon C. Winston. Ann Arbor, MI: University of Michigan Press, 1993.

Bok, Derek. 1992. "Reclaiming the Public Trust." *Change* (July/August): 13–19.

Bok, Derek. 1993. *The Cost of Talent: How Executives and Professionals Are Paid and How It Affects America*. New York: Free Press.

Bowen, Howard. 1980. *The Costs of Higher Education*. San Francisco: Jossey-Bass.

Bowen, Howard, and Jack H. Schuster. 1986. *American Professors: A National Resource Imperiled*. New York: Oxford University Press.

Bowen, William G. 1968. *The Economics of the Major Private Universities*. New York: Carnegie Commission on Higher Education.

———. 1992. Comment. "The Functions and Resources of the American University of the Twenty-First Century." *Minerva* 30 (summer): 175–78.

Bowen, William G., and David W. Breneman. 1993. "Student Aid: Price Discount or Educational Investment?" *Brookings Review* 11 (winter 1993): 28–31.

Bowen, William G., and Neil L. Rudenstine. 1992. *In Pursuit of the PhD*. Princeton, NJ: Princeton University Press.

Bowen, William G., and Julie Ann Sosa. 1989. *Prospects for Faculty in the Arts and Sciences*. Princeton: Princeton University Press.

Boyer, Ernest L. 1987. *College*. New York: Harper and Row.

———. 1990. *Scholarship Reconsidered*. Princeton, NJ: Carnegie Foundation for the Advancement of Teaching.

Breneman, David W. 1994. *Liberal Arts Colleges: Thriving, Surviving, or Endangered?* Washington, DC: Brookings Institution.

Buckles, Stephen. 1978. "Identification of Causes of Increasing Costs in Higher Education." *Southern Economic Journal* (July): 258–65.

Caplow, Theodore, and Reece J. McGee. 1958. *The Academic Marketplace.* New York: Basic Books.

Chaney, Bradford, and Elizabeth Farris. 1990. *The Finances of Higher Education Institutions.* Higher Education Surveys Report, Survey No. 8. Washington, DC: U.S. Department of Education.

Chira, Susan. 1990. "How Stanford, Wealthy and Wise, Is Cutting Costs to Stay that Way." *New York Times,* 8 July, p. 1.

Clark, Burton R. 1987. *The Academic Life: Small Worlds, Different Worlds.* Princeton, NJ: The Carnegie Foundation for the Advancement of Teaching.

Clotfelter, Charles T. 1991. "Demand for Undergraduate Education." Part I in *Economic Challenges in Higher Education,* Charles T. Clotfelter et al. Chicago: University of Chicago Press.

Clotfelter, Charles T., Ronald G. Ehrenberg, Malcolm Getz, and John J. Siegfried. 1991. *Economic Challenges in Higher Education.* Chicago: University of Chicago Press.

Clotfelter, Charles T., and Michael Rothschild (eds.). 1993. *Studies of Supply and Demand in Higher Education.* Chicago: University of Chicago Press.

Cole, Jonathan R. 1993. "Balancing Acts: Dilemmas of Choice Facing Research Universities." *Daedalus* 122 (fall).

Coleman, James S. 1973. "The University and Society's New Demands Upon It." In *Content and Context,* edited by Carl Kaysen. New York: McGraw-Hill.

Committee to Study the Impact of Information Technology on the Performance of Service Activities et al. 1994. *Information Technology in the Service Society.* Washington, DC: National Academy Press.

Consortium on Financing Higher Education. Various years. *Tuition, Student Budgets, and Self-Help at the Consortium Institutions.* Washington, DC: COFHE.

———. 1991. *Growth and Moderation: A Study of COFHE Tuition and Fee Trends from 1976 Through 1991.* Washington, DC: COFHE (July).

———. 1994. *Growth and Moderation: An Update.* Washington, DC: COFHE (March).

Cook, Philip J., and Robert H. Frank. 1993. "The Growing Concentration of Top Students at Elite Schools." In *Studies of Supply and Demand in Higher Education,* edited by Charles T. Clotfelter and Michael Rothschild. Chicago: University of Chicago Press: 121–140.

Davenport, Thomas H. 1993. *Process Innovation: Reengineering Work Through Information Technology.* Boston: Harvard Business School Press.

Ehrenberg, Ronald G. 1991. "Academic Labor Supply." Part II in *Economic Challenges in Higher Education,* edited by Charles T. Clotfelter et al. Chicago: University of Chicago Press.

Ehrenberg, Ronald, and Susan H. Murphy. 1993. Draft. "What Price Diversity?: The Death of Needs-Based Financial Aid at Selective Private Colleges and Universities." 13 January.

Ehrenberg, Ronald, Daniel I. Rees, and Dominic J. Brewer. 1993. "How Would Universities Respond to Increased Federal Support for Graduate Students?" In *Studies of Supply and Demand in Higher Education*, edited by Charles Clotfelter and Michael Rothschild. Chicago: University of Chicago Press: 183–206.

Feldstein, Martin. 1993. "Comment." In *Studies of Supply and Demand in Higher Education*, edited by Charles Clotfelter and Michael Rothschild. Chicago: University of Chicago Press: 37–42.

Feller, Irwin. 1995. "The Changing Academic Research Market." Unpublished paper given at National Bureau of Economic Research Science and Technology Policy Meeting, August 9.

Finkelstein, Martin J. 1984. *The American Academic Profession*. Columbus, OH: Ohio State University Press.

Finn, Chester E. 1984. "Trying Higher Education: An Eight Count Indictment," *Change* 16 (May/June), 29–33, 47–51.

Freeman, Richard. 1976. *The Overeducated American*. New York: Academic Press.

Geiger, Roger L. 1994. "Historical Patterns of Change: The Lessons of the 1980s." Paper delivered at the American Association for the Advancement of Science Meeting, San Francisco. 21 February.

Geiger, Roger L., and Irwin Feller. 1993. Unpublished. "The Dispersion of Academic Research in the 1980s."

Getz, Malcolm, and John J. Siegfried. 1991. "Costs and Productivity in American Colleges and Universities," Part III in *Economic Challenges in Higher Education*, Charles T. Clotfelter et al. Chicago: University of Chicago Press.

Getz, Malcolm, John J. Siegfried, and Kathryn H. Anderson. 1994. Unpublished paper, Vanderbilt University. "Adoption of Innovations in Higher Education." Department of Economics and Business Administration, Vanderbilt University. May.

Goldberger, Marvin L., Brendan A. Maher, and Pamela Ebert Flattau (eds.). 1995. *Research-Doctorate Programs in the United States: Continuity and Change*. Washington, DC: National Academy Press.

Gray, Hanna Holborn. 1992. "Some Reflections on the Commonwealth of Learning." In *AAAS Science and Technology Policy Yearbook, 1992*, edited by Stephen D. Nelson, Kathleen M. Gramp, and Albert H. Teich. Washington, DC: American Association for the Advancement of Science, pp. 229–238.

Griffiths, Phillip. 1984. Statement to the Board of Trustees, Duke University. 28 September.

Guskin, Alan E. 1995. "Reducing Student Costs and Enhancing Student Learning," Association of Governing Boards of Universities and Colleges Occasional Paper No. 27. Washington, DC: Association of Governing Boards.

Halstead, D. Kent. 1983. *Inflation Measures for Schools and Colleges*. Washington, DC: U.S. Department of Education. September.

———. *Higher Education Revenues and Expenditures*. Washington, DC: Research Associates of Washington, n.d.

Hansen, W. Lee. 1986. "Changes in Faculty Salaries." In *American Professors: A National Resource Imperiled*, Howard R. Bowen and Jack H. Schuster. New York: Oxford University Press.

Hansmann, Henry. 1990. "Why Do Universities Have Endowments?" *Journal of Legal Studies* 29 (January): 3–42.

Hauptman, Arthur M. 1990. *The College Tuition Spiral*. Washington, DC: American Council on Education and the College Board.

Hearn, James C. 1990. "Pathways to Attendance at the Elite Colleges." In *The High-Status Track*, edited by Paul William Kingston and Lionel S. Lewis. Albany: State University of New York Press.

Jones, Lyle V., Gardner Lindzey, and Porter E. Coggeshall (eds.). 1982. *An Assessment of Research-Doctorate Programs in the United States*. Washington, DC: National Academy Press.

Kasten, Richard, Frank Sammartino, and Eric Toder. 1992. "Trends in Federal Tax Progressivity: 1980–1993." Paper presented at the Conference on Tax Progressivity, University of Michigan, September 11, 1992. U.S. Congressional Budget Office.

Kennedy, Donald. 1985. "Government Policies and the Cost of Doing Research." *Science* 227 (February 1985): 480–84.

———. 1993. "Making Choices in the Research University." *Daedalus* 122 (fall): 127–57.

Keohane, Nannerl O. 1993. "The Mission of the Research University." *Daedalus* 122 (fall): 101–25.

Kidder, Tracy. 1981. *The Soul of a New Machine*. Boston: Little, Brown.

Kirshstein, Rita J. et al. 1990. *The Escalating Costs of Higher Education*. Washington, DC: Pelavin Associates.

Leibenstein, Harvey. 1966. "Allocative Versus X-Efficiency." *American Economic Review* 61 (June): 392–415.

Lewis, Stephen. 1993. Unpublished typescript. "Report to Alumni." Carleton College. 19 June.

Light, Richard J. 1992. *The Harvard Assessment Seminars, Second Report*. Cambridge, MA: Harvard University.

McNeill, William H. 1991. *Hutchins' University: A Memoir of the University of Chicago 1929–1950*. Chicago: University of Chicago Press.

McPherson, Michael S., and Morton Owen Schapiro. 1991. *Keeping College Affordable*. Washington, DC: Brookings Institution.

McPherson, Michael S., Morton Owen Schapiro, and Gordon C. Winston. 1993. *Paying the Piper: Productivity, Incentives, and Financing in U.S. Higher Education*. Ann Arbor: University of Michigan Press.

McPherson, Michael S., and Gordon C. Winston. 1993a. "The Economics of Academic Tenure: A Relational Perspective." In *Paying the Piper: Productivity, Incentives, and Financing in U.S. Higher Education*, Michael S. McPherson, Morton Owen Schapiro, and Gordon C. Winston. Ann Arbor: University of Michigan Press.

———. 1993b. "The Economics of Cost, Price, and Quality in U.S. Higher Education." In *Paying the Piper: Productivity, Incentives, and Financing in U.S. Higher Education*, Michael S. McPherson, Morton Owen Schapiro, and Gordon C. Winston. Ann Arbor: University of Michigan Press.

Maeroff, Gene I. 1993. "College Teachers, the New Leisure Class." *Wall Street Journal*, 13 September, p. A16.

Massy, William F. 1990. "A New Look at the Academic Department." Palo Alto, CA: Stanford Institute for Higher Education Research. May.

———. 1992. Comment. *Minerva* 30 (summer): 178–80.

Massy, William F., and Timothy R. Warner. 1991. "Causes and Cures of Cost Escalation in College and University Administrative and Support Services." Paper presented at the OERI/NACUBO National Symposium on Strategic Higher Education Finance and Management Issues in the 1990s. Washington, DC: February 24–25, 1991.

Massy, William F., and Andrea K. Wilger. 1992. "Productivity in Postsecondary Education: A New Approach." *Educational Evaluation and Policy Analysis* 14 (winter): 361–76.

Massy, William F., and Robert Zemsky. 1994. "Faculty Discretionary Time: Departments and the Academic Ratchet." *Journal of Higher Education* 65 (January/February): 1–22.

Meisinger, Richard J., and Leroy W. Dubeck. 1984. *College and University Budgeting*. Washington, DC: National Association of College and University Business Officers.

Morison, Samuel Eliot. 1965. *Three Centuries of Harvard*. Cambridge, MA: Harvard University Press.

Murphy, Kevin, and Finis Welch. 1989. "Wage Premiums for College Graduates: Recent Growth and Possible Explanations." *Educational Researcher* 18 (May): 17–26.

Niskanen, William T., Jr. 1971. *Bureaucracy and Representative Government*. Chicago: Aldine.

Noah, Timothy. "Highbrow Robbery: The Colleges Call It Tuition, We Call It Plunder." *Washington Monthly* (July/August 1983): 16–24.

Noll, Roger, and W. Edward Steinmueller. 1992. "An Economic Analysis of Scientific Journal Prices: Preliminary Results." *Serials Review* (spring and summer): 32–37.

O'Keefe, Michael. 1987. "Where Does the Money Really Go?" *Change* 19 (November/December): 12–34.

Parkinson, C. Northcote. 1957. *Parkinson's Law*. New York: Ballantine Books.

Phillips, Kevin. 1990. *The Politics of Rich and Poor*. New York: Random House.

President's Council of Advisors on Science and Technology. 1992. *Renewing the Promise: Research-Intensive Universities and the Nation*. Washington, DC: Government Printing Office. December.

Price, Reynolds. 1993. "Our Half of the Deal." Founders' Day Address, 10 December 1992. Reprinted in *Duke Dialog*, 15 January.

Pye, A. Kenneth. 1978. *Planning for the Eighties*. Unpublished report to the Board of Trustees, Duke University, 8 December.

Ransom, Michael R. 1993. "Seniority and Monopsony in the Academic Labor Market." *American Economic Review* 83 (March): 221–33.

Reagan, Ronald. 1989. *Speaking My Mind*. New York: Simon and Schuster.

Research Associates of Washington. 1994. *Inflation Measures for Schools, Colleges, and Libraries*. Washington: Research Associates of Washington.

Richardson, William C. 1992. Comment. *Minerva* 30 (summer): 180–82.

Riesman, David. 1980. *On Higher Education*. San Francisco: Jossey-Bass Publishers.

Roose, Kenneth D., and Charles J. Anderson. 1970. *A Rating of Graduate Programs*. Washington, DC: American Council on Education.

———. 1990. *The University: An Owner's Manual*. New York: W.W. Norton and Co.

Rosovsky, Henry. 1991. "1990–91 Annual Report from the Dean of the Faculty of Arts and Sciences." *Harvard Gazette* (11 October): 17–19.

———. 1992. Comment. *Minerva* 30 (summer): 183–87.

Rothschild, Michael, and Lawrence J. White. 1993. "The University in the Marketplace: Some Insights and Some Puzzles," In *Studies of Supply and Demand in Higher Education*, edited by Charles T. Clotfelter and Michael Rothschild. Chicago: University of Chicago Press.

Rudolph, Frederick. 1962. *The American College and University: A History*. Athens, GA: University of Georgia Press.

Sills, David L. 1968. "Introduction." In *International Encyclopedia of the Social Sciences*, edited by David L. Sills. Vol. 1. New York: Macmillan and Free Press.

Schmitt, Roland W. 1994. "The Business of Higher Education." *The Bridge* 24 (spring): 17–23.

Shapiro, Harold T. 1992. "The Functions and Resources of the American University of the Twenty-First Century." *Minerva* 30 (summer): 163–74.

———. 1993. "Current Realities and Future Prospects." *Academe* (January/February): 10–16.

Spies, Richard R. 1978. *The Effect of Rising Costs on College Choice*. New York: College Entrance Examination Board.

———. 1992. "The Scandal of College Tuition." *Commentary* (August): 23–26.

Sowell, Thomas. 1993. *Inside American Education*. New York: The Free Press.

Stigler, George. 1992. Comment. *Minerva* 30 (summer): 188.

Stigler, Stephen M. 1993. "Competition and the Research Universities." *Daedalus* 122 (fall): 157–78.

Sykes, Charles J. 1988. *ProfScam: Professors and the Demise of Higher Education*. Washington, DC: Regnergy Gateway.

"Time to Prune the Ivy." 1993. *Business Week*, 24 May, pp. 112–18.

"To Control College Costs." 1993. *Washington Post*, 28 January.

Tompkins, Jane. 1992. "The Way We Live Now." In: Duke University *Faculty Newsletter* 4 (October).

Trajtenberg, Manuel, Rebecca Henderson, and Adam Jaffee. 1992. "Ivory Tower Versus Corporate Lab: An Empirical Study of Basic Research and Appropriability." Cambridge, MA: National Bureau of Economic Research Working Paper No. 4146 (August).

U.S. Congressional Budget Office. September 1993. *The Economic and Budget Outlook: An Update*. Washington, DC: Government Printing Office.

U.S. Council of Economic Advisers. 1991, 1993, 1994. *Economic Report of the President*. Washington, DC: Government Printing Office.

U.S. Department of Commerce. 1960. *Historical Statistics of the United States, Colonial Times to 1957*. Washington, DC: Government Printing Office.

U.S. Department of Education. 1989, 1990, 1992, 1994. *Digest of Education Statistics*. Washington, DC: Government Printing Office.

————. 1991. *Profiles of Faculty in Higher Education Institutions, 1988*. Washington, DC: Government Printing Office.

U.S. House of Representatives, Committee on Energy and Commerce. 1991. *Hearings on Indirect Cost Recovery Practices at U.S. Universities for Federal Research Grants and Contracts*. 102nd Cong., March 13, 1991, serial 102–33. Washington, DC: Government Printing Office.

U.S. House of Representatives, Committee on Ways and Means. 1992a. *Overview of Entitlement Programs, 1992 Green Book*. 102nd Cong. Washington, DC: Government Printing Office.

U.S. House of Representatives, Select Committee on Children, Youth, and Families. September 14, 1992b. *College Education: Paying More and Getting Less*. Hearings, 102nd Cong., typescript.

U.S. Office of Education. 1969, 1973. *Digest of Educational Statistics*. Washington, DC: Government Printing Office.

Vesey, Laurence R. 1965. *The Emergence of the American University*. Chicago: University of Chicago Press.

Wagner, Betsy, and David Bowermaster.1992. "B.S. Economics." *Washington Monthly* (November): 19–21.

Weber, Arnold R., "Colleges Must Begin Weighing Public Perceptions, as Well as Economic Reality, When Setting Tuition." *Chronicle of Higher Education*, October 11, 1989, p. A52.

Charles T. Clotfelter is Z. Smith Reynolds Professor of Public Policy Studies and Professor of Economics at Duke University.